T (partially obscured header/title)

Pete ... ...ambino lieutenant ... ...the homicide cops explained ... Louie's uncle and cousin to a deserted ... school playground in Coney Island under the pretense of having a "sit-down," the Cosa Nostra's version of a corporate board meeting. At the playground they were met by Roy "Roy-Roy" DeMeo. Louie felt his uncle must have realized his life was over the moment DeMeo made his appearance. For Roy-Roy, as everyone knew, was a sociopathic killer whose crew was responsible for over two hundred contract hits. And those didn't include the homicides Roy-Roy did just for fun. Ironically, perhaps a few of the hits had even been ordered by Jimmy Eppolito.

Even the tentative motive, which investigators were already piecing together, carried little surprise. For what the detectives couldn't have known was that Louie had expected the assassinations.

Conversely, what Louie couldn't have known was that the murder of his uncle and cousin would begin a chain reaction that would eventually drive him from the force and back into a world he was sure he had left behind . . . .

MAFIA COP

LOU EPPOLITO & BOB DRURY

POCKET STAR BOOKS
New York   London   Toronto   Sydney

A Pocket Star Book Published by
POCKET BOOKS, a division of Simon & Schuster, Inc.
1230 Avenue of the Americas, New York, NY 10020

ISBN 978-1-4165-1701-6

30 29 28 27 26 25 24 23 22 21

POCKET STAR BOOKS and colophon are registered trademarks of
Simon & Schuster, Inc.

For information regarding special discounts for bulk purchases,
please contact Simon & Schuster Special Sales at
1-800-456-6798 or business@simonandschuster.com

Printed in the U.S.A.

For my father Ralph.
Thanks for making a man
that no other man could break.
—L.E.

For C.A.B.
—B.D.

AUTHORS' NOTES

I AM FOREVER INDEBTED TO A LEGION OF PEOPLE FOR harnessing the thought processes that went into this book. Nick Pileggi provided the inspiration; my agent, Flip Brophy, the manifestation. My editor, Laura Yorke, was a guiding light who wielded her Number 2 pencil like a laser. Michael Korda's deft touch is stamped indelibly on this project.

Among the many who lent me their time, recollections, and analyses, I owe a special thanks to Detective Steve Gardell, Hugh Mo, Esq., District Attorney Charles J. Hynes, Assistant District Attorney Mark Feldman, Theresa (Tess) Mandelino, and the entire Eppolito family. And, with gratitude, I must acknowledge fellow reporters Richard Esposito, Phil Messing, Mike McAlary, and Mark Kriegel for their insight and knowledge of the street. I would also like to thank researcher Christine Baird of the New York *Newsday* library. Finally, I am forever beholden to Detective (Ret.) Doug LeVien, the "fixer" who smoothed my research path too many times to recall.

Ironically, the legend of Detective Louie Eppolito still reverberates ominously throughout the New York City Police Department. For that reason, dozens of current and former police officers granted interviews only on the condition of anonymity. You know who you are, and I thank you. To the goodfellas who shared their thoughts, I, as per our deal, do not remember who you are.

While researching and writing this book I relied on many authors too numerous to name, who hacked previous paths through the thicket of NYPD politics and pierced the veil of secrecy shielding La Cosa Nostra. Yet among those whose works were especially insightful and inspirational, I must acknowledge Herbert Asbury, Jimmy Breslin, Harold Conrad, Nicholas Gage, Robert Lacey, Peter Maas, Mike McAlary, Gene Mustain and Jerry Capeci, Joseph F. O'Brien and Andris Kurins, Joseph D. Pistone and Richard Woodley, Charles Rappleye and Ed Becker, Thomas C. Renner, Nick Pileggi, Claire Sterling, and Gay Talese.

—BOB DRURY

THIS BOOK TELLS A LOT ABOUT LOUIE EPPOLITO. NOW let me acknowledge some others with my gratitude. To my mother—if anyone has earned a place in heaven, it is she. To my sister, Pauline Guarneri, who grew up always covering for her brother. To my wife, Frances, who has put up with me for the past twenty years. Her great love and understanding of me will always be a mystery waiting to be solved.

From my uniform days, I thank all the members of the 71st Precinct for their support and backup. They were the toughest cops with whom I've ever worked. To Sergeant Larry Ponzi and Lieutenant Patrick Flynn, who taught me how to be a detective, I send my respect. And to Captain Anthony Marra, whose knowledge of The Job has, in my eyes, never been equaled, I say thanks.

To my first partner, Sergeant Louie Pioli, and to the detectives who stood behind me in my hour of need—Billy Mulligan, Peter Furtado, Ralph Blasie, and Paul Frommer—you taught me what true friendship is. To Officer Nick Santamaria and the rest of the Capris—Mike, Tommy, Frankie, and Tony—I will be forever in your debt. And to my great good friend Detective Steve Gardell, I offer my heartfelt thanks.

I also offer thanks to Detectives Jimmy Fairchild, Pat Melia, Phil Sciannamia, and Sergeant John Muldoon, who accepted me back on The Job with smiles, understanding, and no doubts. And at no time and in no place did I ever have a friend as supportive as Sergeant James McCoy.

Never in my heart will I forget Jimmy McCafferty. The two of us laughed together. The two of us cried together. And the two of us were always ready to die, if necessary, for the protection of the people of New York City. And there are no words to define my feelings for Detective Steve Caracappa, my closest and dearest friend. And special thanks to my brother-in-law Angelo Todesco for his financial support.

I offer special thanks to Maxi Cohen, who brought my story to the attention of everyone concerned—without her this project would never have come into being; to my agent, Charlotte Sheedy; and to my friend, Nick Pileggi, who grabbed an idea and molded it into reality.

And, finally, to my children, Andrea, Deanna, Tony, and Louie: I love you.

—LOUIE EPPOLITO

PROLOGUE

I stare through the front window of the Brooklyn restaurant as Louie Eppolito unfolds in stages from the front seat of his white Chevy van. A sea breeze skims off the harbor, momentarily brushing aside the folds of his sportcoat. For one instant, the harsh winter sunlight, almost white, glints off Sheepshead Bay and catches the polished black grip of the fourteen-shot Smith & Wesson 9-millimeter automatic pistol riding above his right hip.

I am not alone in noticing the pistol. The maître d' standing beside me raises an eyebrow at the flash of metal and edges closer to the plate glass, the better to scrutinize this man. As this maître d' caters to a regular clientele of Mafia bosses, his health depends upon knowing who is carrying a piece into his establishment.

It is obvious he is not sure what to make of the armed man walking our way. Louie Eppolito is a man who seems larger than his six-foot height. He is plainly powerful, and attractive, though not handsome by the conventional Hollywood standards. Yet there is something deep about his eyes. They are dark brown, slightly hooded. When he stops to talk to a couple of fishermen, his eyes crinkle and sparkle, dominating a broad, open face bisected by a trim black mustache. They are the eyes of someone who can be trusted, which, as we shall see, makes Louie Eppolito's ordeal all the more painful.

There is a nearly undetectable limp to Louie's gait, the one lingering effect of a childhood bout with rheumatic fever. His right leg remains imperceptibly withered. Otherwise, at forty-three years old, he cuts a figure I've watched women of a certain age turn to admire.

His barrel chest descends, V-shaped (when he sucks in his stomach), to a slim waist. Despite the inevitable ravages of gravity, as well as a lifelong diet of bleeding red meat, sausage and peppers, and plates of pasta, the silhouette of a former bodybuilding champion lingers. Louie's jet-black hair, flecked with gray, folds back into a modified pompadour. Those brown eyes flick left and right, shadowed, watchful, patient.

Eppolito projects the aura of a man not to be trifled with, a man slow to anger, but dangerous when threatened. Even his smallest gestures, the regal manner with which he pauses on the sidewalk to smooth the creases from his silk shirt, suggest that this is a person you can come to for help. It becomes easier to see why the helpless and powerless of New York City flocked to Detective Louis John Eppolito for over two decades. His shoulders are wide, literally and metaphorically.

And it is at this moment, sitting in a dockside fishhouse, that I wondered what it had been like to see Louie cry. Not the lone, misty tear that the haunted skirl of a funeral piper can squeeze from even the most case-hardened soul. But the shoulder-heaving, airsucking gasps that his wife, Fran, described to me in such horrible detail. The shudders of a man betrayed by the organization he loved, by people he trusted, by a second family he had nurtured.

I wondered how it had affected this man to have been reduced to uncontrolled sobs in front of his three-year-old son, who had been taught, as Louie had been taught by his father, that "men don't cry." I wondered how the Police Department of New York City managed to break this one good cop.

As we are escorted to a table in the back of the smoky dining room, Louie stops to greet two men. He extends a hand of gnarled and misshapen knuckles, battle scars from the streets. When Louie is deep in conversation, he unconsciously kneads those knuckles, as if trying to pop back into place bones cracked and broken long ago.

"Old friends," he whispers when we are seated. "Lucchese Family associates. And see over there, the guy with the white hair? Peter Gotti. John's brother. The empty table in the corner? Reserved for Carmine Lambordozzi."

The venerable Lambordozzi, a capo in the Gambino Crime Family, is, at eighty-three years of age, the last living link to the heyday of La Cosa Nostra, to the time of the brothers Eppolito, Louie's father and uncles.

Louie, who drinks sparingly, orders a martini with a tall glass of ice water. The maître d', who has subtly taken our station, attempts to read his face. Friend or foe? Cop or robber? Louie is aware of this, and betrays no emotion. He is accustomed to scrutiny. His eyes seem to smile at the man's discomfort.

Drinks ordered, the maître d' departs, and Louie leans conspiratorially over the white linen tablecloth. "I have a friend who eats here, Allie Boy, guy I've known since I was a kid," he begins. "So last year I'm out on the West Coast, looking for an acting job, and Fran gives me a message that Allie Boy called. Turns out he'd seen my bit role in the De Niro picture *Goodfellas*, and wanted an autographed photo of De Niro to hang on the wall of his social club.

"As we're talking, I mention to Allie Boy that I'm up for a part, a truck driver's role. I tell him my agent says I'm supposed to find out the next day, and that the role's come down to a choice between me and some other character actor out there.

"So, after a long pause, Allie Boy says to me: 'Hey, Louie, wait a second. Why don't I just hop on the redeye, fly the fuck out there tonight, and fix it so when you wake up in the morning, their choice is just between you and you.' "

He pauses a beat, awaiting my reaction.

"He was serious," Louie erupts with a laugh. His laugh is hearty, rumbling up from the gut. "It's like the IRA. Once in, never out. Only—contrary to popular opinion—I was never in."

It was good to hear Louie laugh, especially at himself. Not long before, a resentful Louie had written to me that he would eventually forget "the long hours spent in court, the countless days and torrid weather conditions spent out on the street.

"I will forget the hundreds of people I arrested. And my mind will in time erase the jittery feelings you get when you're a cop, whether working or off duty. My eyes will forget so many of the awful things a human being can see; even my nose will forget the daily smells of decaying human flesh or children lying sick in their own excrement, looking up at you for help.

"But never in my heart will I forget all those people who hurt me when I shouldn't have been hurt, all

those who helped ruin my career and my life. I say to all of them: 'You can go to hell.' "

I remind him of that letter, and he laughs again.

"I tend to get a little dramatic sometimes. I guess I inherited it from my father's side of the family."

The late Ralph Eppolito, like Louie's uncles Freddy and Jimmy, was a wiseguy, a made man in the Gambino Crime Family. All three had taken the blood oath of La Cosa Nostra. Ralph Eppolito had taught his son Louie respect with his fists. And though Louie had made the unique career choice of joining the police force, there were several personality traits that bound one generation to the next. For a while, hatred of the New York City Police Department was one. Ralph Eppolito went to his grave despising the sight of a blue uniform.

But time was healing even this wound. And as we sat and talked at that waterfront restaurant, I began to feel sad for the NYPD, and sadder still for the residents of New York City. They could both use more cops like Louie Eppolito.

When we were introduced in the spring of 1990, Detective (Ret.) Louie Eppolito was six months off "The Job," and the first words out of his mouth were, "You know, I didn't do it. Those bastards will tell you I did it. But I didn't do it."

My response was reflexive. After nearly a decade of writing about cops, of patrolling with them and celebrating with them and, yes, of even being the catalyst that put some of them behind bars, I felt jaded enough to know that when a cop blurts out to a journalist that he "didn't do it," the odds are better than even that he *did*.

The accusations leveled against Detective Eppolito

had been harsh—harsher still in light of his heroic career. Louie had been charged with selling his shield to the Mafia. And as I studied this man in the enclosed back porch of his modest Long Island home, my first reaction was to cast my vote with the prosecutor.

Like a lot of wiseguys, Louie was a walking jewelry store, bedecked in diamonds and gold, rings on five fingers, chains shrouding a neck the size of my thigh. A giant gold pendant in the shape of a snake coiled through the underbrush sprouting on his chest. Gold is the charm of the poor. That is why gangsters believe in gold. You can touch it. You cannot touch annuity funds.

And, of course, there was the ubiquitous stream of profanity. I have yet to meet the mobster who can go a paragraph without uttering the F-word. Louie was no exception.

At one point our conversation was interrupted by Louie's two daughters, thirteen-year-old Andrea and twelve-year-old Deanna. They walked in from school, gave their father his requisite kiss, and pulled up a chair. The stream of "cocksuckers," and "motherfuckers" scarcely abated.

"My kids are used to my language," Louie said when he noticed me squirm. "They know their daddy can't help himself."

Yet Louie is graced—redeemed—by his kindness. His friends and acquaintances all speak of an extraordinary person whose generosity far exceeds the customary or typical. This virtue, Louie says, was passed on to him by his grandfather Luigi the Nablidan, and his father, Fat the Gangster, immigrants who, lacking any formal education, did what they could to snatch their portion of the American Dream: joined the Mafia.

A master storyteller, Louie could put you there as if it were *you* who grew up amid the violent schemes, and scams, and midnight meetings that make up life in the Mafia. It was as if *you* were the fifth-grader counting the day's numbers take for "Uncle" Todo, or being taught by "Uncle" Bath Beach the difference between fencing *ice* and *swag*—hot diamonds or hijacked loot.

The newspaper clips had painted a remarkable picture of Officer Louis John Eppolito. He'd survived eight shootouts, killed at least one man, and his heroism was legend among New York's Finest. Yet as he told me about his life, from his formative years to his illustrious career on The Job, Louie seemed most proud when recounting tales about the number of people whose lives he had saved, about how he had broken from the family and gone "the other way," about how good that decision had made him feel.

He spoke of the Welfare mother for whom he took up a collection, the scores of senior citizens rescued from the "barbarians," the crack hooker whose murderer he'd spent his off-duty hours tracking down, "because whores got mothers, too." These were not isolated incidents in the career of Detective Eppolito, and he had a trunkful of thank-you notes to prove it. Louie had worked his job as he had lived his life, always looking out for the little man. And the little man hadn't forgotten, even if the NYPD had.

As if on cue, Fran Eppolito walked in with the mail, and here, eleven years later, was a letter from a woman whose son Louie had kept alive by reaching into the hole in his gut and pinching a severed artery. The note would be added to the others, in the trunk, the manifestation of twenty-some years on The Job.

Yes, Louie admitted, there was a litany of felonies

he had committed while wearing the badge, but they were all in the name of "honor," and "respect." Like most urban cops, Louie's idea of a rational police policy was martial law, even if he had to declare it himself. The sight of a dead "perp" never cost him a moment's sleep, yet he had nightmares for years about the body parts he was ordered to collect following a plane crash in Brooklyn. It was not long after that airline disaster that Louie had forced himself to plunge his hand into the stomach of that mother's son—"The hardest thing," said this complex cop, "that I ever had to do on The Job."

The Department never asked about those sleepless nights, or about those letters in the trunk, when they brought him to trial.

And as Louie vehemently swore vengeance on those whom he felt had besmirched not only his career but the good name of Eppolito, I began to sense the difference between Louie Eppolito and the legions of former police officers who have told their stories in print.

Cops whose careers wind up as books invariably fall into three categories: there are the moralists, like Frank Serpico, who could no longer wade through the cesspool of widespread police corruption; there are the One-Note Wonders, who were part of the Big Case and now feel free to share their squadroom secrets; and there are the kiss-and-tell cops, like the Buddy Boys of Brooklyn, who in the hands of a skilled author can provide to society just the right cautionary note.

Louie Eppolito was none of these. As he sat back and talked with equal ease about his personal experiences with both capo and cop, it became obvious that here was a cop who defied classification.

He had been a child of a Mafia crew, a Crime Family

literally; he became a hero cop, carrying "this stupid sense of honor, this Italian thing," through his career in the New York Police Department, and, then, there was the "betrayal" of that "honor"—suspension, trial, a shattered life.

As Louie and I talked, as afternoon turned to evening and evening to night, a unique story emerged. Louie had straddled two worlds usually closed to the public—the world of the cop and the world of the Cosa Nostra. He was able to give a rare look into each. More important, he refused to glamorize either profession. That *alone* set him apart from most hoods —and cops—I knew.

"Never lose face," his father Ralph had often repeated to young Louie. "Never make what we call *una brutta figura,* a bad showing."

It was Mafia wisdom that Louie never forgot.

It was also one of the last things his Uncle Jimmy said to him eleven years earlier, just days before he was whacked, when everything all started to go wrong.

I

THE HIT

I

THE HIT

I

THE HIT

1

When he took the call from Homicide, Detective Eppolito was seized by the feeling that his belly was dropping out of his body. He clenched the receiver and only a childhood discipline held back the tears. "Men don't cry," Ralph Eppolito had instructed his son over and over, and as the Homicide sergeant suggested that Louie be present to identify the bodies, Detective Eppolito repeated the phrase to himself like a song's refrain.

Men don't cry. Men don't cry. Even when it's your uncle and cousin lying on a slab in the morgue.

Then Louie recalled the ultimate lesson his father had taught him about life in the family business: *Nobody never gets killed for no reason.*

"He had to go," Ralph Eppolito would explain to the twelve-year-old Lou, who reacted with wonderment and awe. "Go where?" he would ask. "To St. Louis? The West Coast?" Ralph Eppolito would merely shrug and turn his back on his son, muttering to his wife that their only boy would never understand "the ways of our world."

But by the time Louie was a teen, old enough to accompany Ralph on policy-slip runs, or a bookmaking pickup, or merely to break down a crap game, he

13

had indeed come to understand the nuances of the family firm, as well as the true meaning of his father's cryptic lessons: when somebody had to go, they stayed gone. Whether it was an ostentatious mobster-turned-informer like John "Johnny Roberts" Robi-lotto, personally dispatched by Louie's father and uncle, or one of the many *capo di tutti capi* toppled by hostile takeovers, Louie learned that, in the lexicon of Organized Crime, "gone" meant "gone forever."

Now Uncle Jimmy and Cousin Jim-Jim were gone. Gone forever. Taken out, "gangland-style" the news-papers would report, behind an elementary school in the Coney Island section of Brooklyn. Three .38-cali-ber slugs in the head had taken Uncle Jimmy, a capo in the Gambino Crime Family; four in the face had dispatched cousin Jim-Jim, a wiseguy wannabe.

Nobody never gets killed for no reason, Louie thought as he fought the image of his dead kinsmen sprawled across a South Brooklyn sidewalk. Child-hood memories welled up inside him. Jimmy Eppolito goading his sickly nephew, who was still recovering from rheumatic fever, to stretch the single into a dou-ble, the double into a triple. The recollection of his father's funeral, and his uncle pulling him aside and draping a beefy arm over his shoulder.

"Always remember, you're an Eppolito," Uncle Jimmy had consoled him. "When one hurts, we all hurt. I'm here to share your pain."

"Our whole lives we've lived with this," Louie said to his mother when he broke the terrible news. "I was stupid to think we'd left it behind." Tess Eppolito was used to Louie's calls at all hours of the night. He'd made it a point to phone her every time a New York City cop was shot, to let his mom know that he was all right. They'd laughed at him in the squad room for his habit. *Big, burly Eppolito, calling his mommy*. But Louie ignored the jeers. He knew about family, and understood a mother's fear.

This time, after Louie found the words for Uncle Jimmy and Jim-Jim, Tess replaced the receiver in its cradle without a response. It was a call she had been expecting for quite some time.

Ironically, one hour earlier, at 5 A.M., October 1, 1979, Louie had been preparing for what he considered the most prestigious detail of his storied twelve-year career in the New York City Police Department: assignment as part of Pope John Paul II's personal bodyguard during the Pontiff's historic visit to the United Nations.

"To me, the Pope represented Christ on earth," Louie would say later. "And I was somewhat overwhelmed knowing that I would be able to see him, even if it just meant trotting alongside his armored car, the Popemobile we called it. It was a very important moment.

"All the medals and citations, they meant nothing compared to the thought of just being next to the Pope. And I was proud to represent the Police Department, proud that everybody could see me with all my medals. Me, the son of an Organized Crime soldier. I could pin all those decorations to my chest and walk down the street with my head held high."

In fact, it was largely because of his cluster of ribbons that Detective Eppolito had been assigned to the detail. That, and his police poster-boy image, for at thirty-two years of age Louie Eppolito was a walking advertisement for the virility of New York's Finest.

Yet Louie—the hero cop, the NYPD's eleventh-most-decorated officer, twice nominated and accepted into the Department's most prestigious Medal of

Honor Society, the recipient of two Presidential Citations, of a slew of official awards, medals, commendations, and plaques, the veteran of countless shootouts—carried two distinct burdens through his life.

One was a devotion, some would say excessive, to an Old World sense of honor. The other was a temper that, as one colleague put it, "never missed an opportunity to miss an opportunity." The detective divided mankind into two categories: those, like himself, who deserved respect; and those who were beneath contempt. When "dishonored," Lou's wrath recognized no rank. The day's subsequent events would serve to throw those values into stark relief.

Louie had been memorizing the Pontiff's route from midtown Manhattan to Yankee Stadium when his desk sergeant pulled him aside. His wife was on the phone. It was an emergency. At four-fifteen that morning, moments after Lou had left their colonial Long Island home for the forty-five-minute drive to his Brooklyn station house, Fran Eppolito had received a frantic call from Lou's Aunt Dolly.

Detectives from the Brooklyn District Attorney's Organized Crime Squad had awakened Dolly Eppolito with dreadful news. Her husband, Jimmy, and her son Jim-Jim were both dead. "I don't believe them," a hysterical Dolly told Fran. "Please, I need Louie to find out what's going on."

Oddly, sitting and shivering at her kitchen table in those predawn autumn hours, Fran Eppolito found her heart aching more for her husband than for his widowed aunt. She felt guilty about her misplaced sympathies, but, she recalled thinking, Louie just didn't deserve this. After the death of his father twelve years before, Louie had vowed to avoid his Uncle Jimmy, to cut himself off from that side of the family and the old friends from the neighborhood.

"We never visited, because Louie didn't want to make it uncomfortable for Uncle Jimmy when 'my nephew the detective' came around," Fran would say. "Louie didn't want to put him on the spot in front of his Mafia friends."

Yet, over the past twelve months, since they had talked and sipped espresso after the funeral of Grandpa Louis Eppolito, Lucky Luciano's old pal, Louie and his uncle had reestablished relations. Lou had surprised even himself, for during that short time span he had come to love, trust, and respect his father's younger brother, the big-shot wiseguy. Fran watched from a distance, pleased. She thought she saw in Jimmy Eppolito a substitute for Lou's lost father, Ralph.

"I knew in Louie's mind he had finally found a father figure again," Fran would recall. "And when that call came in from Aunt Dolly, I was heartbroken for him. I knew he had lost another Ralph. After all those years of hating his father, hating what his family stood for, for this to happen just as they had gotten close . . ." She did not finish the sentence.

"Hoping against hope," yet sensing the inevitable, Detective Eppolito telephoned Brooklyn South Homicide immediately following his conversation with Fran. As a professional courtesy, his call was returned within five minutes. The request to ID the bodies at the morgue was as far as the courtesy extended. What happened next convinced Louie that his father's friends had been correct when they warned him that he would make a great detective but a lousy cop.

"I could take hearing about the hits, after a minute anyway," Louie remembers. "That's the life they chose, and when you choose that life, you run the risk of getting whacked. Nobody knew that better than me. But then I heard people talking in the background, actually giggling and laughing. I identified myself as a police officer—of course, they knew who I was anyway—and asked if it was true my uncle and cousin had been murdered."

Grudgingly, a Homicide sergeant at the other end of the line answered. Yes, two mugs named Eppolito were indeed dead. Louie pressed for details. They did not come. Something was being held back. Finally, he overheard a muffled voice ordering the Homicide sergeant to hang up the phone.

"It was a lieutenant in the background, the guy running the show. I heard him tell the sarge that the investigation was 'none of my fuckin' business.' Talk about fury. My head exploded."

That fury had manifested itself literally hundreds of times on the streets. Louie was, self-admittedly, one hotheaded cop. But he had always before managed to rein in his emotions when it came to dealing with fellow officers, especially superior officers. Now, for the first time, his emotions jumped their brake.

"You tell that cocksucker to get on the phone with me now," he screamed, "because if I start heading down in that direction I guarantee you he'll be shitting through a colostomy bag for a year. You tell him that."

There were children who had lived to be teenagers, and pensioners who still had their life savings and, yes, even cops on The Job who thanked the Good Lord every night for Detective Eppolito's lack of discretion. But to a disembodied voice from the Tenth Homicide Zone, this explosion reeked of insubordination.

Louie heard the sergeant tell his lieutenant that he'd better pick up on an extension, "because I seemed a little upset."

The lieutenant on the line was named Kelly, and his attitude reflected it.

"Okay, Eppolito, whaddaya want?"

Louie calmly tried to explain to Lieutenant Kelly that it was his uncle and cousin who had just been murdered, his family, his blood. If the lieutenant didn't at least have the decency and courtesy to offer condolences, "then perhaps I would be doing the Department a big favor by coming down there and splitting his skull to the base of his spine."

There was a brief silence at the other end of the line. Finally, a shaken Kelly answered. "Let me tell you something, Detective. Do you realize you're speaking to a lieutenant?"

Louie's reply was succinct. "Nice to meet you, Lieutenant. Now I want some information, or else I'm coming down there with bad intentions."

Louie's CO, who had been edging closer to the phone while piecing together the conversation, finally grabbed the receiver from his detective and began a conciliatory conversation with the lieutenant from Homicide. Louie sat and steamed before spotting James Sullivan, Brooklyn's Chief of Detectives. Louie described his predicament and his blowup. Sullivan got on the horn and ordered his Homicide cops to the station house.

When they arrived, Sullivan dragged them all into an interview room and demanded a report on the murders. The scene that followed had more of the feel of an interrogation than a briefing. There was an unease to the conversation. Louie felt it hanging in the air. It was as if, as he put it, "the badge I wore was somehow a mistake."

For the first time in his career, Louie Eppolito, who had adopted the Police Department as a second family, felt like an intruder among cops.

The anatomy of the hit, as laid out by the cops, ran much as Louie had expected. One of the hit men, Lieutenant Robert Kelly said haltingly, was a Gambino soldier named Pete Piacenti. At the mention of the name, Louie's head jerked up. Pete Piacenti had been one of his Uncle Jimmy's oldest and closest associates. Jimmy Eppolito had brought Pete into his crew as a kid. He had served as his sponsor when he "made his bones" at the oath-taking ceremony which formally inducted Piacenti into the Gambino Crime Family. Louie understood well the mores of a Cosa Nostra contract: The shooters come as friends, people who have cared deeply about you your entire life. And they always come when you are the most vulnerable. Still, thought Louie, not Pete Piacenti.

Piacenti and a high-ranking Gambino lieutenant named Nino Gaggi, the Homicide cops explained, had lured Louie's uncle and cousin to a deserted high school playground in Coney Island under the pretense of having a "sit-down," the Cosa Nostra's version of a corporate board meeting. At the playground they were met by Roy "Roy-Roy" DeMeo. Louie felt his uncle must have realized his life was over the moment DeMeo made his appearance. For Roy-Roy, as everyone knew, was a sociopathic killer whose crew was responsible for over two hundred contract hits. And those didn't include the homicides Roy-Roy did just for fun. Ironically, perhaps a few of the hits had even been ordered by Jimmy Eppolito.

Even the tentative motive, which investigators were

already piecing together, carried little surprise. For what the detectives couldn't have known was that Louie had expected the assassinations.

Conversely, what Louie couldn't have known was that the murder of his uncle and cousin would begin a chain reaction that would eventually drive him from the force and back into a world he was sure he had left behind.

2

Several weeks earlier, Louie had dropped in on his Uncle Jimmy at his Bay Ridge home to say hello, sip coffee, and bring Aunt Dolly a box of cannolis. Jimmy Eppolito had begun his career in La Cosa Nostra with his brothers Ralph and Freddy as a policy runner and bookmaker. Ralph and Jimmy had both become made men, had taken the blood oath, after "whacking" Johnny Roberts, who had *turned* and was talking to the Feds.

Under Carlo Gambino's tutelage, Jimmy had worked himself up to the position of capo, or lieutenant, and had retained the position under Gambino's successor, Paul "Big Paulie" Castellano. Jimmy was most likely pulling in a million a year from his gambling, loan-sharking, burglary, and hijacking operations throughout the city. But except for the sprawling white house with the black wrought-iron gate, one would never suspect that the polite, gentle old man was knee-deep in swag. He was always impeccably dressed, and, as even one of his arresting officers was quick to point out, "he never even used the F-word."

"One OC cop gave my uncle the highest compliment a wiseguy can receive when he told me that Uncle Jimmy knew how to take a subpoena like a gentleman," Louie recalls. "My uncle never ran away, never disappeared. He always showed up in the grand jury. He was never a punk. I was proud of that, and in that sense he was so different from my old man. My father hated cops with a passion, had no respect whatsoever for them. I guess that stemmed from the days when he was buying them off for nickels and dimes."

During his visit with his Uncle Jimmy, Louie's cousin Jim-Jim dropped by. Jim-Jim was thirty-four, two years older than Louie, and moved with the arrogant swagger common to the sons of Cosa Nostra bosses. He stayed only for a moment. Nervous and edgy, he whispered something in his father's ear. Louie didn't pay much attention. He thought Jim-Jim, as usual, was just showing off.

Jim-Jim Eppolito cruised through life as if carrying a sign: "My father's a capo in the Gambino Family, the biggest OC Family in the United States, and I have carte blanche." He was under the mistaken impression that his father's Gambino Family standing conferred on the son an invisible armor. "And that," said Louie, "is what got him dead."

"I once heard that Jim-Jim gambled away twelve thousand dollars and then refused to pay the bookmaker, an old Sicilian in his seventies. Called the guy a prick bastard and told him to fuck off when he tried to collect. So the old man called for a sit-down with my Uncle Jimmy, who ended up paying the freight, but still lost respect, because his son was a man without honor. That's the worst thing that can happen to an OC guy, losing respect."

The second-worst thing is hubris. Thus began Jim-Jim's downfall. Through his involvement with a convicted forger named John Ellsworth, Jim-Jim had dealt

23

himself into a phony national charity campaign. Along the way he had conned several national figures, including President Jimmy Carter's wife, Rosalynn, and Senator Edward Kennedy, into fund-raising drives.

The International Children's Appeal was a cash cow for Ellsworth and Jim-Jim Eppolito. Not only were the two skimming money from the campaign, but they used the charity as a front to launder funds from their drug- and gun-running operations.

Their mistake was in aligning themselves with such a high-profile charity. Jim-Jim traveled to Washington and managed to have his picture taken with the President's wife. The photo appeared in papers across the country, including the *Times,* the *Post,* and the *Daily News* in New York. In July of 1978 the television show "20/20" aired a report on how the son of Gambino Family underboss Jimmy "the Clam" Eppolito had insinuated himself into the good graces of Jimmy Carter's wife. The feature ran the picture of Jim-Jim and Rosalynn Carter, showed surveillance photos of Louie's Uncle Jimmy making his rounds, and reported that Ellsworth and Jim-Jim had stolen between three and five million dollars earmarked for destitute children.

"By the time that program was finished, there was a contract out on Jim-Jim. The Justice Department, the FBI, every hick Fed with a pair of white socks and black wingtips was going to be crawling all over South Brooklyn, and the mob doesn't like that kind of publicity. From what I understand, neither did the White House."

So after his cousin left, Lou took his uncle aside to ask, "Just what the hell is happening with Jim-Jim." Jimmy the Clam merely shook his head. "It's going to be very bad for us," he told Louie. He hadn't needed to add more. The message was clear. Jim-Jim, in fact, had been warned by those above his father to avoid any overt associations with politicians. That was standard Cosa Nostra policy. But Jim-Jim felt that by connecting with the President's wife he could become bigger than the bosses who had issued those orders. Lou asked his uncle if there was anything he could do.

"This is a personal thing with us, a family matter," Uncle Jimmy replied. At that moment Lou knew that his cousin Jim-Jim was going to have to be whacked.

"And even though my cousin was a cocky son of a bitch, it still got under my skin. I'm not afraid of death, I could face it in any form. But when you know it's going to happen to your family, and you're helpless to stop it, it makes your blood boil. And I was helpless, both as a cop and as an Eppolito. I had an understanding with my uncle that any talks we had would stay in the family. And there was no way I was going to go back on my word, on my honor, and, say, take this threat to the Organized Crime Division of the Police Department. Nor did Uncle Jimmy want me to get involved personally.

"There wasn't the slightest bit of doubt in my mind that it was over for both of them, because I knew my uncle would never permit his son to be whacked. Did I know it because he told me so? No. I knew it because he was family, he was an Eppolito.

"My father once told me, 'Whether you're right or wrong, I'm going to defend you until my last breath, no matter how wrong you are, because you're family.' My father was the type that if I got drunk and plowed my car into a schoolroom and killed forty-four kids, he'd find the bartender and beat the shit out of him for getting me plastered. And in that sense Uncle Jimmy was nearly a carbon copy of my old man.

"I made it a point to speak to Uncle Jimmy maybe four times after that meeting. I told him that if there was anywhere he needed to go, I was available to help. He gave me a look that said, 'What am I going to do, run to Alaska?' I knew he was right, and I knew he was dead. And when Fran called me that day, I knew he had been whacked trying to bargain for his son's life."

3

As the Homicide detectives narrated the details of the hit on the Eppolitos, Louie's anger turned into amazement that Gaggi and Piacenti were in custody. That is just not supposed to happen in a "professional" mob town like New York City. Gaggi was one of Paulie Castellano's most trusted advisers. It was to Nino, Louie realized, that Uncle Jimmy thought he could plead Cousin Jim-Jim's case, with his old friend Piacenti providing both counsel and backup.

But the shooters hadn't noticed that there was a teenaged couple necking in a parked car behind the school. When the kids heard the shots they ran for a cop. Coincidentally, an off-duty Housing Police officer, moonlighting as a cabby, was at that moment turning the corner. A shootout erupted, Sergeant Paul Roder firing from behind his cab, Gaggi and Piacenti emptying their pistols during a wild dash for safety.

Both hoods were wounded. The third shooter, not yet in custody, escaped in another direction. Lou instinctively knew it was DeMeo. Not only was Roy-Roy Gaggi's main button man, but he fit the teen witnesses' descriptions to a tee.

When the Homicide investigators reached the shootout stage of their narrative, Lieutenant Kelly became apprehensive about disclosing further details. "That's why we didn't want to speak to Detective Eppolito over the phone," he explained to Chief Sullivan. "We didn't want him to know we nabbed two of the shooters. We didn't want anybody to do anything stupid."

As Kelly spoke he shot a glance at Louie. The lieutenant's implication was clear. Blood is thicker than the badge, even the eleventh-most-decorated badge.

Once again, Louie exploded. "I told you on the phone that you're a cocksucker and I'm telling you again," he screamed, startling Chief Sullivan out of his chair. "Chief, can you believe what this guy is saying? That despite all my years on the force, despite all my experience and training, he thought I was going to try and do something stupid. I can't believe he has so little respect for me."

Lieutenant Kelly stammered and tried to apologize. Louie wouldn't accept it. Instead, he stormed from the room, and for the first time in his career he felt nothing but disgust for the New York City Police Department. Sullivan caught him in the hallway and suggested he take some time off. But something told Louie that "it might be important to see the Pope on such a rotten day." But before rejoining his detail, Louie took a detour to the city morgue, fifteen blocks away.

"It was difficult, but I went over to the sheets they had spread over two bodies. I read the two toe tags. The first read 'James Eppolito, Jr.' When I pulled back the sheet, Jim-Jim's head was a mess. It was nothing I hadn't seen before in twelve years on The Job. But all that blood, and Jim-Jim's brain blasted away, it really upset me.

"Then I went to the old man. I don't know how I managed to pull his sheet away, but I did. Uncle Jim-

28

my's face was just absolutely destroyed. His jaw and bottom lip were totally gone, torn off, giving him this long, buck-toothed look.

"And he had tattoos—the gunpowder marks that are left when you're shot at close range—all over what was left of his head. I cleaned him as best I could, combing his hair and washing the blood off his face. But water kept pouring out of his eyes, like he was crying. I asked the morgue attendant if there was something that could be done about that, and turned away. As I walked out I saw the morgue guy with a washcloth, wiping what was left of Uncle Jimmy's cheeks."

Louie Eppolito floated through the rest of his tour in a daze. When it was over, when the Pope had departed and his squad had reconvened back in their Brooklyn station house, he sank down onto a bench behind a pole, out of sight, drained. What should have been the best day of his life had turned into the worst. It was not destined to get any better.

"I saw this big cop walk into the room, a guy named Joe Strano. I had crossed paths with him a few times on the street. He was about six-seven and two hundred and seventy-five pounds, and he had a reputation as being a tough cop. But he always struck me as being a little too impressed with himself. He was one of those cops who was never in the right place at the right time, like his timing in life was always a bit off.

"Whenever Joe had run into me before he had always sucked up to me, complimenting me on my decorations and the like, telling me what a tough guy I was. This time he didn't see me slumped down behind that pole. He walked straight over to my boss, Sergeant Ponzi, and began flapping his gums.

" 'Hey, Ponzi,' he said, 'I heard that a couple of big shots got whacked last night, and guess who on your squad they belonged to? Yeah, they belong to your ace, number one, Mr. Muscles Eppolito. And they whacked 'em good, whacked their fuckin' brains out, both of them, splattered.'

"From my vantage point I could see Ponzi shaking his head, trying to signal Joe to keep his mouth shut. But this big asshole just went right on talking about me and my family. It was a big joke. 'So where's all Eppolito's medals now,' Strano finally asked Ponzi, and I walked out from behind the pole and answered him. 'They're still right here on my chest, Joe.'

"When he spotted me, his face reddened and he dropped his head. 'Lou, Jesus Christ, I'm sorry to hear about your uncle and cousin,' he stammered. 'And I'm sorry I got such a big mouth.' I answered, 'Yeah, Joe, I heard. I heard every word you said. But don't worry about it, because you're just a piece of shit not worth wasting my time on.'

"Then he shuffled around and apologized some more before I finally told him to get out of my sight. For one of the first times in my life, big 'Mr. Muscles Eppolito' resisted the urge to smash in someone's face.

"My father, my uncles, my cousins, they were many things. But two-faced and backstabbing they weren't. From that moment, I knew I could never truly be trusted by the Police Department. I had family members who were also Family members. Yet, at least the mob guys that I knew treated me with respect. Not because I was a cop, but because I was a man of honor. That was the legacy my old man had left me. Not books, not culture. Christ, he could barely read. But he had honor. And I had really been fooling myself about The Job.''

Louie Eppolito left his station house that night and drove directly to the beach, where he often collected his thoughts. As he walked along that Coney Island strip, Louie conversed with a dead man. Strangely, he missed his father more than ever now, missed their conversations, missed even, most surprisingly, Ralph Eppolito's incessant "lectures."

Deep down, he knew, Ralph Eppolito had been wrong. Not all cops could be bought for a song. Not all cops had the ethics of a pack of jackals. Yet, as he remembered his father's contempt for The Job, he began to feel his old man's bitterness.

He was unaware that there were some within the Police Department who viewed the death of Jimmy Eppolito and his son as an opportunity to start a dirty little war against Louie. For twelve years Detective Eppolito had charged through the Department making no effort to hide his disdain for the "three P's: perps, pussies, and the pencil-pushing prigs," who hated his guts because he played by his own set of rules.

Soon, he would be betrayed by these alleged allies, his career and his achievements trashed in the effort to nail a "dirty cop." All because, he would eventually come to realize, he had somehow, subconsciously, never rid himself of that skewed sense of honor passed down by Ralph Eppolito.

II

THE FAMILY

II

THE
FAMILY

4

Until Louie was ten years old he thought his father worked behind a bar. There was no way for a child of the fifties to know that it wasn't part of a bartender's job description to act like Sonny Corleone.

Louis, named in honor of his father's father, was one of the first baby boomers, born on July 22, 1948, in the section of Brooklyn today referred to as East Flatbush. To the locals, however, their neighborhood was Pigtown.

Children on Louie's block were reared among pigs, goats, and even a cow or two tethered to the back fence. Tess Eppolito would often return from wakes in neighbors' homes with hilarious descriptions of chickens running wild through the living rooms, and Louie and his sister Pauline would try to imagine their mom kicking Rhode Island Reds out of her way while paying her final respects.

The Eppolito household, a two-family clapboard building at 660 Midwood Street, was free of farm animals, although the backyard was certainly big enough to hold a sty or a coop. Tess's mother, Philamina Mandelino, owned the building and lived downstairs with Louie's Grandpa John. Ralph and Tess raised their children on the top floor, Philamina charging them twenty-five dollars a month in rent. One of Louie's first memories was watching from his bedroom window as the older kids from the neighborhood chased down runaway farm animals as they trampled the tomato and cabbage patches dotting the block.

Louie was a sickly child, "a skinny runt really," and in that sense he took after Ralph, who stood five-feet-six and weighed 150 pounds dripping wet. Tess was lucky if she topped the five-foot mark. But as the other kids on the block began to grow and fill out, Louie seemed to shrivel, and his parents were afraid he'd contracted polio.

Louie would constantly tell his mother that the bones in his knees hurt, and even after he learned to toddle he found that it hurt a great deal less to crawl across the floor if he needed to get anywhere.

Tess had been trained as a nurse, and by the time her only boy was four years old and weighed no more than thirty pounds, she and Ralph were deeply worried. Louie actually became weaker as he got older. By the time he was five years old, walking was a major accomplishment for him, even when he had the inclination. Nearly every night Louie would lie in bed and listen to his family debating his future in the kitchen. Finally, Philamina, who worked as an aide in nearby Kings County Hospital—where she sewed up cadavers for the morgue at fifty cents a body—convinced her daughter that Louie should be taken in and tested for polio.

"When the doctor took one look at my swollen joints and saw that I couldn't even stand up under my own power, I was diagnosed as having polio and ordered to the fifth floor, the polio ward. Our house was only up the block from Kings County, and on a warm summer night with the windows open we could hear the shrieks coming from that fifth floor. My mom wasn't real happy with the diagnosis."

In fact, to this day Louie recalls the subsequent events in that doctor's office with a vividness that makes him sweat.

"First, Tess began screaming, 'No, don't tell me my son has polio. My son does not have polio.' Then she picked me up, wrapped me in a towel, and ran from the hospital. Of course I was wondering what the hell polio was. But I knew whatever it was, it wasn't good. I looked up at my mother and started crying, 'Don't worry, Ma, I don't have polio.' Turns out I was right."

Two days later Tess Eppolito sought a second opinion, and Dr. Justin Rosenbush, the neighborhood GP, diagnosed rheumatic fever. "Dr. Rosenbush said I had a valve in my heart that was no good, and told my mom he could hear my heart murmur from across the waiting room." His prescription was six months in a wheelchair with absolutely no physical activity, followed by a vigorous regimen of exercise. "That sort of calmed my mother down."

Over the next six months Louie Eppolito was a pampered child. Tess's sisters, and there were nine of them in the neighborhood, spent hours playing with him, reading to him, feeding him, and massaging his legs. In addition, though, Louie had to have blood drawn every three days, which led to a fear of needles that would stay with him for the rest of his life.

When he wasn't being babied by his Aunt Rita, or Aunt Barbara, or Aunt Lucille, Louie would sit at his bedroom window watching the kids outside play ball. To make him happy (and to earn a quarter from

Ralph), they invented a game where they tried to throw the ball up to his second-floor window. If Louie caught it, they were out. If he dropped it, it was their point.

"But what I remember best about being in the wheelchair was my dad coming in every time I had to go to the bathroom. He would put his hands around my waist and lift me out of the chair and carry me to the toilet. When he positioned my feet on the rim of the bowl and put his head under my arm, he always held me on his right side. I thought at the time that it was because he could give me better aim holding my hose with his right hand. I figured he didn't want me pissing all over the walls. Years later I found out that he didn't have a left lung, and that the left side of his body was too weak to brace even a forty-pound child."

After he had been six months "in stir," Tess gave Louie a pair of sneakers, a set of roller skates, and orders to hit the street running. His left leg had withered, and was considerably smaller than his right, and at first the six-year-old had trouble standing, let alone walking. But as time went by he relearned to walk, and then run, and bit by bit began catching up to, and finally passing, the other children his age. "It was as if I had been granted a second chance on life, and I resolved to make the most of it. Frankly, I became an animal."

Louie and his sister Pauline turned Midwood Street into their own personal roller rink. He also made it part of his daily routine to walk up his two flights of stairs fifty times a day. Grandpa John hooked up ropes to the side of their house, like netting on the sides of tall ships, and Louie would spend hours dangling from the contraption. Finally, he reached a point where Dr. Rosenbush could barely hear the murmur in his heart.

As if it were needed, Louie also had an added incentive to get in shape. It was sitting right across from him at the dinner table. "All I had to do was look at my father . . . when I could get the chance."

5

I didn't see much of my dad as a little kid. He worked evenings and nights. He'd wake some time in the afternoon, and I remember watching him shave, shower, and carefully unfold his monogrammed white-on-white shirt, the kind with the collar tabs halfway down his chest. Then he'd don one of his silk suits, smooth the creases, shine his shoes, and come in to kiss us goodbye.

"But despite the outfits my father never could hide the fact that he was the original Mr. Potato Head. And whoever stuck him together must have been in a piss-poor mood. He was born with a bad lung, a bad heart, bad teeth. You name it on him and it was bad.

"He had pyorrhea, a gum disease, and all of his teeth were removed before he was twenty. And he didn't help himself by smoking four packs of Camels, no filter, every day from the time he was about nine years old. He'd get up in the morning and hack and spit huge black gobs of tar into the sink, then turn to me and say, 'Don't ever mooch cigarettes, Louie, you never know what somebody might put in them. You want a cigarette, you ask me.' Yeah, right, Dad. A cigarette was just what I wanted as I watched him turning our kitchen sink into some kind of sump heap.''

About a year after Louie climbed out of his wheelchair, Ralph Eppolito had his first massive heart attack. He was thirty-seven years old. To pay the bills, Tess was forced to go back to work. She took a job working the morning shift at the Jewish Hospital for Chronic Disease, three blocks from their house. She'd leave for work before sunrise and be back by midafternoon to make lunch for the family. Afterward she'd clean the house, care for her husband, prepare dinner, and quite often end up back in the hospital at night working a double shift.

''She was a tough old bird, my mom was, a liberated woman before the term came in vogue.''

It took Ralph Eppolito nearly a year to recuperate. It was during this period that Louie first began to get to know his father, who until then had been no more than a tenant in the house on Midwood Street.

''I honestly can't say I enjoyed the experience. In fact, for the early part of my life, I hated my old man. To say that Ralph Eppolito wasn't easily engaged in conversation, even with his own son, is to say that Tony Bennett can croon a torch song or two. At the dinner table I'd be lucky to get two words out of him. But I guess he made up for that with smacks. I'd get smacked for looking the wrong way at my mother. I'd get smacked for using the wrong tone of voice with my sister. I'd get smacked for being thirty seconds late for dinner.

''And I'm not talking about love taps. My old man would whale the shit out of me at the drop of a hat, with his fists or whatever was handy nearby. You name a kitchen utensil, I'll guarantee it's been bounced off of my forehead. He just missed me once with a bottle of ketchup. And you don't know how evil a loaf of Italian bread can be until you've felt it slammed across your face.''

This violence often occurred under the guise of "lessons," and one of the first things Louie was taught by his father was the Neapolitan ethos of *honor* and *respect*. Ralph Eppolito was no "greaseball," the derogatory name American-born Italians gave to new immigrants from the other side. He had been born in the United States, on Manhattan's Lower East Side. But his father, Louis, was from Naples. Unlike his grandfather and father, Louie just couldn't comprehend, or care enough about, their concept of honor and respect.

"I mean, I was eight years old, I wanted to go out and play with my friends, or watch Davy Crockett on the old black-and-white Philco. Yet here was this madman constantly calling me in off the street to give me lectures on what he called 'the ways of our world.'

"I'd rather play stickball. Unfortunately for me, I was a stubborn kid and my father would think nothing of knocking the shit out of me if I didn't run in off the street quick enough when he decided it was time for one of his man-to-man lectures.

" 'Shut the TV,' he'd say, 'I've got something to tell you.' Then he'd sit down and begin. 'Louie, you know why it's better to have a good name than to have lots of money? Because the name is all you got when you're born, and it's all you got when you die. What you choose to become in between makes that name what it is. When your grandfather came over from the old country they misspelled his name at the docks, changing the "I" to an "E." So he took the new name "Eppolito" in honor of his new country. The most important thing to remember is that when it's time for you to die, your name has acquired respect and honor.' ''

These father-son talks—often ending in physical assaults—became a daily sentence for Louie. Once, when he was a teenager, he decided to grab a quick shower before dinner after an afternoon of playing baseball. While he was in the bathroom, Ralph ordered Pauline to fetch him to the table.

"Louie," she yelled.

"What?" he answered.

"Louie," she said again, and again her brother hollered back.

Ralph Eppolito had heard enough. Yelling was no way to treat a lady. As Louie lathered himself up, the shower curtain suddenly parted.

"The first thing I saw was a two-by-four screaming toward my head. I instinctively threw up my arm and it caught me right on my elbow. I thought for sure it was broken."

"What the hell's going on?" Louie screamed. "I didn't do nothin'."

Ralph Eppolito didn't say a word. Instead, he wound up and slammed the board into his son's stomach. As Louie doubled over, Ralph screamed back, "Is that how you talk to your sister? Let me tell you something. When you yell for someone in this house, their name had better be Spot, or Rex, because no one else in this house gets called like a dog. And if you ever, ever talk to her again like that I'll kill you."

Louie was dumbfounded, and gasping for breath. His father didn't seem to notice.

"What would you do if someone yelled at your sister in the street and you were there?" Ralph demanded of his son.

"I don't know," Louie replied. "I'd probably break his head."

"Exactly," said Ralph, flashing a look of triumph. "That's what I just tried to do to you. That *respect* starts in this house. You *respect* this house and you *respect* your sister. That window is open, isn't it? You want the people downstairs to hear you talk like that? You want them to think Ralph Eppolito's son has no respect?"

But not all of Ralph's lessons ended in abuse. Early on, for instance, there was the "handshake lesson": always shake the hand of any adult male entering the Eppolito household.

"It was amazing, but anyone who walked through our front door, be they stone-cold killers or priests (and there weren't many priests), would be greeted by this six-year-old kid standing at rigid attention and extending his hand. My old man loved it, and it never failed to elicit the same response from his friends: 'Jesus Christ, Ralph, your kid's what, only six? And yet he gets up and walks over and shakes your hand!' My father would beam and say, 'Yeah, Louie's got a lot of respect.' "

All Louie understood of this ritual was that it spared him the ubiquitous smack. And even then, he felt he was being struck more than was necessary. Tess always met his questioning looks with the same refrain: "Louie, your father loves you very much. It will all work out for you." Louie still had his doubts.

There were many rules in the Eppolito house, and they were hard to keep track of. For instance, during meals no one could eat a morsel of food until Ralph had taken the first bite. If Ralph wasn't at the table, if he was talking on the phone or having a conversation with the guy down the block, nobody ate. But if the

Eppolito offspring weren't seated at the dinner table at precisely six o'clock with the rest of the family, they had it coming. Since Pauline was always on time, that left Louie punched out before many meals.

"Once, I must have been eight or nine, I was out in the street playing Scully, a game like hopscotch, except you use bottle caps. I was called for dinner, and no more than two minutes could have elapsed before I got to the table.

"That was two minutes too long. My father beat the balls off me. 'How long do I have to wait for you to come when I call you,' he screamed. Then he'd look in my eyes and I'd throw my hands up around my head and he'd give me a liver shot like you wouldn't believe. It got to the point where I refused to cry. It still hurt like hell. But I refused to show it. Boys don't cry."

Louie's friends would run in from the playground for dinner at 5:30 P.M. and be back fifteen minutes later after a tuna-fish sandwich or a hot dog. Not Louie. A dinner table without piles of pasta, thick cuts of red meat, and a pungent jug of Italian red wine is absolutely foreign to a mafioso. And Ralph Eppolito was mafioso to the core.

"Every single night our dinner table was done and done right, which meant according to my father's specifications. There would be soup, then salad, then a pasta, and then the main course, roast beef, veal, chicken, always a meat. It never varied."

After dinner, Tess and Pauline would clear away the dishes, Ralph would sip his strong Italian coffee, and the family would sit around the kitchen table and relate the events of the day. All, that is, except Ralph, who nonetheless insisted on what he called the Eppolitos' "family time." This was particularly annoying to a boy with friends on the street playing stoopball or Johnny-on-the-pony or ring-a-levio.

Of course, Pauline, the apple of her father's eye, was not subject to such strictures. Ralph doted on his daughter's every move, even to the point of wrapping his best handkerchiefs around his Thumbalina's tiny hand before she went out to draw hopscotch squares in the street. "This," recalls Louie, "from the same guy who would smack me silly for coming to the dinner table with dirty hands. Go figure."

6

One day, when Louie was eight years old, his father walked into his room and asked him if he knew anything about fighting. When Louie replied that he was as tough as any kid on the block, Ralph asked his son for a demonstration.

"Stupid me. I went into my best John L. Sullivan stance, and he reached around my tiny hands and punched me right in the jaw. He didn't pull the punch, either. 'Now listen to me,' he said after helping me up. 'Put your left hand high, up by the bridge of your nose. Okay, now put your right hand a little lower, down by your chin, almost over your throat. Now lower your chin, tighten your muscles and swing your hips to the left a little.' "

So it was that Louie learned the rudiments of the hook and jab. Unfortunately, he soon grew bored—and made the mistake of telling his father so. Ralph erupted.

"What I'm teaching you here is self-preservation, how to live on the street," he bellowed. "And if you think it's more important to go watch cartoons, well, then, go right ahead." Ralph punctuated his outburst with a right-hand sock. Louie's nose began bleeding and his eyes were tearing, but when he looked up at his father, Ralph showed little sympathy. "When you want to learn to fight you come and talk to your father," he said. "When you want to be a pussy you go and watch cartoons."

That evening, Louie listened from his bedroom as his mother and father argued into the night.

"What are you doing, Ralph, the kid's eight years old," Tess screamed at her husband.

"I don't give a shit," Ralph yelled back. "He was jerking me off, and an eight-year-old does not jerk me off. When I talk to Louie, he listens, that's all there is to it, Tessie. He stops what he's doing, he stops who he's doing it with, and he listens to me. That's respect. And it will be that way for as long as he lives under this roof. When I'm not here, Tessie, he's going to have to take this up by himself. He's going to have to remember everything he knew from when he was a small boy and he's going to have to make that work for him until the day he dies. This is how I feel, this is my home, Louie is my son, and he'll listen to me."

Much later Louie realized he had learned something from these bouts.

"My father taught me that fear is an ever present human condition, that every person in the world carries some kind of it within him. He said, once you've learned to deal with fear, you'll have a different perspective on life, and that's how you'll grow as an individual. My dad taught me to control fear, not to be controlled by it.

"He told me that he didn't care if you were the president of Harvard University. He said you could take somebody with all the doctorate degrees in the world, put them in the middle of Bed-Stuy, and watch them wilt, wither, and decay. They'd jump at the sight of their own shadows unless they learned the laws of the street. And my dad was determined to teach me those laws of the street.''

When Louie was nine years old he walked in from school with an ugly bruise on the back of his neck. Unable to avoid the subject, he sheepishly explained to his father that there was an older boy in school, a sixth-grader, who would knock the books out of his hand and pull his hair when he bent down to pick them up.

Ralph asked his son what happened after that, and Louie admitted that he did nothing. He was, he said, afraid of the bully. Ralph asked Tess to leave the room and he sat Louie down at the kitchen table.

''When it comes to a fight,'' he told his son, ''you're always a little scared. And I never want to see you fighting some boy who's younger or smaller than you. But if anybody ever, ever bothers you and you're scared, that's the time when you have to dig down deep and get that adrenaline pumping in your stomach and not take any nonsense. Because if you do fight and lose, that's all you did: fought and lost. You only fight for one reason: to win. So if this kid tries to bully you, you fight to win. Hit him one good shot, bloody his nose, take out a few teeth. A hard shot to the nose will break it all the time. Then this bully will turn tail, he'll worry about how badly he's hurt. And I guarantee you one thing, Louie, no matter how big he is, he'll never bother you again.''

The following afternoon Louie was walking home from school when he was again attacked by the sixth-grader.

''As usual, my books go flying, and this time he tries to throw me into a tree. Without thinking, I grabbed him by the throat, let out a scream, and hit him a shot to the nose so hard I thought my hand was broken. I was so scared I almost wet my pants. The kid screamed, 'My nose. My nose,' and I hit him a second time. And then a third.

"As he covered up, I kept smacking him until I thought he was going to pass out. His blood was all over the place. I had my hand on his belt and was about to punch him again when I heard a loud scream from behind me: 'Louie, Louie.'

"I turned around and saw my father. He looked at me for a split second before yelling, 'Fuck him up, Louie. Break his fucking face.' I couldn't believe it. So I kept on pummeling the kid, trying to break his fucking face."

That night Louie's grammar-school principal called the Eppolitos to complain. Yes, the sixth-grader was a bully, she admitted. But Louie's beating went beyond the bounds of a normal schoolyard tussle. The principal even mentioned the threat of Juvenile Delinquent Court. As Louie recalls, his father's eyes darkened.

"I don't give a shit about a J.D. card," he yelled into the receiver. "My kid defended himself. You know that other kid's a bully. Don't you ever tell me what you're going to do to my son."

Ralph Eppolito, the son of Luigi the Nablidan, followed his outburst with a none-too-subtle warning: "If you got a problem, you come to me. Don't you ever threaten my kid." The principal never mentioned the fight again.

7

Louie still hated the lectures, the smacks, and the peculiar sense of respect his father demanded around the house. But without realizing it, he was becoming imbued with a code of ethics he would carry with him for life. Ralph Eppolito's methods may have been crude, but they achieved the desired results. And it wasn't long before Louie discovered that his father's talent for fighting was not limited to teaching nine-year-olds.

Several months after the schoolyard brawl, Louie, set to make his Confirmation, came home from religious instruction with the red imprint of a hand across his face. An adult hand. Ralph and Tess were outraged.

"So I explained to them that during Confirmation practice we had all been lined up alphabetically and herded into our pews. I had the outside seat in the third row. Some of the kids in the back were fooling around, making a lot of noise during the lesson, and Father Pulio, our instructor and one tough son of a bitch, had blown his top. 'Don't make me come down there,' Father Pulio warned the kids in the back. Then he asked them if they could all see up front. One kid answered, 'Yeah,' and with that Father Pulio swung his hand and smacked me right in the face. 'If I come back there I'm going to break some jaws,' the priest screamed.''

Louie didn't doubt the man. His face ached. Worse, he had done absolutely nothing to deserve the pain.

His explanation complete, Louie watched as his father silently donned his suit and tie, then took his son's hand and led him out to their car. At last he spoke: ''Before we hit the corner, Louie, I'll ask you one more time: Are you telling the truth? Did you do anything wrong?''

''No,'' Louie answered. Ralph didn't say another word for the remainder of the five-minute drive.

''We arrived at the rectory and my father rang the doorbell. Father Pulio answered. He was in his street-clothes, and you could see that the man reeked of toughness. 'Yes, what is it?' he asked, and my father identified himself and began his spiel. 'Father, Louie told me that earlier today in religious instruction . . .' Father Pulio cut him off.

''He told my dad that he was eating dinner, and running late for an appointment, and only had time for a short explanation. The priest said that what with the rowdy kids in the back and all, he hadn't realized the distance between where he was standing and where I was sitting. He said that what he meant to do was grab my chin, turn me around, and use my jaw as an example of the jaw he was going to break if the kids in the back didn't shut up. He admitted that I hadn't done anything wrong, that the entire incident had been an unfortunate mistake.

'' 'Okay, thank you, Father,' my dad said calmly. I never saw the punch coming. My father hit him. His jaw shattered. The teeth, everything, all over the side-walk. I had never seen anything like it, and I was petrified. Then he grabbed the priest by the collar, lifting him up, and started hitting him again.

" 'You're not fucking Jesus Christ,' my dad raged. 'You're nothing but a piece of shit priest. And if you ever, ever put your hands on my son again, I'll fucking kill you.' My father kept screaming and beating the priest. By this time they had tumbled back into the rectory and his oaths were echoing off the walls. The other priests came running. There was blood all over the place.

"The next thing I knew a couple of my uncles, my mother's brothers, were pulling my dad off Father Pulio. I guess my mother had an inkling of what was to come when we left the house, and she had run for help. Just before we turned to go, my father stood over the priest and issued a warning, 'Don't you ever play God with my kid again,' he said. 'If you do, I'll kill ya. I'll kill ya dead.' Then he turned to me and said, 'Come on. Let's go home.' "

During the drive back to Midwood Street, Ralph explained to his son the difference between killing someone—that is, beating them bad—and killing someone dead. Which is exactly what it sounds like. It was another Mafia lesson for Louie.

"I can't explain the mixture of terror and pride I felt over the Father Pulio incident. I mean, you don't even *use* the word 'shit' in front of a priest, and there was my father kicking it out of one. My father didn't say another word about the fight that night until just before I was sent off to bed. 'Louie,' he told me, 'if you're right, you stick to it, I don't care about the consequences. Just never embarrass me. Don't let me go anywhere and have someone say that what you told me isn't so.'

"My old man was the talk of Pigtown for several

months after that. And thereafter Father Pulio always seemed to give the Eppolitos a wide berth."

It was also around this time that Louie began to realize that his father's "job" involved something more than slinging drinks in a tavern. Ralph would often be gone for days, and Louie remembers many mornings sitting at the breakfast table and watching his father walk into the house wearing the wide-brim hat, the cashmere polo coat with those lapels to Secaucus, and carrying the newspaper under his arm. His "bartender" outfit.

"When I was younger, when my friends would tell me about their dads' jobs, how they worked during the day and stayed home at night, I wondered about my old man. But, hey, a bartender's a bartender, and I figured people drink at night. Plus, my dad wasn't exactly the type to pitch in with the kids' civics homework.

"But now I was old enough to begin noticing the strange middle-of-the-night phone calls. On nights when he wasn't 'working,' it wasn't unusual for the phone to jangle off the hook at all hours. These calls would as often as not result in my father hurriedly dressing and disappearing out the door, sometimes for days at a time.

"Then there was the assortment of his fancy-pants friends and relatives dropping by. My uncles Jimmy and Freddy, my dad's brothers, were constant visitors. Pauline and I called them the Three Musketeers.

"Plus, there were men I didn't know, men with gold watches and sparkling pinkie rings who were constantly dropping over to give my father envelopes and satchels. Once, when I was in the fifth grade, Johnny 'Bath Beach' Oddo—I knew him then as 'Uncle Johnny'—walked into the house with a suitcase. He snapped it open and there were stacks and stacks of money, all small bills. 'Louie,' Bath Beach said, 'they tell me you're good at arithmetic. There's a hundred and fifty-two thousand dollars here. Why don't you count it and make sure they didn't shortchange me.'

"It was a big joke, of course. Bath Beach was just showing off for Ralph Eppolito's kid. I learned soon enough that nobody shortchanged Johnny Bath Beach."

In fact, Louie was a quick learner, a quality necessary for survival on the mean streets of Brooklyn. By the age of eleven he was working as a delivery boy for a neighborhood pizza parlor, where a local group of teenagers, the Pigtown Boys, used his pie boxes as cover for their arsenal of zip guns and switchblades in rumbles with the Church Avenue Tigers or the black Jolly Stompers from Bedford-Stuyvesant.

Gambino, Genovese, Profaci, Bonnano; these were the DiMaggios and Nagurskis of Louie's neighborhood, the names that inspired awe. Louie couldn't help but notice that his father and uncles ran with a crowd that was close to these icons.

Invariably, Louie received a rote reply when he pressed his dad about the nature of his job, or the parade of oddly named visitors streaming through the Eppolito household. "I do what I have to do to provide for my family," Ralph would tell his son, and his stare would make it plain that the discussion was over.

Yet, as Louie approached his twelfth birthday, his father realized that his son's inquisitiveness could not be stifled much longer. Ralph, too, had grown up on the streets.

"I got the impression that he'd rather have me find out from him what he did, than hear any bullshit in the neighborhood. There was a kid on the block named

Michael Walsh, and he once told me that my father had saved his father from a beating. It seemed Michael Walsh's old man was behind in his payments to a shylock, and a call from Ralph Eppolito had bought him more time."

The parts of the puzzle were beginning to fall into place. Ralph's constant references to honor. The neighborhood cronies—from Joey the cabbie to Bruno the baker—stopping by the Eppolito home, "just to pay their respects." Louie wasn't shocked when he began figuring it out. It was just something his father did for a living.

Finally, on an afternoon midway through his twelfth year, Ralph announced that he was taking Louie to The Grand Mark, the bar where he "worked." It was on the corner of Grand Avenue and St. Marks Place, in the Bedford-Stuyvesant section of Brooklyn.

The Grand Mark was at the center of an Italian enclave holding out in what was rapidly becoming a black ghetto. Ralph's brother Freddy owned a piece of the joint. Over the next several years, despite the fact that his father was definitely not the bartender, Louie became quite familiar with The Grand Mark, and the "goombahs" who frequented it.

In fact, a street kid from Brooklyn, especially one who had no idea that he was destined to become a cop, couldn't have asked for a better introduction into the closed society of La Cosa Nostra.

III

THE CODE

8

Italians did not invent organized crime. They did not even introduce it to this country. Prior to the great wave of Italian immigration, Jewish and Irish gangs had wrapped a tight fist around America's most profitable illegal schemes, soon to be lumped under the catchall term, "racketeering"—extortion, gambling, loansharking, and prostitution. And the most coveted racket of all, politics, lay firmly in the grip of the WASP.

But what some southern Italians—predominantly Sicilians, Neapolitans, and Calabrians—*did* bring to cities like New York, Providence, Newark, and, later, Chicago, was an unsurpassed organizational proficiency and contempt for the law.

Like the young Italians of an earlier generation who had shipped out to Abyssinia or Argentina to build a better life, the newcomers tended to gather and organize in narrowly defined pockets of these American cities.

One of those urban pockets was a section of Manhattan's Greenwich Village soon to be famous as New York's Little Italy. And one of those who gathered there was Luigi Ippolito, the youngest son of impoverished Neapolitan farmers.

A tramp steamer carrying Ippolito sailed into New York Harbor in 1901. An Irish immigration officer proceeded to anglicize, as well as misspell, Ippolito's name on the Ellis Island entrance rolls. Acceding, or so he thought, to the rules and regulations of his new home, the illiterate fourteen-year-old thus entered the United States as Louis Eppolito.

Like thousands of European children, Louis had been sent to America to live with relatives. He took his first job as a janitor in a Lower East Side shirt factory, at a salary of two dollars a week. Once, after asking for a raise, he was told to find a ladder if he desired to raise his sights. The insult convinced Louis that his future was not in sweeping up linen remnants.

Louis, who was dexterous and mechanically inclined, next apprenticed under an uncle who owned a jewelry store on Manhattan's Mulberry Street. He was soon recognized as one of the neighborhood's more gifted craftsmen. By 1915 he had opened a thriving jewelry shop of his own on Canal Street, attracting a diverse, if not dangerous, clientele.

Louis found that he could supplement his legal income by fencing extorted or stolen jewelry for various Italian gangs who preyed upon their frightened fellow immigrants. These pre–Cosa Nostra rings were known collectively as the organization of the Black Hand, because of the symbol they drew on their threatening extortion letters. Gang members were dubbed "Mustache Petes"* by an observant editorial writer with a flair for the dramatic.

As a result of his criminal connections, Louis Ep-

---

* Future generations of the Cosa Nostra so despised this appellation that mustaches were banned within the organization.

polito was also drawing attention from other quarters. One former New York City Organized Crime investigator who spent forty years infiltrating the Mafia (and is still understandably reluctant to see his name in print) remembered the jeweler well.

"Diamond Louie they used to call him," he recalled. "Charley 'Lucky' Luciano set him up in the jewelry business because he was enamored of his work. Louie was a real money-maker for Luciano. He ran a crew that used to rob the gold from the Hasidim up in Manhattan's old jewelry district on Seventeenth Street. The Jews would pay off the customs agents to look the other way when they smuggled gold over from Europe in their hair and beards. Once they got into town, Diamond Louie's crew would knock them over.

"Then they'd melt down the gold to make watches. I remember Diamond Louie was famous for his watches. All the big wiseguys—Luciano, Vito Genovese, Carlo Gambino—they all used to give an Eppolito watch as a gift. It was kind of a status thing. Everybody wanted an Eppolito watch. He did a nice little business at Christmastime, which is when the bosses handed out expensive gifts like they were candy canes. Loyalty gifts, we called them.

"After the Castellammarese Wars,* when Charley

---

* The Castellammarese Wars, the Mafia's civil war of the early 1930s, was fought between feudal mob contingents loyal to either Giuseppe "Joe the Boss" Masseria or Salvatore Maranzano (whose contingent of thugs hailed from in and around the Sicilian town of Castellammare del Golfo, giving the conflict its name). Maranzano won, declared himself Boss of Bosses, and set up the Five Family Mafia structure in New York City that exists to this day. The Mangano Crime Family eventually evolved into the Gambino Crime

Lucky codified the Cosa Nostra and set up the Mafia Commission, Diamond Louie hooked up with Gambino's crew, working under the Family headed by the Mangano brothers, Vincent and Phillip. The Mad Hatter, Albert Anastasia, was one of the Manganos' lieutenants, and he was tight with Don Carlo. Eppolito branched out with Gambino, into rackets, bookmaking, the numbers. And though they never got him for it, word had it he remained one of Charley Lucky's premier pimps until they nailed the big guy.* Eventually, he brought his kids into the rackets. But he always kept the jewelry operation going on the side."

Louis Eppolito had along the way married a New York girl named Pauline Malardi, who bore him seven children. Of his four boys, Ralph, Jimmy, and Freddy showed a natural inclination toward the family business. Only the eldest, Joe, walked away from the underworld of organized crime. Like his brothers, Louis's second son, Ralph, dropped out of grammar school early, and began doing odd jobs for his father. Those errands included delivering watches to the likes of Luciano, Gambino, Genovese, and Joe Profaci, boss of what would later become the Colombo Family.

The prewar period was a heady time for young racketeers on the make in New York City. Mario Puzo had yet to introduce Don Corleone into the public consciousness. Joe Valachi had yet to spill his guts. And

---

Family. Maranzano's victory was shortlived, however. He was eliminated on the orders of Charley Luciano, the Thomas Jefferson of the modern Mafia, who abolished the title Boss of Bosses and further codified the faction-ridden Cosa Nostra.

* In 1936, Lucky Luciano was convicted of compulsory prostitution and sentenced to thirty to fifty years in prison. In 1945 he was paroled and deported to Italy, where he died in 1962.

even to local and federal investigators, La Cosa Nostra—loosely translated as "Our Thing" or "This thing of ours"—was a relatively unknown phenomenon outside its own small circle of members.

The three Eppolito boys quickly became favorites of their father's notorious clients. And it was not long before the enterprising Eppolitos were offered jobs of their own within the Gambino organization. The handsome Freddy combined his ambition with a flair for the ostentatious. "His women always wear mink," reads one law-enforcement profile, which may indicate why Freddy gravitated naturally toward the mob's nascent foothold on the entertainment industry. While Freddy soon owned a piece of Manhattan's Peppermint Lounge, Jimmy and Ralph were a more workmanlike duo, eager yet not too curious, adept at following orders.

Ralph, whose Roman nose and high forehead suggested a passing resemblance to George Raft, the film star who portrayed hot gangsters of the era, exhibited a special aptitude for figures. Thus, it was only natural that he should be taken into the Gambino policy operation. Ralph began his criminal career as a numbers runner in Lower Manhattan, but his routes soon expanded into Brooklyn.

There, in 1939, he met a waitress named Tess Mandelino. To Tess, Ralph Eppolito was, initially, just another knockaround guy, the escort who would take her dancing at one of the many supper clubs that honeycombed the borough.

9

TESS EPPOLITO: "When I married into the Eppolito clan I can honestly say I didn't know what the hell I was getting into. I was Italian, but I was fourth-generation Italian, as American as a Roosevelt or a Whitney. My mother's side, the Fenimores, were descended from the writer James Fenimore Cooper. And even though my paternal grandfather's people, the Mandelinos, had come from Italy, I didn't know a cannoli from a can of beans.

"Well, the first thing I notice about Ralph's people is this heavy emphasis on *honor* and *respect*. I mean, we were brought up to show respect to our elders, don't get me wrong. But not to the point where it was sickening. It was shocking to me in the beginning. I mean, my father walked into a room, it was 'Hi, Pa.' Nobody got up and kissed him.

"But with the Eppolitos, Christ, old man Louis would enter a room and stand there waiting for his kisses. Sons and daughters rose as one and formed a line. You'd think the Pope had just breezed in. Once, I asked my sister-in-law, Louise, 'What happens if you don't get up and kiss him?' A solemn look spread over her face. 'Very disrespectful,' she whispered. It was like a bad movie.

"When I told Ralph I thought this whole honor thing was a little silly—I mean, we'd go to a family gathering and it took a half an hour to say hello and a goddamn hour to say goodbye—he said I didn't understand because I wasn't brought up with respect. 'This kissing is respect?' I asked him. 'Half the time it's the goddamn kiss of death. You kiss these guys before you blow their brains out. Killing is respect?' He was steamed, but he didn't have an answer.

"At any rate, I didn't figure out this whole honor thing until much later on. I was seventeen when I met Ralph. He was an older man, going on twenty-six, and my parents weren't thrilled about me seeing a man eight years my senior. I used to love to go dancing, but Ralph couldn't dance a step. Yet he'd bring me to the clubs and watch as I danced with everyone else. We'd go to the Ansonia Ballroom and the Roseland in Manhattan, and there were two or three dance clubs alone along Brooklyn's Dekalb Avenue that we'd hit all the time.

"Before I met Ralph, all the girls would meet and head down to the cellar clubs in Brownsville. We danced with guys from Murder Incorporated. I remember Abie Reles* in particular. He could trip the

---

* Abe "Kid Twist" Reles was one of Murder Incorporated's most proficient practitioners. Known as the best "shiv man" in the business, he perfected the art of approaching a victim on the street with his knife folded into the *Daily News*. After accidentally "bumping" his target with the tabloid and shivving him through the heart, Reles would be around the corner before the unfortunate hit the sidewalk. He was arrested in 1940 and provided investigators with information that led to convictions in numerous previously unsolved gangland slayings. He died on November 12, 1941, following a mysterious plunge from the sixth floor of the Half Moon Hotel in Coney Island

light fantastic. But with these guys there was never a problem. We were young, we were carefree, and my group wouldn't have known a Mafia man from a matador. If the guy was dressed up, had a decent haircut, and sprung for a hot dog and a Coke afterward, we honestly weren't all that inquisitive. I danced with Sonny Francese* almost every Saturday night in Big Ralph's Cabaret, a supper club between Myrtle and Broadway, and I never had any idea what he did for a living.

"I was working part-time as a waitress in a pizzeria on Utica Avenue where Ralph used to come in and order a pie. He was usually with his brothers, and sometimes his father—they called him Luigi the Nablidan. I'd see one of the Eppolitos at least once or twice a week. One night we closed late, and Ralph offered to take me home. He was from Greenwich Village, and I was just a farm girl from Pigtown, but to be quite honest, at first I wasn't all that interested.

"I was a hellion, a gypsy, and he was so quiet. I thought of Ralph as the old reliable. He wasn't a big man, in fact he was small and wiry. And he was involved with the numbers when I met him, although I wasn't sure specifically what he did. He would mention names like Vito Genovese and Joe Profaci, but,

---

while under the protective custody of half a dozen police officers. "Abie tried to go out a six-story window with a six-foot sheet," was how Tess remembered the incident.

* John "Sonny" Francese rose from soldier in the then-named Profaci Organized Crime Family to head that organization in 1978. By that time the Family was named after one of Profaci's successors, Joe Colombo. Francese ruled the Colombo Family for two years before giving way to Carmine Persico in 1980, when Persico was released from jail.

to me, they might as well have been men in the moon. I never gave his job a second thought, except to notice that sometimes the money wasn't so steady. At that time there were certain things a girl just didn't ask about.

"We dated on and off for four years, one thing led to another, and eventually he proposed. He didn't sweep me off my feet or anything like that. But he was a good man, and with the war on, good men were getting scarce. We were married on October 23, 1943. The night we wed he took me to Ernie's Three Ring Circus, a club in the Village owned by one of his cousins. I think his brother Freddy may have had a piece of it, too. Vito Genovese was at the bar, and when he found out that we had just been married, he closed the bar and ordered champagne drinks for everybody. We had an all-night party.

"I had no idea who Vito Genovese was personally, but I certainly got the impression that he was some kind of important guy. Don't misunderstand me—I wasn't naive. But also don't forget, this was in the 1940s, when the Mafia wasn't as well-known as it is today. New York wasn't like Chicago, with Al Capone's gang driving down the street with machine guns blazing. There were murders and such, but they were more hush-hush.

"Later on, when Vito Genovese's name began appearing in the papers and I realized he was wanted for ordering murders and dealing drugs, for being a Mafia don, it was very hard to make the connection that this was the same man who threw us the party on my wedding night.

"After we were married, Ralph tried working a straight job, as a longshoreman. But he couldn't take the labor because of his bad lungs. See, he was a four-pack-a-day smoker. The whole family smoked heavy, the mother, the father, all the brothers. Ralph's mother died at forty-six, before I met him. She had complications from diabetes. The only other legit work he ever did after that was on and off, mostly off, as a bartender at a place my family owned in Pigtown, or sometimes over at his brother Freddy's Bed-Stuy place, The Grand Mark.

"As for my father-in-law, I knew him as a jeweler, always with the watches. He didn't display anything, but if some mob big's daughter was getting married, he'd say, 'Send the bride down to such and such an address.' By this time he had closed his shop in the Village, remarried, and moved to Brooklyn. He was operating out of his home. But he still had connections. Watches in one place, rings in another, bracelets in yet another. He'd get you a good deal. He knew stones, and he knew jewelry. Even my sisters went to him for their rings. He had a nice business going until the day he died.

"My father-in-law adored his grandchildren, although I must admit that Louie got on his nerves a little bit as a boy. Every time Grandpa Louis gave Louie a watch it would be broken within the week. One day he took a broken watch and threw it out the window and told Louie, 'No more watches. All you do is break them.'

"It dawned on me early in my marriage that my father-in-law was somehow involved with the rackets, most probably the numbers, and that his kids were looking to inherit the family trade. Every Sunday Louis had to go pick something up, and my husband would always drive him. I knew that what they were doing wasn't kosher, because they treated it like some military secret. But I never understood the big mystery. Everybody played the numbers.

"Ralph never accounted to me for his whereabouts. And I never asked. There were times he didn't come home all night, and if he said anything at all by way of explanation it usually involved dice or cards. God knows where he was. But he always gave me his 'winnings,' and when he'd throw seven hundred dollars, eight hundred dollars down on the bed, who was I to argue? As time went on, I realized what business he was in. But by then it was too late. I had the kids, Pauline and Louie. What was I going to do, walk out?

"Ralph and his brother Jimmy were sedate, just like their father. Always immaculately dressed, always very presentable, never talked out of turn. People thought that Jimmy looked a little bit like Tyrone Power, but Freddy was the flashy one. He was handsome, taller than his brothers, about six-one, with jet-black hair and pale-blue Paul Newman eyes. Eyes to die for. More than a few did, I think, in both senses of the word. Freddy was a real lady-killer, with a devil-may-care, I-don't-give-a-shit attitude. It was always wine, women, and song with Freddy.

"Our household did not lead what you would call a normal life-style. There were the phone calls in the middle of the night, for one thing. Then the word would be passed: 'Somebody got hung in the Sahara Club,' and my living room would turn into Grand Central Station. My brothers-in-law would come over, the phone would be ringing off the hook, then the next day, sure enough, you'd pick up the paper and read about a murder in the Sahara Club. It still boggles my mind.

"In my house, when the phone started ringing at two or three in the morning, I could almost guarantee you that somebody had been dropped. When my husband would get up and get dressed in the middle of the night and go out with his gun, I knew there was real trouble.

"Freddy was getting bigger in the Mafia, and he was dragging Jimmy and Ralph along with him. They started a shylocking business to go along with their numbers operation. And they all did a little bookmaking on the side. But Freddy was always the point man. Neither Ralph nor Jimmy were the type of men to cabaret at night, to run with the uptown crowd. Freddy was the big wheel.

"It really began after the war, when Freddy and Jimmy returned from the service. The Army had rejected Ralph because of his lungs. The older brother, Joey, was never involved in any of this stuff. Nobody ever talked about him. It was like he was a black sheep because he'd gotten an honest job as a longshoreman. When Freddy returned from overseas, he said he was working as a bartender. But you had to figure that with the women, and the flashy clothes, and the fancy cars, he wasn't working for tips serving Seven and Sevens.

"Freddy got the big car first, he got the big house first, he was always the first in the family to get the goodies. And he was involved in an awful lot of trouble. If there was a murder, they'd pick Freddy up, then they'd pick Jimmy up, and Ralph would be the last man on the totem pole.

"Freddy got in trouble a couple of times. He'd go out and be missing for a week. Maybe he was shacked up. Maybe he killed somebody. Who knew? Then he was caught that time at that big upstate meeting, in

Apalachin.* God, did the phone calls start after that. Jimmy had to go up and get him. 'What the hell is he doing up there?' I asked my husband. 'There's all gangsters up there.' Ralph's answer: 'Well, Tessie, you know Freddy, he goes all over.' You had to be really stupid not to know what these brothers were into, but Ralph would never admit it.

"One night there was a family meeting at our house —it was like these guys had radar—and the next day I read that some mug took five bullets in the Joy Lounge over in Flatbush. Freddy disappeared for six or eight months after that. Ralph said he was 'on vacation.' Three weeks after he returned, the phone rang again, and again Freddy couldn't be found. There was always a 'dropout' when somebody got killed. And it was always Freddy doing the dropping out. I'd hear Ralph on the phone saying, 'That crazy bastard is at it again.' And the next day, sure enough, there'd be a story in the papers about a murder.

"Except for when they killed Johnny Roberts,† then

---

* In November of 1957, near the bucolic upstate New York hamlet of Apalachin, an unprecedented nationwide convocation of the Cosa Nostra leadership was called. Its agenda, in part, was to confirm Carlo Gambino's ascension to the throne of the Family previously headed by the late Albert Anastasia, who had succeeded the Mangano brothers. Three weeks earlier, Anastasia had been the victim of a hostile corporate takeover, engineered by Gambino and Vito Genovese and carried out in the barbershop of New York City's Park Sheraton Hotel. The number of delegates, henchmen, and drivers arrested during a police raid of the meeting totaled sixty. Among them was Alfred Eppolito.

† John "Johnny Roberts" Robilotto, a flashy restaurateur with nightclubs in both Brooklyn and Manhattan, was a made man in the Gambino Organized Crime Family. He was shot to death on September 7, 1958, after being lured out of Sam Shell's, a Canarsie

it was Jimmy who had to drop out. Ralph never told me in so many words, but it was Jimmy and Ralph who did Johnny Roberts. I think Ralph went along just to make sure his kid brother would be safe. And that's what got him his button. You might even say Ralph became a made man by accident, looking out for his little brother. They said Johnny Roberts was a rat, and if there was anything Ralph couldn't stand, it was a rat. They were all that way. I guess to them, that made murder okay.

"The cops eventually picked up Jimmy for the Johnny Roberts killing. The story went that Jimmy and Johnny Roberts were having a drink in one of Johnny's clubs, when Jimmy invited him for a ride. They left the club together, and five minutes later Jimmy came running back in, shouting that someone had shot Johnny Roberts. No one ever knew who shot him.

"My most vivid memory of Johnny Roberts is of him walking through the Italian feast, handing out dollars to the kids flocking around him. It was hard to believe that someone put five in his head. It was even harder to believe that my Ralph had been part of it.

"After the killing the newspapers ran a picture of Jimmy, called him 'the Sleeper' because he snored through his entire arraignment.

"But to his friends Jimmy was known as 'the Clam.'

---

nightclub and notorious Mafia hangout. Joe Valachi told author Peter Maas in 1968 that Robilotto had been killed because, as an Anastasia loyalist, he was plotting a counter-coup against Gambino. That may have been true, but subsequent intelligence sources have confirmed that Robilotto was also supplying information to federal agents. His assassins were never found, and the Robilotto murder remains an open file in the New York City Police Department.

Christ, they all had to have nicknames. There was 'the Blood,' and 'the Bug,' and more goddamn 'Sheiks' than you'd find in a harem. Every guy who knew how to comb his hair and brush his teeth was a 'Sheik.' Every neighborhood had a 'Sheik,' sometimes two. I think Freddy may have been a 'Sheik.' Even Ralph had a nickname, though he never told me about it. I found out accidentally from one of his pals.

"Once, at a wedding, some crum-bum from Greenwich Village came up to me and asked about 'Fat the Gangster.' I asked him what the hell he was talking about, and he said, 'Well, aren't you married to Ralph Eppolito?' When I nodded yes, he exclaimed, 'That's Fat the Gangster.' I almost doubled over laughing. Imagine me, Mrs. Fat the Gangster. Ralph must have picked up the name before he lost all his teeth, which I guess cut down on his appetite.

"Except for the pyorrhea, Ralph was a fairly healthy man when I met him. It wasn't until about five years after we were married that his health really began going downhill. The lungs went first. He had such trouble breathing that he couldn't lie down at night, and he took to sleeping in a chair, choking until dawn. Finally, while I was pregnant with Pauline, he had the left lung removed. They wouldn't let him smoke in the hospital, so five days after the operation he walked home in the snow just so he could have a cigarette.

"Then there was the heart attack, when Louie was recovering from the rheumatic fever. That was followed by more lung problems, but they couldn't do surgery because of his heart condition. And, of course, the man refused to stop smoking. Oh, he was a terribly stubborn bastard. I said to him once, 'Do me a favor and just drop dead now and stop putting me through this anxiety.' But each time he got sick, it wasn't more than a few weeks before he was back to work with his brothers.

"I guess they picked Jimmy up for a couple of murders, but they could never pin anything on him. You'd read about one of these killings, and it would just make you feel unreal. I never knew Ralph to kill anybody personally, to actually pull the trigger. But he may, like in the Johnny Roberts thing, have been along for the ride. Word would get around of a murder, and I'd say to myself, 'It couldn't be my Ralph involved. He was here all afternoon. And so was his brother Jimmy.' But then you'd realize that these guys were night crawlers, and who knows what was going on while the kids and I were asleep. I sure as hell didn't want to know.

"I'm telling you, I met some of the supposedly meanest, cruelest guys, men who would end up doing life in prison, but to us they were always nice people. Take Joe Profaci. He was a real gentleman. He'd stop over the house, always polite, respectable. Maybe he'd bring a little present for the kids. He'd have his black coffee, talk to Ralph in the kitchen, and then leave. Carlo Gambino used to like to dip his goddamn Graham crackers in milk, for chrissake.

"I can't say it didn't bother me that my husband might be involved in some of these killings. I mean, the guy who got killed might have a wife, a couple of kids. Okay, I know the code: 'Nobody never gets killed for no reason.' But nobody has a right to take a life. I'd mention that to Ralph. He'd just shrug me off, or say it was a 'matter of honor.'

"But all this big talk about respect and honor just boiled down to one thing. Easy money. These guys were always on the lookout for the quick scam, and if you threw five dollars on the sidewalk you could watch that honor go south real quick. I knew some of these big, macho Mafia guys who would drive to the factories in Secaucus, New Jersey, or to Orchard Street on the Lower East Side, and fill up the trunk of their cars with wholesale shirts, belts, scarves, whatever.

"Then they'd come back to Flatbush with this load of shit, spread the word that it's hot stuff, swag, and the neighborhood would go crazy for it. Maybe they'd make a buck or two on each item. This is the big Cosa Nostra Code of Honor? Give me a break. I'd call them glorified peddlers. And half the take would eventually wind up as kickbacks to the cops.

"The cops were crumbs, and that's why Ralph detested them so. I don't know who he hated more, cops or rats. Cops were always looking for a payoff, yet their take was so minute it was laughable. I mean, if they caught one of Ralph's numbers runners, two dollars was all it took to make them look the other way."

Tess Mandelino did not need Ralph Eppolito to educate her about the ethics of New York City's "Finest." The horrors of the trenches at Verdun had driven her father into an alcoholic stupor, and she had often watched her mother slip five dollars to an arresting officer to spare John Mandelino a night in the drunk tank.

And once, when she was in her mid-twenties, her younger brother, Mike, was arrested in Flatbush on charges of possession of stolen property. Moments after the arrest, Tess opened her door to a uniformed police officer approaching the front stoop. "Look," the cop said, "tell your mother that if she buys the captain a hat, we won't press charges against your brother.''

Tess dutifully informed her mother of the proposed trade-off, and her mother sent Tess to the corner bar to hand an envelope containing twenty-five dollars to a waiting detective. That night the bar owner called and informed the Mandelinos that the detective had returned. The captain, he said, wears a more expensive hat. "Now they're getting shifty," Tess's mother replied. "Tell them to forget it. They can lock him up.''

Years later, another detective, investigating the Robilotto killing, appeared at the Eppolito home with a search warrant. He was looking for the murder weapon. Eyeing the sixteen-inch television in Ralph's living room, he casually remarked that his children would be delighted if they, too, could afford to watch cartoons. For the price of a new TV set, the cop intimated, he just might forget to search the house. Tess exploded.

"I'm going to save you the trouble, Officer," she told the detective. Then she emptied out every drawer in the Eppolito household. She even woke Louie and Pauline and pulled their mattresses up off their beds. "How dare you make an offer to my husband not to search this house for the price of a goddamn television," she screamed. "I'll search the goddamn house for you. We have nothing to hide.''

Even to Ralph Eppolito, who despised the police, this was an embarrassment. He sheepishly informed the detective that his wife was "a nut.''

Despite periodic "housecleanings," the New York City Police Department, particularly the South Brooklyn Division, remained a veritable sewer of police pads and payoffs until well into the 1970s. Taxpayers and mobsters alike could buy their way out of nearly any predicament, from parking tickets to racketeering. It was not unusual, for instance, for truck hijackers caught in the act to offer half of their swag to intruding investigators who happened to stumble across their stickup. Ralph Eppolito avoided jail several times in this manner.

And for all of the hype surrounding such gangbusters as Chicago's Eliot Ness and New York's Thomas E. Dewey, the government had discovered that the surest way to put a crimp in the Mafia's style was to hit them in their accounting ledgers. It worked with Al Capone, who beat several murder raps but went to jail on an income-tax-evasion count. And it would continue to work against others. Even the foot soldiers.

Ten years into the Eppolitos' marriage, while Pauline and Louie were still small children, federal agents began snooping around the house.

"Ralph had no legitimate job," Tess explained. "And they'd come in—one day it was the IRS, the next it was the FBI—asking all these questions: 'Who paid the rent? Who bought the food? Who made the payments on the car?' But I had a job as a private-duty nurse, with the pay stubs to prove it, so I'd throw it right back in their faces. Ralph was always telling me not to talk to them, to throw the bums out of the house, but I had nothing to hide."

As her children began to grow, Tess felt trapped by her role as a Mafia wife. Five years into their marriage she had threatened Ralph with divorce over "this nonsense, your stupid job and these stupid telephone calls in the middle of the night." But she lacked the resolve to follow through.

* * *

TESS EPPOLITO: "My major concern was raising my kids in this kind of atmosphere. After a while, it became embarrassing to read your name in the paper every time you went to the corner market. It was Eppolito this and Eppolito that. Freddy, Jimmy, Ralph, whoever, one of them was always getting locked up, although the most they ever got Ralph for was bookmaking. I wondered what kind of an effect it would have on the little ones when they were old enough to understand.

"Plus, there was the general annoyance of a working stiff—namely, me—trying to make an honest buck while being part of a family that was getting a reputation as the second coming of the James gang.

"I was embarrassed for my kids, too, and not just because of the mob stuff. The Eppolitos were known throughout the neighborhood as wild men, although I must admit that I think my son Louie loved that. There was that incident with that priest, for example. Father Pulio was his name. Christ, I could have died. But by that time I was used to Ralph's moods.

"Once, just after Pauline was born, I was out in the neighborhood walking her in the baby carriage. One of the neighborhood drunks accosted me, an older guy named Sal D'Antoni, who had bothered me since I was a kid. He came up to me and said the nastiest thing a man could say. He said that since the baby had been born I was looking pretty good again, and maybe it was about time I got laid. He said he was willing to do the job.

"I saw black. I turned the baby carriage around, ran home, and woke Ralph up. It was about one in the afternoon. Well, after I hysterically blurted out Sal D'Antoni's insult, Ralph was so calm you'd think he was going to church. 'Don't get excited, Tessie,' he said. 'I'll take care of it.' Then he took his time showering and shaving. He even asked me to make him some breakfast.

"By now I'm boiling, both at Sal and at my husband, who doesn't appear all that interested in rushing out to defend my honor. I was insulted that he wasn't going crazy. Eventually he puts on his suit and tie and walks out the door without saying a word.

"Ralph found Sal D'Antoni stone drunk asleep, his head resting on the bar of my aunt's joint down the street. He walked into the bar, picked Sal's head up, and hit him in the face so hard he knocked him across the room. Sal was out cold. Just as Ralph hit Sal, another neighborhood guy, Louie LaBaun, entered the bar. Louie made the mistake of asking Ralph what the hell he was doing beating up a drunk. So Ralph hauled off and smashed LaBaun's face. Louie was tough, nobody in the neighborhood messed with Louie LaBaun, but when Ralph got lathered up into that rage of his—although it may have taken a while—there was no holding him back.

"Anyway, Louie LaBaun wore false teeth, and after Ralph's punch, his teeth went sailing out the door, into the hedges that surrounded the bar. Word flew around the neighborhood that Ralph Eppolito had knocked Louie LaBaun's teeth out of his mouth. Within twenty minutes there was a crowd at the bar, and it continued to grow as the afternoon wore on.

"Freddy gets the word. Jimmy gets the word. And that night there must have been fifty guys, all mafiosi, milling around the neighborhood looking for Sal D'Antoni and Louie LaBaun. 'My God, what have I done?' I thought, 'this is going to turn into a catastrophe.' Anyway, LaBaun made himself scarce, and someone hid out Sal D'Antoni until a sit-down could be called and tempers cooled down. It was explained to Sal that he had done a very bad thing, and that it wouldn't be tolerated again. It was also taken into consideration that he was a hopeless drunk. From that day on it was 'Why, hello there, Tess, are you having a nice day?' whenever I ran into Sal D'Antoni. Louie LaBaun wasn't given so much as an apology. I think he felt he was lucky to be alive.

"That episode taught me a lesson. Ralph Eppolito didn't handle slights and insults like ninety-nine percent of the world. He had to avenge his *honor*. And his brothers were no different, no matter the opposition.

"Freddy once had a beef over a girl with a neighborhood guy named Sonny "Scans" Scandiffia. Now all five Scandiffia brothers were about six-foot-five and three hundred pounds, and they took the jobs even the Polacks would sniff at. Loading cement trucks, hauling beef, anything that required sheer strength from gigantic people. Sonny had once thrown a punch at a guy, who held up one of those old-time wooden milk cartons to block it, and the punch had shattered the box.

"Freddy had terrible ulcers, and at the time of this insult—Sonny Scans threw a drink in his face—he had just gotten out of the hospital and had a drain attached to his belly.

"Freddy left the bar telling Sonny he couldn't fight him, because one punch in the stomach would kill him. Then he returned an hour later attempting to smooth things over. 'Let's go for coffee,' he said to Sonny Scans, and the two of them drove off in Freddy's car. On Troy Avenue, a dead-end street down by the Boys High athletic field, Freddy pulled over and said, 'Gee, Sonny, I think I got a flat and I'm not going to be able to change it myself.' When Sonny bent over the wheel, Freddy caved in the back of his skull with a lug wrench. Then he hit him again. And again. He just massacred the guy's face. Beat him to a bloody pulp.

"Freddy left Sonny Scans for dead. But like I said, none of the Scandiffia brothers went out that easily, and Sonny managed to crawl down the sidewalk. After a block of crawling he was right in front of our house. I hadn't any idea what had happened. All I knew was that Sonny Scans's brains were leaking out all over our front porch.

"Ralph was home, but he wanted nothing to do with this situation. 'Let the fucker bleed to death,' was his advice. Thank God he didn't know his brother was involved or he would have finished him off. So I called a neighbor to bring a car around, and together we got Sonny to Kings County Hospital.

"Sonny lived, and I ended up mediating the proposed war between the Scandiffias and Eppolitos. It was all settled when Ralph, Jimmy, and Freddy agreed to fork over fifteen hundred dollars for Sonny's plastic surgery. But I continued to be amazed at the mere fact that someone throwing a drink in someone else's face could constitute an insult that called for this kind of retaliation. After that there was a saying around the neighborhood: 'Be careful or you'll be asked to go for coffee with an Eppolito.' Some honor, huh?

"Now all this stuff might have been easier to take if we were living the life of Riley in a twelve-room mansion with servants and chauffeur. But we weren't. Sure, there were weeks when Ralph would saunter in with a score, maybe twenty-five hundred dollars or so, and that was damn good money in the 1950s. But there were also long stretches when we were living off my paycheck because too many numbers came in, or a loan went south, or the dice rolled the wrong way. People think being married to a Mafia guy is all hot cash and swag. It ain't always so. And I had kids to raise.

"From the time he recovered from his heart murmur, we knew Louie was going to be a smart kid. Personally, I think he would have made a terrific member of the Mafia. He was fearless, and he loved to fight. If his brain had been challenged in the other direction, he would have made his Uncle Freddy look like a Christian Brother.

"Even though I would never hit my children, I must admit that most of the time when Ralph would smack Louie, the kid deserved it. Let me tell you, he was no bargain to raise. I loved him dearly, but sometimes I'd just have to sit in the kitchen and shake my head when he'd purposely go out of his way to piss Ralph off. Louie would go into the refrigerator and break six eggs looking for just the right one to fry sunny-side up. 'I was looking for the perfect egg,' he would explain with this shit-eating grin on his face. Little things like that would agitate Ralph. Pauline you could put on a pedestal right now. The girl was a saint.

"But sometimes Ralph would hit Louie and it would make me furious. I wish I had a penny for every time I almost chopped his head off. But he'd just turn to me and say, 'Don't worry, Tessie, I know what I'm doing.' He wasn't a mean man, but he had what I thought was an odd way of showing his affection. Yet that kind of upbringing may have worked, for even as a child Louie always stood straight and tall, and never whimpered when Ralph would knock the crap out of him.

"From the day Louie learned to comprehend English, Ralph tried to impress upon him this need to have respect. It must have been something in the Eppolito genes. As a youngster, Louie was a defiant sort of kid, always getting in some kind of trouble, usually fights. He was fearless, and had this tendency to think he was the toughest guy in the world. He had this I-don't-take-shit-from-anybody attitude. And the irony was, I think his father molded that into him.

"But I know my husband never wanted Louie to follow him in his line of business. Christ, he cried like a baby when Louie graduated high school. And from the looks of things early on, Ralph got his wish. You see, Ralph was the fussiest dresser in the world. He wouldn't leave the house to go down to the corner for a newspaper without his white shirt, suit, and tie. It could be one hundred and fifty degrees out and Ralph would be buttoned up like Lord Astor. Now that I think of it, I'm surprised he wasn't a 'Sheik.' One to a family, I guess, since Freddy already had the nickname nailed down.

"Anyway, Louie was the sloppiest kid God ever put on earth. And that aggravated his father no end. He'd throw his jacket on the chair, and his shoes were always in the middle of the floor. Once, his Grandfather Louis even made him a shoeshine box. It was a hint, I think. But it never came out of his closet. So I figured, if they were so different in their attitude toward outward appearances, maybe there was hope for Louie.

"As Louie got older his father drilled the same lecture into him over and over. 'Respect everyone's rights,' he would say. 'No matter what color they are, no matter what religion they are. But be a man at all times, and stand up for *your* rights at all times. Don't take shit from no one.' Then one day, I guess Louie was about twelve, they walked out the door together. I was heartsick. Like every other father, Ralph was taking his kid to the office: The Grand Mark.''

10

The Grand Mark Tavern, on the northeastern corner of St. Marks Place and Grand Avenue in the heart of Brooklyn, was more like a social club than a gin mill. Sure, working men off the street were known to drop in for the occasional boilermaker, the odd longshoreman could be found waiting for a vodka pick-me-up at one of the faded and cracked red vinyl booths. And there would even sometimes appear a poolshooter from Za-Za's across the street, slugging back a Ballantine or Schaeffer. But, like most bars, The Grand Mark had its own subtle personality. And the aura that personality projected was: Members Only. Strangers were eyed with caution. The regulars had good reason to be wary.

For, adjacent to The Grand Mark, at 612 St. Marks Place, there was a nondescript whitewashed door that appeared to be a long-bolted entrance to an abandoned warehouse. Behind that door was an ill-lit staircase that led to a windowless second-story loft. It was here that the Eppolito brothers staged their dice games and all-night poker fests. It was also here that Louie Eppolito's Mafia education began in earnest.

After Louie's twelfth birthday, he began accompanying Ralph on his afternoon trips to this mysterious place. He set up crap tables. He swept out the butts and bottles. And he would often remain well into the evening, listening to the tales of the "Bugs" and the "Tongues" who populated his father's world.

"That's how my father would introduce them: 'Louie, meet a friend of mine, Frankie the Tongue.' Never a last name. I'd shake hands, and the Tongue would turn to my old man and say something like, 'Good-lookin' fuckin' kid you got there, Ralph. Shows a lot of fuckin' respect.' I'd be amazed that my father would let a guy get away with that kind of language in front of me. Not that my old man didn't swear like a drunken sailor himself. But that was different. It was his prerogative. Anybody else would have to watch his mouth in front of Ralph's kid, or any kid, for that matter. Except for the Tongue. Dad would just shrug it off when the Tongue swore. And, eventually, I got used to it. Especially when Dad began taking me to Bensonhurst."

Twice a week Ralph would pack his son into the family's black Chrysler New Yorker for the drive across Brooklyn to Bensonhurst. Louie would marvel at the ropes of sausage and wheels of Parmigiano hanging in the windows of the *pizzicherie,* or delicatessens. His eyes would widen at the rows of marbled funeral parlors and Italian catering halls. But most of all, even at his age, Louie knew Bensonhurst was notorious for one thing. The neighborhood was to the mob what Vatican City is to Roman Catholics. In the vernacular, Bensonhurst was—and remains—the mob's "sit-down central."

People said, "I'm from Bensonhurst," with a swagger. When the kids from Pigtown ran across their rivals from Bensonhurst, they all walked taller and struck a tougher pose. In fact, Louie remembers how embarrassing it was to have to tell his peers from across the borough exactly where he hailed from. The reaction to Pigtown was inevitably a sneer:

"Eh, where da fuck is dat? East Flatbush? Oh, you mean over near all da jungle bunnies?"

Nonetheless, the trips to Bensonhurst were akin to attending an Italian street festival for Louie. Ralph would lug his briefcase full of policy slips into one of the coffeehouses along Eighteenth Avenue and tote up his weekly take while someone like "Uncle Todo" Marino or "Uncle Johnny" Oddo sent Louie out to the sidewalk for all the dirty-water franks and Italian ices he could eat. Free of charge.

"And, Christ," Louie still says today, with a hint of wonderment, "the people I'd meet."

There was Petey "Big Head," who looked like an artichoke with eyes. And Pete "the Blood," who operated a butcher shop near The Grand Mark, when he wasn't setting shylock interest rates over espresso in Spiro's Bath Avenue Cafe. The Blood's specialty was the disposal of bodies, and to the twelve-year-old Louie he looked like a cinderblock with arms.

"And we usually ran into Joe Profaci, the olive-oil king who had been named head of a Family by Lucky Luciano himself. Joe looked like he used vats of his stuff on his hair. 'You got to grow up and have a lot of honor like your father,' Profaci would say to me. 'If you want to grow up right, grow up like your daddy.'

"But best of all I remember a walking scar named Bang Bang Brandefino. The story went that Bang Bang was a stone killer who had been shot five times in the face during one of the intermittent skirmishes that sometimes erupted within the Families. But Bang Bang didn't die. He became a legend instead. And this is the guy who used to sit me on his knee and tell me,

'I eat bullets, Louie, I eat 'em for fucking break-fast.' "

Louie was still too young to discern exactly what his father's friends did for a living. But he sensed that "my old man and his cronies sure as hell weren't Ward Cleaver spinning sermons to the Beav."

There were times when Louie would whoop in from the playground only to be shushed by his mother. "Don't disturb your father," Tess would warn. "He's busy with his bookkeeping."

"So naturally I'd peek into the living room and there would be my old man, hunched over one of those old-time adding machines with the slot-machine handle, surrounded by what seemed like millions of slips of paper and sacks full of small bills. He was oblivious, just punching that machine like he was adding up the national debt."

By the time Louie was a teen, Ralph was talking to him as an adult, being a bit more explicit in describing how his world worked.

Take, for instance, hijacking. Louie thought the word applied only to airplanes until one night his father broke down the components of what to this day remains one of the Mafia's most lucrative activities: ripping off trailers full of sable coats, Maytag washing machines, whatever was around.

"He'd explain about the guy at the airport tipping you to the swag. The driver's route. The best places to intercept. If the truck wasn't scheduled to take a dark side street, then you'd send somebody out the night before to shoot out the street lights. 'You never have to hurt the driver,' he'd tell me. And it was true, you'd never hear of a hijacking where the trucker was killed."

"The driver, what is he?" Ralph would ask his son.

"Nothing but a poor working stiff doing a job. If you do it right, there's no reason for anyone to get hurt."

And whenever Louie asked just what his father was doing associating with men who could reel off the contents of every airport cargo bay but didn't know where Staten Island was, Ralph's reply was always the same. "I do what I have to do to take care of my family. I work numbers. I loan money. I do a lot of illegal things, and that makes me a hoodlum. But when you think that's so terrible, remind yourself of the guy who's breaking concrete. You'll hear a lot of people talking about me, about my two-hundred-dollar suits and star-sapphire pinkie ring and manicured hands. But when you hear that gossip, just think of that guy pounding a sledgehammer. He's got a steady job, and he's got responsibilities, and I got both of those, too. But I also got fucking honor and respect."

Louie was being programmed. His father and his father's associates were fearless. Louie couldn't miss that. They'd fight for what they believed was right. And they were loyal. Family was everything to them. Both of those qualities would one day attach themselves to Detective Louie Eppolito, who was not adverse to charging into the middle of a shootout and putting his life on the line if another cop was in trouble.

Finally, one other odd irony was at work as Ralph Eppolito imparted his life's lessons to his only son. The Italian gangsters of La Cosa Nostra liked to perpetuate the myth that they were really a band of Robin Hoods, merry men lifting swag from the rich and redistributing it among the more deserving poor. As ludicrous as this idea has proven in reality, it stuck in the mind of an impressionable teenager. And on more than one occasion far in the future, some unfortunate citizen would find that he or she had an ally in Officer Louie Eppolito, simply because he had been taught by his father that it was up to an Eppolito "to do the right thing" for those less fortunate.

Of course, there was the inevitable downside to Mafia membership, a side that no number of home-spun platitudes could mask. There was murder, for instance, an act with which Ralph Eppolito obliquely admitted he was not unfamiliar.

"Once, when I must have been about twelve, my dad and I were having a conversation on the drive to The Grand Mark when he began a sentence with, 'When I got made . . .'

"I interrupted to ask what that meant.

" 'It means when you take the blood oath of the organization,' he answered. When I asked him which organization, he kind of scrunched up his face and said, 'The Cosa Nostra.'

" 'Me and your Uncle Jimmy, we had to take care of some rat bastard one time,' he continued. 'This rat stool pigeon bastard had to go. And after that I got made.' Stupid me. I wondered where the rat bastard had to go.

"He explained some of the rules, as it were, to me. For instance, he said, it was disrespectful to have a guy killed in front of his family, or to even think about fucking another guy's wife. And one made man never lays hands on another. Arguments were always settled at sit-downs. And he tried to impress upon me that patience was more than a virtue. It could also keep you out of jail. 'If somebody does something to hurt you or embarrasses you,' he preached, 'don't ever retaliate right in front of witnesses. It's stupid, and it's not classy.'

"He said he was telling me this because he'd never

lie to me, and not because he thought I should follow
in his footsteps. 'I have to do this,' he would warn me,
'so you won't have to fucking do it too.' He didn't
have to worry about that. There have been plenty of
times in my life when I knew I could kill somebody.
When I wanted to kill somebody. But never because
some guy stuck a pin in my finger, drew a little blood,
and said it was my legacy.''

By the early 1960s, the brothers Eppolito, with the
ambitious Freddy nominally in charge, ran a thriving
policy, shylocking, and bookmaking operation that
stretched from the Queens County border into the
middle of Brooklyn, encompassing three police precincts.

Ralph had proven himself something of a mathemat-
ical whiz within the Gambino organization and had
risen to the position of policy banker. Ralph and his
brothers had more than a dozen controllers working
their territory, and they in turn had more than one
hundred runners reporting to them.

"Ralph could look at a supermarket receipt two feet
long and total it in his head before the guy on the cash
register was halfway through," says one mob associate of the Eppolitos, open in his admiration these
many years later, yet still circumspect about revealing
his identity.

"Most of the bankers had their controllers acting as
bookkeepers, Jewish guys mainly, but not the Eppolitos. Freddy and Jimmy left all the bookkeeping up to
Ralph," the wiseguy continued. "I don't know how
he did it. I don't think the guy made it past third grade.
But he could smoke with a bag of policy slips and an
adding machine. And don't forget, this was before
Lotto, before OTB. Gambino's bookmaking and num-

bers operations were bringing him heavy, heavy income. Ralph's policy bank was a big contributor. And that contribution was regular. Don Carlo liked regular.''

Cosa Nostra accounting methods are by their nature specious. Yet Ralph Eppolito's former co-worker, as well as several former police investigators, put the brothers' weekly policy bank and bookmaking take at close to $15,000.

Even after deducting the occasional winning bet or numbers hit, police payoffs, salaries for their runners, controllers, and, of course, themselves, the Eppolitos ran a big-time operation by any standard. In the mid-1950s, for instance, a police lieutenant's yearly salary was $5,000. In contrast, perhaps half of Ralph Eppolito's average weekly take would pay his rent for a year.

The policy game derived its name from a cheap and legal form of life insurance sold during the Depression. But it was commonly known to the masses as "playing the numbers." Bettors could put up anywhere from a quarter to a dollar, wagering that their three-digit figure would hit in sequence and pay off at odds ranging from 100–1 to 500–1. The winning number was often pegged to the last three numbers to the left of the decimal point of the total pari-mutuel handle at a specified racetrack.

Local shopkeepers, barbers, say, or candy-store owners doubled as runners, collecting from the bettors. They then turned their take over to controllers, who delivered it to bankers. And nowhere was playing the numbers more institutionalized than in the city's poor black neighborhoods.

Harlem numbers players had made Dutch Schultz a millionaire during the Roaring Twenties. In fact, one of the reasons Lucky Luciano and Vito Genovese had ordered the contract killing of the Dutchman was that La Cosa Nostra coveted his policy bank. So, as Manhattan blacks migrated across the East River after the war, transforming entire Brooklyn neighborhoods such as Bedford-Stuyvesant, East New York, and Crown Heights, the Gambino organization seized the opportunity. Taunts about living near "jungle bunnies" may have shamed Louie, but the proximity of Pigtown to these new "Negro" neighborhoods meant lots of money to his father.

"In one respect my old man was unlike any other wiseguy I've ever met: the guy didn't have a racist bone in his body. People in organized crime are notorious, and rightly so, for spewing out the epithets 'nigger,' 'spic,' 'kike,' 'mick,' and the like at the drop of a hat. There's usually a 'bastard' attached, as in 'that fucking sheeny bastard. . . .'

"But I never heard those words used in our house. My father would tell me day after day after day, 'Louie, you treat everybody as you want to be treated.' I remember that during the Jewish High Holy Days the Orthodox would walk down the street wearing their hats. Sometimes as kids we used to run along beside them flipping the hats off. Kids, you know, just trying to break balls.

"But once, after my old man heard I was involved, he sat me down for another of his lectures. 'That man believes in his God,' he said. 'And he's proud enough of his religion to wear that ceremonial garb. If he's proud enough of it, then you have to respect him as a man.' I couldn't believe that this was my father speaking. I thought he hated the whole world.

"Same with the blacks. I came home from a baseball game once and told him how a nigger had won it for us with a home run. He stopped me in my tracks. He wanted to know why I was calling them names. And when I gave him the classic kid's response—because that's what everybody else calls them—he blew up.

"Louie, you're not everybody else. I deal with a lot of colored people at my job, and they're the nicest people in the world. You're going to find that there's low-life Italians, Polacks, Jews, the works. But don't ever start off as a racist. Make each individual earn your disdain. Once they earn your contempt, then you can disrespect them. But skin color and what God they pray to have nothing to do with it."

And to Louie's recollection, his father was true to his word.

"Two of my best friends in grammar school were Macho Rodriguez and Andrew Ball. They were as welcome in our house as anyone else. Of course, this was unheard of. A Puerto Rican and a black going into an Italian house in Pigtown!"

Louie had no misconceptions about his father's formal education. "I don't think the man could read or write much more than his name, although he could get by enough to eventually piece out, say, the general idea of what a newspaper article might be about."

Yet when Ralph would preach to Louie about the sanctity of a man's religion, or the foolhardiness of judging someone by his skin color, "he showed me more wisdom than any man I've ever met in my life." So it was that Louie began to lose his disdain for his father, and began to understand, almost through osmosis, what Ralph had been getting at during those interminable sermons about "honor" and "respect."

Ralph would often invite Louie to accompany him on his "rounds," and together they'd cruise the black

neighborhoods to check in on his crew's policy operation. "Mr. Ralph," his runners would call him when
they'd drop in on one of his numbers sites, perhaps a
candy store, or a local bar.

"These coloreds are just out there making a living,
just like me," Ralph would repeat to Louie as they
climbed back into the black New Yorker. "Try to always remember that."

As if to drive home the idea, Ralph made it a point
to have his son associate with the "coloreds." He
hired one of his East New York controllers, a black
man called Tipsy, to show up at his house every Saturday afternoon and clean out the garage.

"Of course my old man was a cleanliness nut, so
Tipsy would get to Pigtown and there'd be nothing for
him to do. But Ralph would hand Tipsy twenty-five
dollars for sweeping the floor, or something like that,
which in those days was a lot of money."

And like every kid in Brooklyn, Louie was a big
fight fan. His idol was Sugar Ray Robinson. So in the
early 1960s Ralph hired another black man, a broken-
down welterweight named Johnny Saxton, to instruct
his son.

Saxton, a rugged 147-pounder, had once taken the
Championship Belt from Kid Gavilan. But three title
fights with the banging Carmen Basilio had left his
brain damaged. The wiseguys had controlled Saxton's
career, and when he retired and went looking for all
the big purses they had "invested" for him, he was
told to take a hike. Ralph Eppolito disdainfully repeated the sad story to his son, thirteen years old and
weighing in at 150 pounds, when Saxton began coming
around to put on the gloves.

Louie's wheelchair experience had never really left
him. He wanted a body beautiful, and he wanted peo-

ple to know it. So four hours every night were set aside for weight training in Grandpa John's basement gymnasium.

"Now my old man wouldn't have known a weight bar from a crowbar. But he came down once and said to me, 'You know, Louie, I watch you come down here every night and kill yourself, and it makes me proud. Now me, I'd be down here for half an hour, looking for a way to steal those goddamn weights. And you know what? I could do it, too.' Then he went back upstairs. He was a schemer, I'll give him that, a great schemer."

It ran in the family. Louie knew what the girls went for, and as his hormones surged, he became, in his words, "a little fucking Casanova." But as much as the girls loved his pectorals, the boys hated his swagger. It led to trouble. Johnny Saxton notwithstanding, sometimes there was only so much two fists could handle. One of those occasions led to a merciless pummeling from a rival gang whose girl Louie had been angling to date.

"I took a major beating. After they stopped I couldn't stand straight, and several times on the way home I had to drop to one knee to let the dizziness pass. I crawled up our front porch, knocked on our door, and heard my mother coming. 'It's me, Ma,' I said. 'Is Dad home?'

"She knew immediately that something was wrong, but I wouldn't let her pull open the door. 'Stay inside, Ma,' I yelled. 'Let Dad come to the door.' My father didn't even bring me into the house. When he saw me he grabbed a towel, wrapped it around my head, and drove me straight to Kings County Hospital. I took seventy stitches in my face, another fifty in my hands, and had a quarter of my tongue sewn back in."

As Louie recuperated at home over the next several weeks, he found it strange that his father never once asked him about the particulars of the brawl. Eventually the stitches came out, the wounds began closing, and one afternoon a friend called with word that the leader of the gang who had beaten him, a boy named Charlie Francis, had been spotted alone in nearby Prospect Park.

" 'Great,' I answered, 'what time does it start?' Then I turned to my dad and asked to borrow a couple of bucks for the movies. He threw me the money and I was out the door."

Louie found Charlie Francis sitting on a swing. It was dusk. The two parried and feinted with small talk, each sizing up the other. Finally, laughing, Charlie Francis mentioned that he had heard Louie had messed with the wrong crowd's girl. "How bad did you get it?" Charlie wanted to know.

Louie was wearing sunglasses, so he doffed them, "and that stupid son of a bitch just sat there and laughed and never noticed me planting my feet. 'Wow,' he said, looking at my black-and-blue shiner, 'that really must have hurt.'

" 'Just like this,' I answered and blasted that motherfucker backward off that swing. I grabbed him by the throat, pushed him against a wall, and kept pounding his face. A fight seems longer in memory than in reality, but I knew at the moment that I was punching out this kid that I was hurting him bad. I also knew that I was going to kill him. He was unconscious. I was holding him up and smashing his face. Suddenly, a hand grabbed my fist in mid-flight.

"I wheeled with a full fist to throw a left-handed punch, and came face to face with my old man. Suit.

Tie. Monogrammed shirt, the whole bit. 'That's it,' he said. 'You gave him enough.'

"To this day I don't know how he knew where I was going. I do know that if he hadn't been there to step in I would have killed Charlie Francis. Now I'm shitting in my pants because I lied to my old man, telling him I was going to the movies. But instead of a whack, he wrapped his arm around my neck and told me how proud of me he was, how I'd reacted 'just like a man.'

"I had never told my old man the circumstances surrounding the first fight, and he had never asked, yet he continued, 'Another guy would have been so scared that three guys beat him up, he may have never gone looking for this guy Charlie Francis. Or he may have been afraid that the next time there would be five guys on his ass. But you're no pussy, you blasted his face off and he never saw it coming.'

"I was dumbfounded. 'But, Dad,' I said. 'How did you know?'

" 'Because I'm a father,' he answered. 'Someday, when you're a dad, you'll know too.'

"Now *that* was something I'd expect Ward Cleaver to say to the Beaver. Though I doubted if he'd utter the words under similar circumstances."

By the time Louie reached high school he was a junior Schwarzenegger. Erasmus Hall in Flatbush is the alma mater of Barbra Streisand, Elliot Gould, Woody Allen, and a host of Brooklyn celebrities. But Louie, in his words, "was the biggest stud they ever had. I was a football player, a baseball player, I boxed constantly. In general, I was a physical fitness nut.

"If I was inclined toward any bad health habits, I only needed to resurrect the memories of the rheumatic fever. And cigarettes were out, my old man's black lungs saw to that. Even though a lot of the kids from my neighborhood dabbled in drugs, most knew better than to even approach me with the stuff.

"I was bodybuilding competitively at the time—some stupid Hercules movie had set me off and Steve Reeves had replaced Sugar Ray Robinson as my idol—and my father used to love to bring me into a bar and show me off. One of his friends would need only say hello, or ask how old I was, and my old man would order me to take off my shirt. My pecs would be out to here and my abdominals would be in to there and my dad would beam and say something like, 'Not bad for a sixteen-year-old, eh Frankie?' What the hell, I liked the attention, too."

Which, naturally, resulted in more than his share of fights. One typical adventure began when Louie beat the crap out of a classmate dealing Seconals at a Sweet Sixteen party. The combat escalated when the boy's older brother showed up for revenge. Louie dispatched him, also. Finally, a cousin of the duo arrived, a twenty-three-year-old named Booty Romano. Booty kicked Louie through a plate-glass window.

With typical aplomb, Louie got to his feet, dusted the shards of glass from his clothes, "and knocked every single tooth out of the front of this guy's mouth."

When the police arrived, Louie was taken into custody and offered the customary phone call. He dialed home.

"It was against my better judgment, but the cops gave me no choice. I was hoping to get my mother. No such luck. My father answered, and to my surprise, when I apprised him of the situation he began laughing hysterically. It turned out that, thirty years earlier, Booty Romano's old man had slugged my dad with a baseball bat, and my father had turned around and knocked the teeth out of *his* mouth. Like father, like son."

By the late 1950s, the intruding lower class had gotten the better of even the semi-enlightened Ralph Eppolito, who moved his family several miles, from Pigtown to a Flatbush apartment house. The neighborhood had less character, but better sanitation.

"My mom's people had moved with us, into the same building, and my Grandpa John set up a full gym in the basement. Johnny Saxton taught me more about fighting than I ever could have picked up on the street, about training, about feinting, about the proper way to get the most power out of a punch. It would come in very handy.

"But I think for my old man the fight lessons were secondary. He was showing me the human side of a black guy. I guess Johnny Saxton and Tipsy were walking, talking classrooms on race relations. I carried those lessons for the rest of my life."

11

For all of Ralph Eppolito's racial enlightenment, there was one color he couldn't stand. Blue. He despised cops. Hated the way they walked. Hated the way they talked. The mere sight of a police officer's uniform was enough to drive him into an uncontrollable rage.

Once Ralph began allowing Louie to accompany him to "work," he never tried to hide that disdain. "I guess he figured that even a dumb teenager like me would have had to have been pretty stupid not to catch on."

Along with the crap games, one of the most popular card games played above The Grand Mark was an Italian version of baccarat called Ziganet. Louie would sit and watch as Ziganet stakes rose as high as $2,000 a hand. He also noticed that every four hours, like clockwork, during these Ziganet marathons, officers from the 80th Precinct, Serpico's old station house, would park outside the door.

"They'd make like they were having coffee, just passing the time of day. But cops never just pass the time. Pretty soon one of my jobs was to bring them their payoff."

Ralph Eppolito would slip a five-dollar bill into an

envelope and hand it to his son. "Here's the money," he'd say. "Go give it to those bloodsuckers." Louie would run downstairs, casually lean into the radio patrol car, and drop the envelope on the front seat. It would never pass from hand to hand, and the police wouldn't even acknowledge the graft, much less say thanks.

"They'd just pull out and drive off. I guess my father despised them so much because they could be bought so cheap. I learned just how cheap a couple of days after my thirteenth birthday.

"I was standing on the corner of St. Marks and Grand Avenue, in front of Za-Za's poolroom. Jimmy the Bug ran Za-Za's. One of my dad's controllers named Frankie Chi-Chi walked up and told him that a black runner named Floyd had been coming up short in his weekly accounts. Moments later Floyd turned the corner. 'Come with me,' my dad said. 'I want to teach you how to talk to people when they're not doing the right thing.' My father led Floyd into the hallway of an abandoned brownstone next door to The Grand Mark.

"He backed Floyd up against the wall and let him have it. 'Let me tell you something, you black motherfucker,' he said very evenly. 'You pay the fucking money to the fucking people you owe and you stop putting that shit into your veins.' Floyd started stuttering, 'No, no, Ralph, it ain't like that. I ain't using. It's probably my counting is wrong.' Then my father reached into Floyd's jacket pocket and pulled out a set of works, a needle, and a bottlecap. He screamed, 'I'll put a fucking hole in your fucking head, you black cocksucker.'

"Floyd began babbling another excuse just as a cop came through the door from the sidewalk. When the cop opened the door I nearly shit in my pants. I envisioned all three of us behind bars. But my old man just looked at the cop and spit out, 'What the fuck do you want?' The cop started in with a, 'Ralph, I thought I . . .' but my father cut him off.

" 'Get the fuck out of here and don't ever, ever bother me when I'm talking to someone,' he said to the cop. And the guy turned around and left! My heart was beating a mile a minute. Floyd, Dad, and I all walked out together. The cop was leaning against his patrol car. My father reached into his pocket and handed him two bucks. Two lousy dollars! 'Red,' he said, 'don't ever interrupt me again.' The cop apologized and walked away. I was flabbergasted. My old man sneered that he knew every cop in the precinct. He added that he hated every one of them.

"I was ambivalent about police at the time, but years later I vowed that I'd rip a new asshole in the first prick who ever offered me a bribe."

On the streets of New York City, then, as today, there were cops, and there were *cops*. And what produced the most disdain among the goodfellas of Brooklyn was that special breed known as the "fucking Feds." Feds didn't play the game right. They didn't know how. To the mobsters (and even to most members of the NYPD), the Feds were from "out there"—Montana, or Georgia, or Arkansas.

The Feds hassled you for no good reason. They didn't care about tradition. And, worst of all, they lacked that vital give-and-take between cops and robbers: courtesy. Even to Louie, who had to hide from his father the fact that he didn't despise every single soul in a blue uniform and badge, the Feds were a special pain in the ass.

"The FBI used to break balls just for the hell of it.

My old man taught me early that the initials stood for 'Forever Bother the Italians.' They'd show up at our house with their Ozark accents and, I swear, the confrontation between my old man and the 'G' would be like something out of a television sit-com.

" 'You Mr. Eppalata?' one would ask.

" 'The name's Eppolito.'

" 'Excuse me, Mr. Eppalata.'

"Now I'd see the smoke pluming out of my father's ears. 'Eppolit-O. Eppolit-O. If you guys can't even get the name right, then I don't even want to talk to you.'

" 'Well, Mr. Eppalata, you have to talk to us, because we're here investigating certain federal statutes of the United States government that we believe your brother Freddy has broken.' Then one of them would turn to me and ask me to leave the room.

" 'Whatever has to do with me has to do with my son,' my father would answer. 'We'll talk in front of Louie. As a matter of fact, fellas, you'd better talk fast, because if you want to talk about Freddy, then you go talk to Freddy. I want you out of my house. Unless you got a warrant for my arrest, get the fuck out.' Then he'd slam the door in their faces.

"Two, three days later I'd head outside to play ball and see those same two agents sitting in their car. It was easy to spot them. They never hid. I think they thought they could scare you better that way.

" 'Come here, boy,' one of them would say, and I'd feel like fucking Mandingo the cotton picker. 'You'd better watch it, son, because you could be locked up federally.'

" 'For what?'

" 'For withholding information.'

"For chrissake, I was fourteen years old. 'Fuck

you,' I'd tell them, because that's what my father had taught me.

"Incidents like this happened all the time, and it followed me right into high school. I was coming out of class during my sophomore year once when I was stopped by two Feds. I remember it like it was yesterday. I was holding hands with a girl named Gloria Salmona, and the agent's name was Thompson, Federal Agent Thompson.

"I told Federal Agent Thompson to go fuck himself, but Gloria Salmona would never walk home with me again. Fucking Feds.

"At any rate, you can see how my father's irrational loathing of anyone with a badge could wear off on his son. My old man called it harassment, but for me it was a bizarre learning experience."

Louie also learned—the hard way—just how cautious he had to be around his father when the subject was the police. A few months after his thirteenth birthday he was playing handball in a vest-pocket park around the corner from his home when he heard a woman scream. Turning, he saw a white kid on a bicycle making off with an elderly woman's purse. The purse snatcher had knocked the woman down and dragged her a few steps before she let go, which gave Louie just enough of a running start.

"I bolted through a hole in the chain-link fence and threw myself at this motherfucker like a guided missile. Direct hit. The bike kept rolling in one direction as he flew through the air in the other. I rammed him right into a firebox. There were a couple of cops down the street, so I gave them a wave, and I remember how excited I was as I explained how I foiled the purse snatching."

Naturally, the cops clapped Louie on the back and

told him what a wonderful job he had done. Then they offered to drive him home. "I sat in the back of that squad car feeling like Eliot Ness. I had stopped a robbery. I had caught the perp. I was a hero. It was one of the proudest moments of my life."

Both of the officers escorted Louie to the door of the family's second-floor apartment. He stood between them, beaming, as one knocked on the door. Ralph answered.

"Is this your son, Mr. Eppolito?" the cop asked.

Nobody saw it coming. Ralph smashed Louie with an overhand right that sent him dribbling down the stairs. He bounced off a wall at the bottom, into a radiator, and lost consciousness. His lip was split open, his nose was gushing blood, and the right side of his face was already swelling up.

The incredulous officers pushed Ralph back into his apartment and tried to calm him down. "What's the problem with my kid?" he finally asked them.

"Mr. Eppolito," one replied, "the *problem* is that your son is a hero. He grabbed a guy who robbed a woman and held him until we arrived."

By the time the officers had calmed Ralph down to a mild rage, Louie, though woozy, had regained consciousness. As his eyes focused, he looked up the stairway and saw his father standing at the landing. In a measured tone, Ralph addressed the police, although Louie knew the message was really meant for him.

"Yeah, why don't you go across the street and tell every one of my neighbors that that's the reason you brought my son home?" Ralph said. "Why don't you do that? Because everybody sees a police car in front of my door, and you two come out with my son between you, you know what they all think. They all think he did something wrong. They all think he was brought home because he disgraced his parents. I don't want to be embarrassed by my children, and I'm embarrassed now. You goddamn cops don't ever get it right."

The officers looked at each other in amazement. "Mr. Eppolito," said one, "you're crazy. What the hell did you hit the kid for?"

"He's my kid," Ralph growled. "If he had called and told me that the police were bringing him home for saving an old woman from being robbed, I would have been waiting outside with bells on. But because you brought him up here, the neighbors now think he's a creep. And I blame you two as much as I blame him. I'm an Eppolito, and no cop will ever bring my son home to my house."

As the pair of officers walked down the stairs one patted Louie on the shoulder. "I pity you, kid," he said. "Life's going to be tough living with that guy."

After they left Louie looked up at his father, whose face was a mask of disgust. Louie knew Ralph would never apologize. That night, lying in bed, he recalled what his mother had told him years before. "Louie," Tess said, "if you're ever arrested and they give you one call, make sure it's not to here. Your father goes crazy at the sight of a cop."

He was angry at himself for not remembering that sooner.

12

In September 1963, when Louie was fifteen, the Mafia turncoat Joe Valachi appeared before Arkansas Senator John McClellan's investigative subcommittee on Organized Crime. The televised proceedings were required viewing in the Eppolito household.

"Valachi was everything my father hated in a man. Ralph would sit in front of the television and have apoplexy as Valachi named names, lots of them friends of my father's. Even I recognized a few of them as men who had been to our house, or as guys I knew from the trips to Bensonhurst. Johnny "Bath Beach" Oddo in particular was singled out a couple of times.

"Anyway, my old man used the Valachi hearings as a kind of teaching tool on what not to do. He drilled both Pauline and me over and over that whatever was said in our home stayed in our home. I never bragged about any 'connections' in high school. I was beginning to learn what kind of pull my old man did have. Man, I was fifteen years old, and sitting on top of the world. I thought the Eppolitos were invincible.

"Then my Uncle Freddy died."

His Uncle Freddy's death was not only a blow to the fifteen-year-old Louie, but to the entire Eppolito clan. Freddy Eppolito was, in essence, their spiritual leader. Despite being the youngest, he was the brother who had taken Ralph and Jimmy under his wing. It was his schemes and scams that had inflated the family business from a mom-and-pop operation into an efficient, Brooklyn-wide concern. But Freddy Eppolito made the classic mob mistake of overstepping his bounds. In his case, that boundary was the Gambino edict against dealing drugs.

The Gambino Family orders to steer clear of the heroin trade were strictly pragmatic. Drug busts meant heavy sentences, and heavy sentences bred vermin. Mobsters hate rats like the devil hates holy water, and drugs posed a threat to Omerta, the Mafia's heretofore unbreakable code of silence.

This fear of leaking to the authorities was capsulized in a joke known to every wiseguy of the era that was repeated often in the Eppolito household:

The courtroom is packed on the day Joey from Sicily is to become an American citizen. The judge asks Joey, "Who is the Father of our country?" When he answers, "George Washington," whoops and hollers emanate from the viewing section. "Thatta Joey, he'sa some smarta kid," yells one Italian-accented voice. The same pandemonium breaks loose when Joey correctly answers the judge's question regarding the Declaration of Independence.

But when the judge asks Joey, "Who shot and killed Abraham Lincoln?" an eerie silence falls over the courtroom. It is broken at last by a warning from the back row: "Joey, shut uppa you fuckin' mout. Don't say nuttin'."

Wily veterans like Gambino, Vito Genovese, and Joe Profaci failed to see the humor in busted capos and soldiers who, faced with harsh life sentences, would undoubtedly sing like canaries and turn in their bosses in exchange for a sweeter deal. Despite the huge profits to be made in the illicit drug market, there was only so much a man could do with cash in a federal prison.

Of course, no edict could stop the ambitious. The Lucchese and Bonnano Crime Families jumped into the heroin business with both feet, and Joe Valachi admitted to author Peter Maas that even Genovese himself was not above ignoring his own antidrug pronunciamentos if *his* skim off the top was creamy enough.

Further, Freddy Eppolito had a genealogical connection. The Camorra, a centuries-old confederation of Neapolitan gangsters, had for years possessed the most extensive smuggling routes. When the Camorra put together a consortium of Turkish pashas, Corsican chemists and American distributors to form a heroin chain stretching across the Atlantic, the youngest son of Luigi the Nablidan recognized his opportunity.

In certain mob circles it was then believed that Freddy Eppolito was actually vying with Gambino's son-in-law and cousin, Paul "Big Paulie" Castellano, for the title of heir apparent to the Don. Whether or not that was the case, there is no doubt that he was rapidly rising in the Mafia hierarchy.

Unlike his brothers Ralph and Jimmy, whose rap sheets were mainly limited to long strings of bookmaking and policy busts (aptly enough, a partial list of Ralph's arresting officers reads like the Tipperary phone book: McAuley, Murphy, Fitzgerald, Sutton), Freddy Eppolito had, from the start of his gangland career, been willing to stretch the envelope.

Freddy's first arrest occurred in 1936, at the age of sixteen. He was nailed by the Police Commissioner's special Organized Crime Squad for taking part in the armed robbery of a Manhattan warehouse, and he served two years in a state reformatory. Freddy's rap sheet thereafter provided an eclectic reflection of Cosa Nostra concerns, with busts ranging from hijacking to counterfeiting to felonious assault.

It should therefore have come as no surprise to his family when he attempted to become a player in the Camorra's heroin pipeline, a pipeline that would shortly become notorious as the French Connection.

Freddy was brought in and questioned by agents from both the FBI and the old Federal Bureau of Narcotics. And though he was never charged with any crime, word hit the streets that he was "pulling a Valachi," or cooperating with the law.

"Let's put it this way," says one former FBI agent familiar with the case. "It didn't hurt our cause to have a guy with Freddy's weight suspected of being a rat."

Freddy's stock plunged in the Gambino Family, and the subsequent contract put out on his life confirmed the dictum that the Mafia had no friends, only interests.

"Ralph and Jimmy didn't know what to do," recalls Tess Eppolito. "Freddy, who had once been one of the biggest guys in the Family, was now afraid to come out of his house. There'd be all-night meetings at our place trying to come up with an alternative to having him killed. For a while we thought my father-in-law could pull a few strings, use all that influence he built up over the years, but even Grandpa Louis was helpless. Ralph was beside himself, as mad at Freddy for getting involved with that junk as he was at Gambino and the other bosses for ordering him dead."

Tess would watch each evening as her husband

paced their living-room floor, or made futile calls to associates who owed him favors. But, deep down, the Eppolitos all knew that no last-minute reprieve would be handed down to Freddy.

"Finally, Freddy put everyone out of misery by killing himself," Tess remembers. "He drank himself to death. Of course, he didn't have much choice. If he had walked out on the street he would have been blown away. He was the next man on the hit parade.

"So he stayed in his house and drank two bottles of Chivas Regal a day. The man had terrible stomach problems, ulcers on top of ulcers. So, in a sense, he was really committing suicide. His wife called one day to say the ambulance had come to get him. He was dead before they hit the hospital."

Freddy's death seemed to hit brother Ralph the hardest. It was as if, Louie recalls, his father lived out some of life's vicarious thrills through his brother. But, Louie emphasized, Freddy's life-style would never have suited Ralph, the plodding, mechanical policy banker who was more than satisfied with the middle-class foundation he had laid for his family.

"My Uncle Freddy made my old man look like Mother Theresa. He was only forty-three when he drank himself to death, and, afterward, my father didn't say much about it around the house. But I could sense that there was more to the story than just another rummy losing the battle of the bottle. All I knew was that Freddy had gotten in some big trouble with the Family. Too bad, too, because all you needed were a good pair of eyes to see that Freddy was on the Mafia fast track. Even I knew that he had risen to the position of underboss when things suddenly went sour. The FBI put out the word that Freddy was in-

volved with drugs, that he had a piece of the heroin
shipments coming over from Marseilles.

"Whether this was true or not, I don't know. My
father always believed that it was a smear campaign
started by the Feds, designed to undercut the obvious
successor to Carlo Gambino. But I have to believe
that even Ralph wasn't aware of all the scams his
younger brother had going.

"You see, Uncle Freddy was first and foremost a
treacherous guy, the kind who'd kill you as soon as
look at you. And he didn't bother to hide it from anyone."

Louie will never forget the thirteenth-birthday bash
his Uncle Freddy and Aunt Millie threw for their son
Lou. Louie was eleven at the time. The family was
just about to cut the cake when Uncle Freddy received
a phone call.

"I don't know what was said on the other end of the
line, but it set him off like a firecracker. He was curs-
ing and screaming, 'I'll kill that fuck, I'll kill him dead
and take his eyes out myself. I'll rip his fucking eyes
out of his fucking head.' This was right in front of all
the kids. I was kind of embarrassed for my aunt and
cousin. I could see they were squirming.

"Uncle Jimmy and my father tried to quiet him
down. 'Hey, Freddy, we got people, we got children
around here.' But that didn't bother him a whit. He
just went right on screaming, and eventually some of
the little ones started to cry. But Uncle Freddy just
railed right on. Finally, in front of everyone, he said
something about someone 'having to go.' I watched
Uncle Jimmy and my father turn white.

"Jimmy and my father were the quiet type. They
plotted their revenge, all right, but they kept it low

key. Not Freddy. He didn't care who knew what he was doing.

Louie was the one who broke the news of Freddy's death to his father. "He was upstairs sitting at his work desk. And for the first time in my life I saw the man break down. He was just devastated. Perhaps, in hindsight, you can say that maybe he saw a portent in Uncle Freddy's death, because he was getting sicker and sicker by this time. At any rate, it took him several days to really get over it.

"The funeral was out of a bad mobster movie, with about twenty-three flower cars and some eighty-odd limousines, befitting, I suppose, the man who would liked to have been king."

After the shock of Freddy's death, life went on for the Eppolitos. Ralph and Jimmy picked up the slack and resumed running their numbers and gambling operations. But it was never the same. It may have been that Freddy's death threw the symbiosis of their organization out of whack. It may simply have been that Ralph's lungs and heart were slowly giving out on him. In either case, the fifteen-year-old Louie couldn't help but notice that his father "didn't seem to take the same joy out of life anymore."

There were exceptions. In June of 1966 Louie was one of two thousand students to graduate from Erasmus Hall High School. It was one of the proudest moments of his father's life, "although he sure as hell wasn't admitting it."

On the morning of his son's graduation Ralph teased his wife unmercifully. "Tessie, if that son of a bitch embarrasses me and doesn't graduate today, I'll kill him dead." Louie not only graduated, he was honored with the school's top Physical Fitness Award. Louie, his black, wavy hair peeking out from under his blue cap, his V-shaped physique discernible even under the folds of his graduation gown, strode to the podium to accept his award.

"After I went onstage to accept it, I was supposed to return to my seat with the seniors. But I said, 'Forget that,' and walked fifteen rows past the student section and into the grandstand. I handed my father the trophy and kissed him on the cheeks. 'This is for you,' I told him, and he started to cry."

Louis had had a feeling for some time that his father wasn't going to be with him for much longer. Ralph's breathing was becoming more labored, his body had turned puffy, and although he was just over fifty years old, he moved with a gait of a man walking slowly toward the grave.

"Just getting him to the bathroom was becoming a major project. And as I lifted him into the can I thought how we had come full circle from the days when he carried me out of my wheelchair. I wanted my father to know how much I cared, how much I finally understood all those lessons he had tried to teach me. But it just wasn't in my nature to verbalize those emotions. Deep down I also knew that it wasn't in his nature to want to hear them."

Throughout his senior year Louie had steadily dated a local girl named Teresa Gallipani. A month after graduation he proposed, and Teresa accepted. Only then did he inform his father that he was getting married. They took a walk along the beach.

"Is she pregnant?" Ralph asked.

"No, she isn't," Louie replied, and Ralph tried his damnedest to impart one, final lesson to his only son.

"You're still growing," Ralph said. "Physically and emotionally. In a couple of years you'll be ready for marriage. But not now."

Louie didn't listen. Louie and Teresa were married on July 7, 1967, in the Flatbush Church of the Holy Innocents. He was nineteen. She was eighteen. Ralph Eppolito attended, under mild protest. Their union produced a son, Louis, Jr., and lasted a little over two years. Louie's father was not around to tell him, "I told you so" when they separated in 1969.

After graduation, Louie found work in a Flatbush pet store. He had always had a way with animals—in fact, he liked them better than most humans—and though his grades had been fair, college had no appeal. The Army had rejected him because of his heart murmur, and he needed a steady job to keep the baby in diapers and formula.

Louie had several opportunities to jump into the family business—he recalls his Uncle Jimmy making a couple of cryptic offers—but he sensed that his father was against it. Besides, Louie told himself, he wanted a straight job, a job where he didn't end up like Uncle Freddy. "It's a privilege in your line of work to die of old age," he had once jokingly told his father, who failed to catch the humor. Seeing little future in the pet-store business, he applied for work with the phone company, and was hired as a breaker and installer. He and his bride moved into an apartment three floors below his parents.

On March 8, 1968, as he was walking home after installing a new phone line, Louie spotted his grandfather John Mandelino in front of his apartment building. "You better head inside fast, Louie," his grandfather told him. "Everybody's crying, and I think your father's dead." John Mandelino had seen too much death in the trenches, and he was afraid to enter the apartment himself.

"I ran up the stairs and opened the door. My mother

met me in the hallway. 'Daddy's gone, Louie,' she said. 'He died in his sleep.'

"I walked into their bedroom, and his body looked disfigured, as if he was fighting death to the very end. His left hand was up in the air, and his pinky and ring finger were bent down. His left foot was twisted toward his right foot. It looked like he had suffered a massive heart attack or stroke. Later, the autopsy said both.

"I closed the door, went over to him, and ran my fingers through his hair. I was nineteen, yet I began to moan, 'Daddy, Daddy, Daddy, why did you have to die? There's so much more you could have taught me.' I had flashbacks of all those times he wanted to lecture me, times I'd get so annoyed because I hated to be dragged away from my friends.

"I felt as if I only had my father for a short period of time, between the ages twelve and nineteen. Prior to that, I hated his guts. And now I was racked with guilt. It was funny, like that old Mark Twain line, but now it seemed to me that as I had gotten older, my old man had gotten smarter.

"I guess I talked to him alone, for about an hour. I wasn't speaking to a racketeer, or a cop-hater, or a murderer. I was speaking to a man I loved. Finally, my mother came in. She didn't think it was healthy for me to stay in there like that. 'Look at him in that bed, Ma,' I muttered. 'A young man, fifty-two years old, sickly most of his life; a devoted husband, a father who put two kids through school, provided for his family, and a member of organized crime. God, will I miss him.'

"I was the one who broke the news to my Grandpa Louis. I left the apartment and went straight to his house, knocked on his door, and with his big heavy

Italian accent he greeted me with, 'Hey, Mr. Big Shot, now you come to see me. To what do I owe this visit?'

"I stammered and stuttered, but the simple words wouldn't come out. Finally Grandpa Louis asked me what the hell I was trying to say. 'My father died today,' I told him."

It wasn't as if the news was unexpected. Ralph's father had a weekly table setting at Tess's Sunday dinners, and had seen for himself his son's deterioration. Nonetheless, when Louie broke the news he turned white, and sank back in his chair. After a stunned moment or two, he began weeping.

He told Louie how he had always put more pressure on Ralph than on Jimmy or Freddy, because Ralph was the oldest boy to follow him into the business. Then he began talking about Joey, how he wasn't like the other three, and how only Jimmy was left to him now. Louie's heart was broken all over again as he sat silently, watching his grandfather weep.

On March 10, 1968, a team of undercover FBI agents stood by as a fleet of black limousines sailed down Brooklyn's Flatbush Avenue. The agents, disguised as utility repairmen, counted a total of eighteen cars. Five alone were needed to haul the flowers and wreaths. The limos were trailed into a parking lot adjacent to the Vigilante Funeral Parlor by an endless motorcade of boxy, American-made automobiles.

Although not quite up to his brother Freddy's standards, thus began a fitting, if slightly cinematic, sendoff for the racketeer Ralph Eppolito.

The funeral parlor was closed to all other customers, and Chapels A, B, C, and D were reserved for the family and friends of Ralph Eppolito. As their hidden video cameras whirred, the undercover team recorded a veritable constellation of New York City's Organized Crime world. When they couldn't identify men by surnames, they made do with nicknames and aliases.

Blank stares, for instance, from agents and mourners alike, may have greeted any mention of Ralph Eppolito's good friend Joey Llongo, a small-time Brooklyn haberdasher whose most striking feature was a pair of gigantic hands. But everyone recognized Joey the Hammer, who had once abruptly concluded a tavern brawl by wrapping those same hands around a twelve-pound sledgehammer and smashing his opponent's skull.

Into the Vigilante filed "Hammers," and "Bloods," and a myriad of "Sheiks." Had the agents been able to follow this snaking caravan of bookmakers, hijackers, and leg-breakers into the main viewing room of the Vigilante, they would have seen nineteen-year-old Louie Eppolito forming a one-man honor guard over his father's brass casket.

Periodically, between accepting Mass cards and condolences, Louie would glance over at his mother. Tess, flanked by Pauline and Uncle Jimmy, was seated at the foot of the casket. Louie watched as his uncle intermittently left his mother's elbow to hold whispered conversations, moving from corner to corner, from room to room, the better, Louie realized, to circumvent any hidden recording devices.

By ten-thirty that evening the Vigilante had emptied, and the agents dispersed. "Where's all the big shots?" one of them joked. "They ain't showing Ralphie no respect."

But the Fed had spoken too soon. Shortly before midnight, Jimmy Eppolito returned to the Vigilante with a small group of associates who wished to pay their final respects to his brother under less public circumstances. A solitary limousine deposited them behind the funeral home. They were escorted through a side entrance by Louie, who greeted each with a kiss on the cheek.

The mourners included the legendary Carlo Gambino, accompanied by his white-haired *consigliere*, Joe N. Gallo. Of the old-time bosses, Gambino alone remained, and though he was ancient and frail, Louie remembers thinking that even his trembling handshake could not mask the treachery that had allowed him to outlive his compatriots.

Don Carlo's train that night also included two of his father's oldest and dearest friends, Thomas "Todo" Marino, a capo in the Genovese Crime Family, and Johnny "Bath Beach" Oddo, the Colombo Crime Family capo who possessed a stare "that could make faces bleed." None had entered the home with bodyguards.

After a moment of silence, this small group settled down in the viewing room's vestibule to reminisce, their conversation, as always, laced with the words "honor" and "respect."

And along with the ubiquitous Mass cards, several of these late-night mourners passed on to Ralph's son small slips of paper bearing telephone numbers; numbers to call for jobs on city piers, in the garment district, or on construction sites. It was, thought Louie, the Mafia's way of saying the Eppolito family would never want.

"One by one the old-timers came up to me. 'I want to tell you stories about your father, how he loved you and wanted you to become something,' I would hear. 'So come down to the piers Friday, and we'll talk about your future.' Or the garment center. Or some construction site. Then I'd be given a number to call.

"After the funeral I told my mother about the offers, specifically about a post office job Johnny Bath Beach had mentioned. She reacted kind of peculiar. Considering everything my father had taught me, she asked, did I really think he'd want me to pursue a job in the Family business?

"But I had my own family to consider. And I thought Johnny Bath Beach's post office connection might be the beginning of a solid career. It was, after all, a federal job. I was thinking about security, a pension, all that. On the surface, I had never really given much thought to being a junior wiseguy. I just assumed that I'd never have to make the decision. Now I was faced with Bath Beach's offer, and I guess I deluded myself into hoping that there were no strings attached. But subconsciously, I think I realized the choice I was making.

"I mean, the man who had just offered me a job was the same guy who bought cars based on how many bodies would fit in the trunk."

At nine o'clock on the morning of March 12, 1968, the day after Ralph Eppolito was interred in the Evergreen Cemetery in Queens, Louie walked into Manhattan's Central Post Office carrying a card bearing Johnny Bath Beach's name and telephone number. A union foreman was expecting him. He was given a perfunctory application to fill out for an entry-level position, paying $175 per week. When he asked what kind of work he'd be doing, the foreman smiled.

The question was answered after lunch, when the foreman flipped him a coin and ordered him to run to the corner newsstand for coffee and the afternoon paper.

"Who the fuck you throwing a quarter at?" Louie demanded.

"What the fuck you think you're here for?" the foreman answered. "Everybody in this business starts as a gofer. Now go get me my joe."

"Well, Ralph Eppolito's kid don't start out as no gofer. So why don't you take this quarter and shove it up your ass."

Thus ended Louie's brief career as a postal employee, and, effectively, as a junior mobster.

"I rode the subway home to Brooklyn that afternoon squeezing the straps with both hands, wondering what the hell to do with my life. But what I really think aggravated me the most was the idea that Ralph Eppolito's son was thought of as no better than some low-life gofer, fit only to fetch coffee.

"Back at the apartment house I complained to my mother about being treated like some greenhorn just off the boat from Italy. 'I took that job because I wanted to work,' I said. 'But they think they can buy your soul, these motherfuckers. They buy it and chew it up, just like they did to Daddy, and Uncle Freddy. Uncle Jimmy's probably in for the same. Frankly, Ma, my soul's not for sale."

Tess said nothing to her son, who had finished his tirade and sat stewing at her kitchen table. Before padding out of the room, she pushed a cup of coffee and a plate of anisette-flavored *biscotti* in front of her only son. Louie, ignoring the cookies, absent-mindedly stirred his coffee. He stared into space. And in that moment, he gave his first thought to becoming a cop.

IV

THE COP

13

Patrolman Louis Eppolito adored the battle but despised the bureaucracy of his new profession. He had been taught by his father to care about people, to respect their feelings, to go out of his way to *help* others in need. He had also been primed to be combat-ready at all times. When murderers and rapists were banging on your door, Officer Louie Eppolito was the cop you wanted answering your 911 call.

In fact, the features Louie found most attractive about The Job were, ironically, many of the same that had drawn his father into the world of organized crime. Men could be men in this uniformed fraternal order. If you wanted to scream "shit," at the top of your lungs, you screamed it without worrying about antagonizing the "prude filing memos at the desk across the aisle."

Better yet, if the occasion arose where it was necessary to "beat the shit" out of someone—a husband who battered his wife, a pimp who slashed his hooker, a purse snatcher who'd run down an old woman—those opportunities availed themselves regularly, as the New York City Police Department of the late 1960s was by no means a bastion of civil rights.

But, best of all, Louie recalls, "you could swear

and you could brawl and it was all in the name of helping other people. I liked that. It was honorable. You shit on the perps and protected the citizens, and got paid pretty good to do it."

Eight thousand dollars a year, plus overtime.

It was the "chickenshit," the petty injustices and everlasting grudges rampant in the Department, that Louie found so devastating. The son of Ralph Eppolito had no heart for what that term signified: the open scrimmage for power and prestige at the expense of solid police work; the behind-the-scenes settling of old scores; the petty harassment of the weak by the strong. That's why the cops on the beat called it "chickenshit." It wasn't even important enough to be bullshit.

Had Ralph Eppolito's heart remained healthy, Louie's calling would have been out of the question. "He wouldn't have had to hire somebody to whack me, he would have killed me himself for even thinking about it." But the son had not inherited the father's absolute contempt for The Job. Louie even calculated that if the rest of the Eppolito family initially gave him the cold shoulder, blood would eventually tell.

"Personally, I had no problem with Louie joining the force, except the normal fears a mother has for her son," says Tess. "He was a big boy, and Ralph and I had taught him to make his own decisions. And I knew he'd be good for the streets. The philosophical problem, I think, came from Ralph's people. It was like treason, like going over to the other side. That's the subtle feeling I got, anyway. At family parties, even talking to the relatives and Ralph's old friends over the phone, it was like someone was always holding something back. But, of course, no one was going to say anything to me to my face."

The Cop

It was Louie's brother-in-law, Al Guarneri, who really put the idea in his head to become a cop. After Ralph's death, Pauline's husband had taken the Department's written test, and passed it. But he'd flunked the physical. In an attempt to improve his stamina, he began training with Louie in Grandpa John Mandelino's basement gym.

Al and Pauline had married three years earlier, and the brothers-in-law were fairly close. Al realized Louie was "basically groping around in life, not looking forward to installing phones for the next forty years," yet hesitant to throw in with Uncle Jimmy or "Uncle" Bath Beach. In fact, Louie had no idea for which type of career he was best suited. So Al suggested he give the police exam a try.

"Of course, I thought he was nuts. I told him they'd take one look at my family tree and throw me out on my ass."

But the hell-raiser from Pigtown was intrigued by Al's flights of fancy. While pumping iron together they'd wax poetic about shootouts; about being the first on the scene of a robbery; about "the different insight on life you'd get from a cop's point of view." When Louie was a child he used to play cops and robbers. The older kids from the neighborhood would hog the robber roles, leaving the squirts like Louie to pick up the badge. Al's enthusiasm was infectious, "and I guess I was still playing that game in my head."

In the end, however, it came down to the fact that Louie had nothing better to look forward to. So, as much for a lark as anything else, he drove into Manhattan and signed up for the police written entrance examination. "I figured I'd flunk the thing anyway, and that would be that. Two months later the results were in. I got a 94."

On August 1, 1968, nine days after his twentieth birthday, Louis John Eppolito was called to the Police Academy for a formal interview. Before the interrogation process, each prospective cadet was ordered to write a short biographical essay. Louie pulled no punches. When he turned in his eleven-page report (longer by half than the hopefuls seated around him), the investigating officer was astounded not only by the essay's length, but by its content.

"Christ, you've got a lot of balls writing down this history," the recruiter told Louie during his oral interview. "There isn't anybody in your family who hasn't been in jail."

"Except for me," Louie shot back. "And since when did the NYPD begin judging a man by his relations?"

In fact, as Louie well knew, nepotism was practically an application requirement for a post in the NYPD. Yet Ralph Eppolito's son went on to explain with such conviction how he'd never even received so much as a traffic summons, how he'd been reared in a strict Italian household, and how, in all honesty, he thought he was cut out to be a good cop, that he struck a sympathetic chord.

"I think the interviewer admired my audacity, because he passed me on with a recommendation. Also, the fact that Ralph and Freddy were both out of the picture probably didn't hurt my chances."

Despite her denials, Louie sensed that Tess was not exactly ecstatic over his decision. He was sure that lingering memories of buying off the men in blue at the behest of her father and brother still made her feel queasy about The Job. "And I'm pretty sure some of my father's attitude toward cops had rubbed off on her. But mostly she was afraid for me. Police officers were being shot left and right in those days.

"I spent six months in the Academy, and at times it got pretty weird. Once, during homicide class, the instructor unveiled a chart full of mug shots signifying the Gambino Crime Family tree. He was trying to explain how difficult it was to pin a murder on a capo or a boss, whose pictures were aligned at the top of the chart, when there was no link to the actual hit men, whose faces were arrayed along the bottom.

"After the bell rang, one of my classmates called me over to the blackboard and pointed to a mug shot of one of the button men. This cadet was a gung-ho hick from Long Island, and I could read the excitement in his face. 'Look, Lou, this guy has the same last name as you.' His mouth dropped open when I told him that he was pointing to my old man."

Upon graduation, Louie was assigned to the 63rd Precinct, in the Marine Park section of Brooklyn, not far from his old Pigtown neighborhood. He wasn't stupid. He knew what he could be getting himself into, and the night before reporting for duty he took a walk along the beach "to get things straight in my head."

"I told myself that there was going to be some time or another when I'd cross paths with the people from my past, and I decided then and there that I would show them the same respect I had been taught to exhibit all my life. I wouldn't go out of my way, but every time I had to deal with a mobster from my old world, I'd try to think of my father, to remember what he taught me about honor. Show them respect, I figured, and they'll show it to me. It worked, too. Whenever I'd bump into one of the old goombahs, I'd always stop to talk. Just chit-chat."

For instance there was one goodfellow, named

Jimmy "Jim Brown" Clemenza, who lived in the Six-three. Although Clemenza was a capo in the Colombo Family and had spent his career overseeing shakedowns in Manhattan's garment district, he had known Ralph Eppolito well. Clemenza was an old man now, and forever working in the vegetable garden out in his yard. Whenever Louie passed by in his patrol car, he'd stop, get out, and dutifully ask after "Jim Brown" 's three boys, Anthony, Charley, and Jerry.

"Consequently, he'd always offer me iced tea, and he always told me how much his back hurt. I found it odd that, whereas we both came from the same kind of family, here I was sitting in a police car, about the last place "Jim Brown" Clemenza or my old man would have figured I'd end up.

"Now, informal meetings like this were strictly forbidden by the rules and regs. But hell, I figured, who was it going to hurt to stop and commiserate with an old Mustache Pete about his lumbago?"

After he'd been on The Job for about a year, Louie ran into his Uncle Jimmy at a family wedding. He had tried as best he could to avoid family gatherings since entering the force. There was, after all, no use asking for trouble. But the pull of the clan proved just too strong in some cases. This was one of those occasions. On the church steps, Jimmy Eppolito told his nephew how proud he was of him. Louie didn't know what his uncle was talking about until Jimmy mentioned the good reports he was getting from his friend "Jim Brown" Clemenza.

"All I hear is that Ralphie's son the cop is such a respectful person." Jimmy Eppolito beamed. "I hear you never turn your back on nobody."

And, in truth, Louie didn't think his actions conflicted in any way with being, in his phrase, "one hundred percent tough cop."

"From day one, I was out on the street making arrests. I caught them for drugs, I caught them for burglaries. I caught them for running traffic lights. Believe it or not, it got so that I hated to see anyone breaking the law. But that didn't mean I was going to disown my heritage."

The Police Department's red tape was, sooner or later, bound to prove frustrating to Patrolman Louie Eppolito. It wasn't long before the young cop found himself using vigilante justice if he felt the situation called for it. Family habits, after all, die hard. Louie liked to think of it as the Cosa Nostra interpretation of police procedures. The public certainly had no complaints.

"Once I was called to a house where a husband was really knocking the crap out of his wife, a little Irish girl named Katie. She had bruises all over her body, and deep, vicious bite marks on her breasts. I knew that arresting this scumbag would only earn Katie another beating, so I devised a plan my old man would have been proud of.

"After showing up at her house twice and telling Katie's husband I was investigating reports of a prowler, I snuck into her backyard after my shift one night and began rattling a garbage pail. I wore a ski mask over my face. When the wife beater came out to investigate, I cracked him six or eight times in the throat with a lead pipe. I even had a story prerehearsed to cover my tracks.

" 'Look, motherfucker,' I told him, 'my kid goes to school with your kid, and I hear you've been beating your wife. My father beat my mother to death, and

any man who beats his wife has got to answer to me.'
Then I knocked him out and sneaked off.

"Three days later I returned, in uniform, investigating further reports of a 'prowler' in the area. The wife beater was a mess. He couldn't get out of bed. But on my way out Katie thanked me and gave me a peck on the cheek. She knew it was me, she said, adding that she hadn't been battered or bitten since."

There is an adage on The Job—and adages must start with some grain of truth—that a cop can spend twenty years patrolling the streets without ever unholstering his piece. Not this cop. In Louie's rookie year alone he was involved in two shootouts.

"The first time, a rapist and I threw shots at each other in a vacant lot. Neither of us were hit, but I collared the guy and he was sentenced to fifteen years in the can. It wasn't so much an exhilarating feeling, like in the war movies, as a scared-shit feeling. Scared and pissed off. I mean, I really wanted to kill this guy. He was shooting at me, for chrissake. The second was an armed robbery. Two perps running out of a bodega began blasting away like it was Dodge City. I blasted right back and cornered them until the cavalry arrived. They were lucky I didn't shoot them in the head right there. But I was young and green and had yet to learn Custer's advice, updated for New York City: the only good perp is a dead perp.

"The awards and accolades began piling up, and there were times when I felt, ironically, that I was born to be a cop. I had some kind of sixth sense that allowed me to merely look at a person, or a situation, and smell something wrong. Once, my partner and I were stopped for a light when I saw this guy loping across the street. It wasn't a particularly hot day, but there were beads of sweat caught in a fold in the back of his neck.

" 'See any buses coming?' I asked my partner. There weren't, nor were there any taxicabs, nor was the light about to change. There was no reason for him to be running. 'Let's grab that guy,' I said, and my partner wanted to know just what the hell for. I told him I just had a feeling. He thought I was crazy, of course, but we jumped from the car, yelled, 'Halt!' and the guy spins and drops a pistol. I swear to God, not one split second later a bank alarm went off on the opposite corner. This guy had done the bank, and we had nabbed him. I was all over the television news that night explaining my 'sixth sense' to the tabloid and TV reporters. The newsmen in New York like to think of themselves as a cynical bunch, but, in truth, they eat that stuff up."

In 1969, the Six-three had a reputation as a quiet house in a well-kept, middle-class neighborhood. But Patrolman Eppolito was setting it on fire. And he wasn't learning anything by example. Most of the old-timers who walked into work carried their pajamas and a pillow under their arms. "Cooping" is a time-honored police tradition. Lazy cops find a dark playground, or a dead-end street, where they can park their patrol car and spend their shift sleeping. The boys in the Six-three had it down to a science, down to the nightclothes, which Louie thought were a bit much.

The veterans were also more than willing to bend the departmental rules—but in a different way, and for different reasons than Louie. Louie once rode with a sergeant who would ignore felony calls coming over the police radio, yet would turn into A. J. Foyt at the report of a fender bender in order to palm the ten-dollar bribe the garage truckers would lay out to secure the tow.

"I thought of my old man every time I saw these 'public servants' screwing off. It was like working with Ali Baba and the Forty Thieves. A supermarket was knocked off once and my partner and I were the first on the scene. The robbers were long gone, but the joint was a wreck. The first thing my partner did was call the owner and ask him where he kept his secret emergency stash of money.

"When the owner told him about a hidden drawer behind one of the freezers, my partner told him to hang on, went and pocketed the cash, returned to the phone, and said, 'Yeah, the motherfuckers got that, too.' Even I had to laugh, although when I thought about it later it made me a little sick to my stomach.

"But these kind of things only made me more determined to become a Wyatt Earp. If I was going to do that kind of shit I may as well have gone to work for my Uncle Jimmy. Believe it or not, my old man's code of ethics probably made me a better cop than most— I had too much self-respect to steal."

By the time he was three months into his rookie tour, Louie and his new partner, another young cop named Lou Pioli, had reached a mutual agreement with "these lazy bastards just waiting for their pension." The two rookies agreed to catch every call covering the southern half of the entire precinct. The other officers willing to work handled the northern half. The arrangement benefited all sides.

Eight months into his first year, Louie broke the Six-three's rookie arrest record. Superiors from the Brooklyn Borough Command were beginning to sniff out the hot young prospect, and Louie was soon fielding promises of transfer to a higher-crime-rate area.

Basking in the attention, anticipating his transfer, Louie told his mother he was in "seventh cop heaven."

Unfortunately for Patrolman Eppolito, things weren't quite so celestial on the home front. After two years, his marriage to Teresa had fallen apart. As Ralph Eppolito had predicted, the two teens from Flatbush had outgrown each other. Nor was Teresa thrilled with the hours her husband devoted to his new job. At Louie's urging, the two agreed to separate.

Teresa packed up Louis, Jr., and moved out of their Flatbush apartment. Louie gave up the flat and moved back in with his mother. Within a year, Teresa had met another man from the neighborhood, and was soon remarried. Louie, meanwhile, graduated from Casanova to Don Juan. "Perps and pussy" were his only goals. There was more of Uncle Freddy in him than he had ever stopped to consider.

14

It started after I left Teresa, a game really, how many girls could I screw? How many hours a day could I stay up? How many times could I get laid on the same tour by different women? My partner would be in a diner on break having coffee, and I'd be getting a blow job out in the parking lot. I don't know if it was a sickness or what, but I was good at it. And women loved the uniform. Every time we went on a call where a husband smacked his wife, I went back that night and smacked it to her, too.

"Battered wives were the most vulnerable. They needed a crutch to lean on, especially if that crutch just put the fear of God in their husbands. I'm not proud of it now. But it meant nothing to me then.

"By this time I was also bodybuilding professionally. I won the Mr. New York City title. Then Mr. East Coast. And it seemed like each time I'd come to a door a woman would answer, look me up and down, and I'd be back banging her that night.

"As often happens when you let your little head do all your thinking, I ran into problems. I once answered a wife-beating call at a sanitation worker's house, and this guy made the worst mistake a man can make with me: while trying to get at his wife, a girl named Kathy, he put his hands on me and ripped my uniform shirt. I proceeded to show him what respect for the law was all about.

"Then he sued.

"The case went on for about four months. In the interim, the garbage man was calling and making all kinds of threats, to kill my family, to kill me, that kind of stuff. Finally I'd had enough, and went to see him. I took off my badge and gun and suggested we settle our differences man-to-man in a nearby park. To my astonishment, he agreed.

"He was a tough sonofabitch, I'll give him that, and we went at it for a good four or five minutes. I got my shots in, and he got his. I had a busted lip and couldn't hear right for a couple of weeks because of his punches to my ear. But in the end I got my hands around his neck and nearly choked him to death. That was the last I heard of the lawsuit. His wife, however, was another story.

"Kathy, who had a body she loved to show off, became a Playboy Bunny. She'd wear skirts about two inches longer than her garter belt, and when I'd meet her in a bar she'd come and sit on my lap and make sure I noticed that she was wearing see-through panties. She was a cop's dream—until she'd cry and tell me how much she loved me. I knew deep down that there was no way in the world I'd consider throwing a ring on this one's finger. She was a hard girl, not the type you'd bring home to Mom. I'd still drop by her house on the way to a night shift for a quick bang, but that was as far as it got. That was as far as it got with scores of them."

After several years of watching her son's whoring, Tess Eppolito could stay silent no longer. She sat Louie down one night and told him, literally, that he

EPPOLITO DOES IT AGAIN

Irene McCall a barmaid in Jeffrey's Playhouse at 1221 Nostrand Avenue saw two men armed with a 12 gauge shotgun placed the gun against the head of 18 year old Mark Barcey, quickly pressed a ... which alerted the ... and Police ... Ca...

Lisier fired at the policemen, but the gun ... fired and officers captured ... Eppolito was ... he noticed ... deadly holding ... with a shot...

... holdup ... as Miki ... were warn... ... till then ... Eppo... ... shot... ... re... ... the ... ...

who had gathered outside the store. Eppolito finally persuaded Peres to give himself up. At the stationhouse, the records revealed a previous charge of first degree robbery and rape, charged with robbery and grand larceny auto and was on parole.

They were indicted, charged with five counts of robbery, first degree, possession of a deadly weapon, two counts and reckless endangerment, first degree (formerly called attempted murder). The were held on $20,000 bail.

* * *

For Eppolito this was just another day of duty. On November 6 he was involved in three robbery arrests, on November 21 he apprehended a man with a gun and had completed the paperwork on him at 7 p.m. At 7:10 p.m. he went back on the street and arrested another man with a gun. In November scoreboard for ... dedicated policemen shows ... felony arrests, 2 misde... or arrests and the keeping ... gun off the quiet streets ... bush.

... officer, Hope Com... ... Cawley recognize ... police work.

For Louie Eppolito, Tin Turns to Gold

The Devastation of Flatbush -
Coverage Next Week

(Photo by Nick Federovitch)

... the NYPD, which has reached in his promise to ... ... July 1st. For story on the new ... ...

DAILY⊕NEWS

New York's Picture Newspaper

... Saturday, November 24, 1984

MOB BIG GOT DATA FROM COP

Story on page 3

By MURRAY WEISS
Police Bureau Chief

Detective passed confidential Police intelligence reports to a member of the ... who was convicted last month as ... trafficker. The Daily ...

... who ... identified ... last De... Intelligence ... files on mob figure Eberto Gambino while he was under federal investigation, according to an informed source in the Police Department. Gambino, a nephew of Carlo Gambino, the late "boss of all bosses" who reputedly was the most powerful crime figure in the United States before his death in 1976.

The detective, a 36-year ... assigned to a Brook... ... ouse is being in... ... Internal Affairs ... ... the degr...

May when FBI agents with a search warrant entere... ranch home in Cherry H... N.J.

The agents found copies of the files and ... them over to the Poli... ... investigation, which foc... ... Department inve... checked records ... copies of the ... ... the Intelligence ... ... headquarters on ... ... entries ... Brooklyn ... ... through Dec...

The sour... detective's ... ... the ... ... hind t...

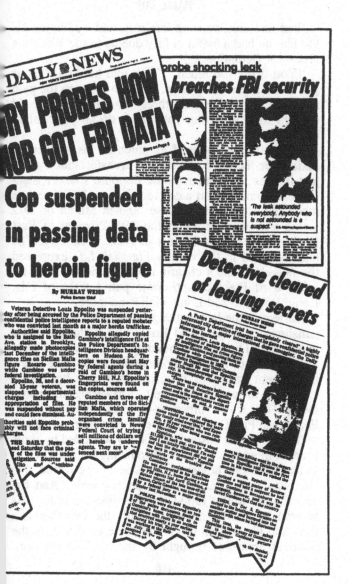

RY PROBES HOW
OB GOT FBI DATA

Story on Page 5

probe shocking leak
breaches FBI security

'The leak astounded
everybody. Anybody who
is not astounded is a
suspect.' U.S. Attorney Raymond Dearie

Cop suspended in passing data to heroin figure

By MURRAY WEISS
Police Bureau Chief

Veteran Detective Louis Eppolito was suspended yesterday after being accused by the Police Department of passing confidential police intelligence reports to a reputed mobster who was convicted last month as a major heroin trafficker.

Authorities said Eppolito, who is assigned to the Bath Ave. station in Brooklyn, allegedly made photocopies last December of the intelligence file on Sicilian Mafia figure Rosario Gambino while Gambino was under federal investigation.

Eppolito, 36, and a decorated 15-year veteran, was slapped with departmental charges including misappropriation of files. He was suspended without pay and could face dismissal. Authorities said Eppolito probably will not face criminal charges.

THE DAILY News disclosed Saturday that the passe of the files was under investigation. Sources said lito and Gambino

Eppolito allegedly copied Gambino's intelligence file at the Police Department's Intelligence Division headquarters on Hudson St. The copies were found last May by federal agents during a raid of Gambino's home in Cherry Hill, N.J. Eppolito's fingerprints were found on the copies, sources said.

Gambino and three other reputed members of the Sicilian Mafia, which operated independently of the five organized crime families, were convicted in Newark Federal Court of trying to sell millions of dollars worth of heroin to undercover agents. They are to be sentenced next month.

Detective cleared of leaking secrets

by MURRAY WEISS

A Police Department trial has "completely cleared" a highly decorated city detective of charges that he gave confidential police information to a major international dope smuggler, the Daily News has learned.

The veteran, Louis Eppolito, 37,

looked like shit, smelled like shit, and was living his life like he had a fistful of fifty dollars in the Women's House of Detention.

"You drink too much," Tess told her son. "Your gut looks like a sand dune. You never go to the gym anymore. You're twenty-three years old, Louie, old enough to stop letting your prick do all your thinking."

Louie stunned himself as much as his mother by taking her lecture to heart. His transformation came just in time: Patrolman Louie Eppolito's next assignment was not the sort a cop took lightly. His superiors made good on their promise, and in March of 1972 Louie was transferred to the 25th Precinct in East Harlem, one of the busiest in New York City. The lead editorial in the weekly *Flatbush Life* expressed the neighborhood's chagrin over the move: "The famous 63rd Precinct anti-crime patrol team of Ptls. Louie Eppolito and Louis Pioli is no more."

Harlem in the late sixties and early seventies was a gunslinger's dream. And Louie was nothing if not a gunslinger. The neighborhood had yet to recover from its vicious race riots, and one month into Louie's new assignment an event occurred that cast his career choice in an entire new light. Answering an anonymous "10-13," or officer-in-distress, telephone call, Patrolman Phil Cardillo entered a Harlem mosque and in the melee that ensued was fatally wounded by shots fired from what was believed to be his own revolver.

The weapon, however, was never recovered. No one was ever charged with the homicide. And the unorthodox investigation into Cardillo's murder was viewed by many—most especially the Department's rank and file—as so shoddy as to be a rollover to the political pressures brought by the city's black com-

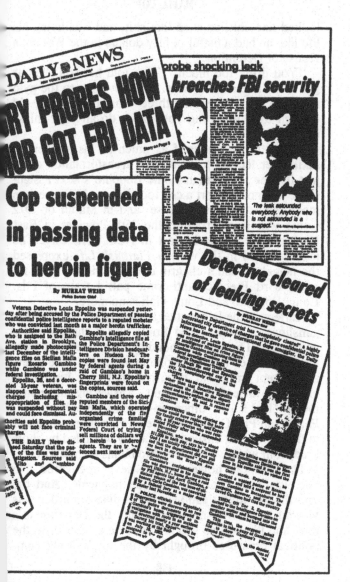

DAILY ● NEWS
NEW YORK'S PICTURE NEWSPAPER

RY PROBES HOW
OB GOT FBI DATA

Story on Page 3

probe shocking leak
breaches FBI security

'The leak astounded everybody. Anybody who is not astounded is a suspect.' — U.S. Attorney Raymond Dearie

Cop suspended
in passing data
to heroin figure

By MURRAY WEISS
Police Bureau Chief

Veteran Detective Louis Eppolito was suspended yesterday after being accused by the Police Department of passing confidential police intelligence reports to a reputed mobster who was convicted last month as a major heroin trafficker.

Authorities said Eppolito, who is assigned to the Bath Ave. station in Brooklyn, allegedly made photocopies last December of the intelligence files on Sicilian Mafia figure Rosario Gambino while Gambino was under federal investigation.

Eppolito, 38, and a decorated 15-year veteran, was slapped with departmental charges including misappropriation of files. He was suspended without pay and could face dismissal. Authorities said Eppolito probably will not face criminal charges.

THE DAILY News disclosed Saturday that the passing of the files was under investigation. Sources said Eppolito and Gambino con...

Eppolito allegedly copied Gambino's intelligence file at the Police Department's Intelligence Division headquarters on Hudson St. The copies were found last May by federal agents during a raid of Gambino's home in Cherry Hill, N.J. Eppolito's fingerprints were found on the copies, sources said.

Gambino and three other reputed members of the Sicilian Mafia, which operated independently of the five organized crime families, were convicted in Newark Federal Court of trying to sell millions of dollars worth of heroin to undercover agents. They are to be sentenced next mon...

Detective cleared
of leaking secrets

by MURRAY WEISS

A Police Department trial has "completely cleared" a highly decorated city Detective of charges that he gave confidential police information to a major international dope smuggler, the Daily News has learned.

The decorated Detective Louis Eppolito...

looked like shit, smelled like shit, and was living his life like he had a fistful of fifty dollars in the Women's House of Detention.

"You drink too much," Tess told her son. "Your gut looks like a sand dune. You never go to the gym anymore. You're twenty-three years old, Louie, old enough to stop letting your prick do all your thinking."

Louie stunned himself as much as his mother by taking her lecture to heart. His transformation came just in time: Patrolman Louie Eppolito's next assignment was not the sort a cop took lightly. His superiors made good on their promise, and in March of 1972 Louie was transferred to the 25th Precinct in East Harlem, one of the busiest in New York City. The lead editorial in the weekly *Flatbush Life* expressed the neighborhood's chagrin over the move: "The famous 63rd Precinct anti-crime patrol team of Ptls. Louie Eppolito and Louis Pioli is no more."

Harlem in the late sixties and early seventies was a gunslinger's dream. And Louie was nothing if not a gunslinger. The neighborhood had yet to recover from its vicious race riots, and one month into Louie's new assignment an event occurred that cast his career choice in an entire new light. Answering an anonymous "10-13," or officer-in-distress, telephone call, Patrolman Phil Cardillo entered a Harlem mosque and in the melee that ensued was fatally wounded by shots fired from what was believed to be his own revolver.

The weapon, however, was never recovered. No one was ever charged with the homicide. And the unorthodox investigation into Cardillo's murder was viewed by many—most especially the Department's rank and file—as so shoddy as to be a rollover to the political pressures brought by the city's black community, particularly the mosque's fiery spiritual leader, the Reverend Louis Farrakhan.

"I was in the second or third squad car on the scene after the Muslims attacked and killed Cardillo in the mosque. That day was one of the toughest in my life, because it was a massacre and it was a one-way deal. The brass botched the investigation and that poor cop died in vain. If the incident taught me anything, it taught me about the politics of the Police Department.

"If my bosses were going to back down every time there was pressure from a special-interest group, then my policy would be to shoot first and ask questions later. In truth, that had always been my policy, but now it was, like, official.

"Harlem was a whole new world anyway. You can only imagine the misconceptions an Italian kid from Brooklyn, even one with a semi-enlightened father, had about the 'nigger capital' of the country. Despite my old man's lessons, after the race riots, and especially after the Cardillo shooting, I thought the blacks were the lowest form of human beings.

"But, strange as it sounds, when I got to know my way around up there, I did find so many people who were *human*. When I was first transferred, I imagined that they'd be shooting at me from the rooftops. It was just the opposite. Maybe because they needed the law more than most."

Nonetheless, Harlem was a far cry from Louie's dream-world days of the shuffling Tipsy or the stoic Johnny Saxton. He saw a bleak and destitute side to the ghetto that Ralph had never shown him.

"True, the community was filled with junkies and prostitutes. But these people were victims more than anything. I was also a little ashamed about my father's people's role in turning the area into such a shithole. I mean, who was bringing in the junk the entire neighborhood was using as an anesthesia?

"But believe it or not, I started to take a liking to the African culture. I had my bedroom back in Brooklyn done up in an African motif, filling it with masks, shields, all kinds of artifacts. My mother thought I'd gone loony. Yet I enjoyed sitting on corner stoops, letting neighborhood people explain their history, their beliefs.

"Harlem was also a world of extremes, where the good were very good and the bad were motherfuckers. It wasn't long before the shooting began. I was coming out of the precinct one day during my first week when a guy ran in yelling that his wife had caught him with another woman and was going to kill him. Not two seconds later the wife burst into the station house and blasted him in the face with a little twenty-five automatic. The bullet lodged between his two front teeth. He was only stunned. Must have been bad ammo. I was used to wives wielding frying pans, not automatic weapons.

"Another time we were called to a domestic dispute on the twenty-fifth floor of a housing project. The husband swore he was going to throw his wife out the window. But the woman ordered us out of their apartment. She said she could take care of him with a broom handle. As he hadn't laid a hand on her, we had no choice but to back off into the elevator.

"Sure enough, she hit the courtyard about the same time we did. Three cops standing with clipboards gave her a ten for the dive. It's not so much that we laughed at their tragedies . . . well, yeah, okay, it was that we laughed at the tragedies. But it was only an outlet for all the degradation you'd come across. As I would tell Fran after a shift, 'You can't make this shit up.'

"Three weeks into my tour we interrupted a bank robbery that turned into the goddamn OK Corral. Instead of surrendering, this stupid perp decides to shoot it out with six of us. Then he stands on the hood of a parked car to get a better shot. By the time the smoke cleared he had about thirty holes in him. I was sure I was the one that fired the killing shot, but the dead guy's body was so ventilated that ballistics couldn't, or wouldn't, say who made the official kill.

"The police psychiatrists don't like to tell cops when they kill somebody. They don't want to make the cop upset. But really, who gives a fuck? We aren't out there shooting priests. I learned something about myself during that gunfight. I not only had the capacity to kill, I had the capacity to forget about it, to not let it bother me.

"I would spend my last dime buying food for hungry little kids on the street, the cutest and sweetest things you ever wanted to see, and for weeks afterward I'd agonize over them, and sometimes even dream about them. But a perp in a gunfight? Forget about it. He was forgotten as soon as he hit the pavement."

Louie's next Harlem gunfight proved to be more frightening, as well as a lot more personal. After the mosque killing, the FBI passed the word to the NYPD that a home-grown terrorist organization calling itself the Black Liberation Army had concocted an alarming agenda: they planned to kill a cop a month. So there was an added element of urgency as duty sergeants warned their patrolmen at daily briefings, and every cop took the threat seriously. It was, as Louie soon discovered, literally a matter of life and death.

"One rainy morning my partner, John O'Halloran, and I were cruising East 125th Street at about three-thirty when a white guy came tearing down Madison

Avenue, on foot, screaming that his hack had been stolen. The cabbie told us the car thieves had driven north, and when we reached 132nd and Madison, sure enough, there was his taxi, just idling at the curb. Four black guys were still in it.

"O'Halloran was about to pull up alongside the cab when I suddenly got a clammy feeling. 'Stop the fucking car,' I screamed. 'Right now.' When he jammed on the brakes we were still about three car lengths behind the cab, and O'Halloran wanted to know what was the matter. I told him I thought we were about to get ambushed and reached for the radio to call for backup.

"Just as I had the words out of my mouth, John opened the car door and our overhead light went on. Immediately a skel—a lowlife—jumped from that cab and threw two shotgun blasts at our patrol car, blowing out the windshield. By that time we had both rolled into the street and were emptying our service revolvers.

"As we exchanged shots, the four blacks split up. I chased two of them north, while John took off south. I heard gunfire coming from his direction, but I was kind of busy to be thinking too much about him. One of the perps I was chasing stopped and turned, got off four shots that, I swear, whizzed past my ears, and I pumped two thirty-eight-caliber slugs into his gut. He died a few days later in the hospital. I never gave it a second thought. The other I treed on a nearby roof. My adrenaline was such that the paramedics had to pry my radio out of his forehead."

For his heroism, Louie was nominated for the Medal of Honor, the highest award the NYPD confers. He was also invited to a public awards ceremony at City Hall, where Mayor John Lindsay hung a Bravery Commendation around his neck. But what Louie took the most pride in was his instincts, the fact that he had sensed the trouble, "and saved two more cop families from hearing those goddamn bagpipes they play at every police funeral."

If there was anything lacking in Louie Eppolito's life, it was the most important thing: a sense of family. Given his background, that deprivation was almost more than he could handle. He did manage to see Tess almost daily. And when he wasn't working holiday tours he squeezed in the occasional visit to Al and Pauline. But as Teresa and her new fiancé drifted from his orbit, his visits to Louie, Jr., became few and further between. The death of his father, he had begun to realize, had left more of a void than he expected.

Although Louie's initial resolution to avoid his Uncle Jimmy, his cousins, even his Grandpa Louis had been made largely on instinct, it became a practical necessity when a friendly supervisor advised Louie that he had been caught in an FBI surveillance tape chatting with some "goombah capo" outside a Brooklyn church wedding. Louie immediately recalled his "Jim Brown" Clemenza conversation with his Uncle Jimmy.

Despite a police career that was reaching nearly mythical proportions, he knew that The Job was really one huge hen party. Any blunder, any gaffe, any misstep at the top of the North Bronx would fuel gossip at the bottom of South Brooklyn within hours. It was the natural order of things, especially in the clique-ridden NYPD bureaucracy, for the brass to converge on a wayward hero.

But Louie had an Achilles' heel: music. Specifically, music from the fifties. The golden oldies were his passion, and, unfortunately, most of the New York City clubs booking these nostalgia acts were owned and operated by mobsters. Some of them Louie knew personally, through his father. Some he knew only by reputation. It didn't matter. When there was a group in town he wanted to see, Louie would stride right into a club, flash his badge, and take a seat in the front row. The hell with the brass. They might be able to keep him away from his family, but he was not going to let them drive a stake between him and his music.

Doo-wop, however, could only carry a man so far. There were nights when Louie found himself stretched across his bed envisioning the holiday feasts of his childhood. He missed the cacophony of bawling cousins, nieces, nephews; the pungent aroma of deep-fried calamari and scungilli, even the stomach-turning odor of the *baccalata,* the codfish dish that was an Italian household's Christmas staple. What he'd give for a slice of homemade Easter pie; a mixture of sweet and hot sausage, hard-boiled eggs, and cheeses. But the risk wasn't worth the investment, and he stuck to his guns as best he could.

When he attended family weddings with Tess, for instance, he sat in a back pew and skipped the receptions afterward, asking his mother to proffer his congratulations, as well as his envelope, to the bride and groom. At family funerals he said a perfunctory prayer over the body at the wake before slipping out some side door, forgoing the church service.

On the occasion when he inevitably bumped into his uncle, or Bath Beach, or old Todo Marino, he was polite, respectful. But that was as far as it went. There could be no mix and match of the old mob with his new career. He had dozens of friends from The Job, guys with whom to play cards and drink beer and whore around. But, on the whole, life on the force was beginning to get pretty lonely.

Then, in the spring of 1972, just prior to his reassignment to Harlem, he met his match. Her name was Frances Todisco. In an extremely un-Louie-like turn of phrase, he told his mother that Fran "filled some kind of hole in my soul."

15

Louie met Fran in the elevator of the El San Juan Hotel, at Isla Verda, in Puerto Rico. He and two fellow cops had flown to the island for ten days of rays and babes. By the second day of their vacation, they had their pickup routine down to a science: every morning, while Officers Pat Bafardi and Frank Intiri were dressing, Louie would head downstairs to the lobby, or the coffee shop, or the beach, and arrange the day's scores.

"I had a rap of bullshit a mile wide, and I managed to set up those two hellhounds with a couple of señoritas the first three days we were on the island."

On the morning of their fourth day, Louie was waiting for the elevator when the doors opened and standing in front of him was Fran.

"She was gorgeous. I kind of walked into the elevator with my eyes glazing over and said to her, 'Please tell me you're from New York.' When she said she was from the Bronx, and asked why, I told her 'Because I'm going to marry you.' It was Easter Sunday, 1971, her birthday. She had just turned twenty. So I called her Bunny."

* * *

FRAN: "Louie came on with that I'm-going-to-marry-you stuff and I said to myself, *Oh yeah, just you*. From the moment I met him I had a feeling the guy wasn't being honest with me. Just intuition. To tell you the truth, I really didn't care, because I wasn't all that interested.

"He was very handsome, and built like an Adonis. But there was something in his eyes, a craziness, that scared me a little. But my girlfriend and I had gone down there to have some fun, and I had nothing planned for that night, so I decided to take a flyer. I mean, what's an island vacation for if you don't take a risk every once in a while. We had dinner and he was the perfect gentleman. He didn't even make one move. I didn't know whether to be angry or not."

LOUIE: "Fran was the best-built girl I had ever seen, a bod that just knocked my socks off. As far as I was concerned, I was in love. I wasn't going to screw up this relationship by trying to get into her pants. I took her out that night, and again a few nights later, and finally told her that I was a cop back in New York. She didn't believe that I was only twenty-three until I showed her some identification. I promised I'd call her as soon as my flight touched down in New York.

"I kept that promise. But once back in familiar surroundings she became a little leery. I told her I'd been married, and she explained that she came from a strict Italian family, and would never think of becoming involved with someone who had already been married, much less someone who had any children. I figured it wasn't the best time to bring up Louis, Jr.

"So here I was, separated, with a child, and in love from the first moment I saw her. Under the circumstances, she left me no choice. I started with my line.

She was seeing a guy from the Bronx, but I knew she wasn't happy. I played on that theme.

"I asked her if she could see the difference between a boyfriend who treated her like crap, yet who was single, and a divorced boyfriend who worshiped the ground she walked on. I told her I'd treat her like gold, smother her with love, honor her, trust her, do everything right by her. I said I couldn't believe all that meant nothing because I had once been married.

"After about three weeks of this, I took her to a park and told her the whole story. About Teresa. About Louis, Jr. I remember it was the day Joe Colombo* was shot and paralyzed. And she came to a decision. She told me she couldn't see me anymore."

FRAN: "When Louie finally told me that he was in fact separated, and had a little boy, I saw that as an excuse to break it off. I was seeing another guy who I thought was a little more, say, stable, than this wild bear. Of course I knew by this time that he was a cop. It was funny, but when he told me, I didn't believe him, and made him show me his badge. But he wasn't real forthcoming about the rest of his background.

"I honestly didn't feel like he was trying to hide anything from me. It's just that we never got around to talking about his family, except for maybe his mother. You know how Italian boys feel about their mothers. But anything about his father, what kind of

---

* June 28, 1971. Joe Colombo, head of the crime family that still bears his name, became one of the oddest protest leaders of the civil rights era. Founder of the Italian-American Civil Rights League, he was the target of an attempted assassination at a Manhattan rally. He was shot in the head and neck, incapacitated, and died in bed in 1978.

Patrolman Louie Eppolito's first day on "The Job,"
August 22, 1969. By Christmas the rookie cop was
leading the 63rd Precinct in arrests.

The last thing turncoat Gambino soldier Johnny Robilotto saw before being "whacked" was the faces of his hitmen, Louie's dad, Ralph "Fat The Gangster" Eppolito (left) and his Uncle Jimmy "The Clam" Eppolito. Three decades later, in 1980, Louie's Uncle Jimmy and his cousin, Jimmy Jr., were blown away in a Brooklyn hit.

Louie Eppolito in 1956, recovered from rheumatic fever and "ready to take on the world."

Louie's father as a "mobster-about-town" before he met his wife Tess, who remembers Ralph cutting this picture in half when the Feds knocked on the door.

Mr. New York City,
1967.

Ralph and Tess at their
daughter Paula's wedding.
Two years later, "Fat The
Gangster" was dead.

Louie Eppolito weds Frances Todisco, August 26, 1973. Fran's family never knew why the band played the theme from *The Godfather*.

Patrol partners Louie Eppolito and Lou Pioli, "The Starsky and Hutch" of the Six-three Precinct.

"The two Godfathers of the NYPD," Louie and his Robbery Squad partner Steve Caracappa. Steve saved Louie from a homicide rap by pulling him off a beaten "perp."

Louie receiving his first Medal of Honor, the Department's highest award, from Police Commissioner Michael Codd and Mayor Abraham Beame in 1973.

Louie and Commissioner Codd on Medal Day, 1973.

(Left to right) Detectives Steve Gardell, Jimmy McCafferty, and Jack Healy. Cancer took McCafferty six weeks later.

Fran and Louie on his first day as a detective, July 1, 1977.

The first time Tony saw his dad in uniform. He wanted to play with the gun.

Detective Louie Eppolito, "always ready to go."

(Left to right) Tony, Andrea, Deanna and Fran in 1991.

Louie Eppolito, Jr., in 1984, about the time he made the call that made his father cry. "I love you, Dad. I'm in your corner."

work he did, was very sketchy. All I knew was that his father had been a bartender who died young. So I figured I really didn't need to know any more. I guess I had a passing thought that maybe Louie didn't get along with his father's side of the family.

"None of this really seemed to matter, though. Because, as far as I was concerned, Louie was history."

LOUIE: "I respected her for her decision, but I died a little bit the day Fran dumped me. And then my brains moved back into my shorts. My little black book quickly expanded to the size of an encyclopedia. In fact, it became so large that about six months later I had to redo it, and as I was copying telephone numbers into a new directory, I came across Bunny's. So out of the blue I decided to give her a call.

"And lo and behold, if she hadn't broken up with the Bronx guy. She also had a change of heart about previously married men, me in particular. She told me she had made a mistake, and we made a dinner date."

FRAN: "I can't describe how good Louie was to me when we began dating again. He was so concerned, so attentive, so caring. He was very open with his feelings, and I wasn't used to that coming from a guy. He would think nothing of telling me, 'I'm falling in love with you.' And I'd tell myself, 'Oh my God, it's too soon.'

"And I tell you, not one time did he try to get sexual. He was like Mr. Goody-Two-Shoes. I felt it was too good to be true. By now I was beginning to get to know a little bit about his background, or so I thought. He took me to a party at his sister's house, and I met Tess and about four of her sisters.

"But all the friends I met of his were cops. We only

went out with other cops and their wives. One night, after about six months of dating, as we were driving he turned to me and said, 'I told you in Puerto Rico that I was going to marry you.' I paused, then answered: 'You know, you're right.' I think I shocked him. Within two weeks his divorce had come through and he had given me an engagement ring. But first he went and asked my father for his daughter's hand.''

LOUIE: ''From that time on it was Fran and only Fran in my life. She wanted to hold our wedding reception at a fancy Bronx restaurant named the Marina Del Rey. It was top shelf, I suppose, with a large meadow that overlooked the East River. But when we went to check it out, it just did nothing for me.

''One of the restaurant managers who showed us around kept raving about how beautiful the lawn was, and how we weren't going to believe how pretty the grass would look in the spring with the sun coming off the water. It was the grass this and the grass that until after ten minutes I finally cut him off. 'You know, my family aren't cows,' I said. 'They're not going to eat the goddamned grass. How's the food in this place?'

''After that Fran and I thanked the man and left. By the time we reached the car Fran was laughing so hard she could barely blurt out that she had been wondering how long it would take before I'd had enough of that guy's grass nonsense.

''So we drove to Brooklyn and started checking out different catering halls. We came across one called the Pisa, in Bensonhurst. The Pisa was more to my liking. When the gentleman showing us the place took down my name, he looked a little stunned. 'Any relation to Jimmy Eppolito?' he asked. My uncle, I said. 'My

God,' he stammered, 'why didn't you tell me that when you walked in.'

"Out went the old price list; in came the new. What was originally going to cost us around seven thousand dollars was now slashed to three thousand dollars, while the spread had mysteriously tripled. It was like the miracle of the loaves and fishes.

"The odd thing is that I honestly hadn't planned any of this. We had merely stopped in there while making the rounds of these catering halls. I had no idea that Uncle Jimmy pulled such weight with the owner. Now I had a moral dilemma. Fran and I walked outside and I told her that, on the one hand, renting out this place could hurt my career. But on the other hand, the Pisa had been recommended to me by another cop, and I knew for a fact that other cops had rented out the place. We walked back in, hand-in-hand, and booked the joint on the spot."

FRAN: "Throughout our engagement, I never met the Eppolito side of Louie's family. Every once in a while if we were at his mother's for dinner a name might come up. Or an event. One of the aunts might say, 'Remember the time Freddy had to disappear?' or make some other reference to some shady deal. But, truth be told, most of it went right over my head. There was no way these nice people could be involved with all that nasty stuff the newspapers were printing about the Mafia.

"I wasn't stupid. I knew what the Mafia was. But it was all from television and the papers. It's not like I ran into Mafia men all the time on the street. When Tess or her sisters would talk about Ralph, or Jimmy, or Freddy, I found the stories interesting. Yet it never dawned on me that these guys had been full-fledged gangsters. Until that day in the Pisa.

"I mean, when Louie said the name 'Eppolito,' the red carpet was rolled out. I'd be lying if I said that I wasn't a little excited. It gave you a tingle up your back to have some snooty maître d' suddenly fawning all over you. But I was just as thrilled by the power Louie wielded as a cop. We'd go to a club, for instance, Louie would show his badge, and—boom!— we were right in. We also went to clubs that were operated by the Mafia, only I didn't realize it at the time.

"Louie loved the oldies groups from the fifties, the Mellow Kings, the Platters, and they were always booked into this one club on Flatbush Avenue called El Dante's. Whenever we went to El Dante's there'd be a long line, and Louie and I would stroll right up to the front and meet the manager working the door.

"The guy would always be really dapper. Silk suit. White-on-white shirt. Matching tie and breast-pocket handkerchief. The works. And he'd get all excited at seeing Louie, asking about his uncle, his cousins, talking about the old neighborhood. I'd watch Louie light up as he was talking about his family. Even though he couldn't see them, they still meant the world to him. That's just the kind of person Louie is. Family means more to him than anything else in the world. And it was almost as if he got some kind of family feeling from meeting and talking to these old friends of his father's and uncles'. The kisses on the cheeks were always next. Then we'd go right in. Front-row table.

"Once, I said to Louie—again, being very naive— 'Is he a cop or something?' And Louie would answer, 'No, you don't want to know what he does.' Louie never bragged about his connections. And when he did bother to explain anything, it was always in an offhand manner: 'He's just one of the wiseguys. I've known him for years.'

"I never asked anything else, and he never told me anything else. But I did see the respect there. And, deep down, I saw the longing in Louie. He was trying to be a good cop, he was trying to stay away, but the pull was sometimes just too strong.

"We'd be in some club and they'd come over to our table to sit and talk. They'd send drinks over. And by the end of the night there'd be no check. I thought it was great.

"I finally met his Uncle Jimmy, and Jim-Jim, and Aunt Dolly, at the wake for his father's oldest brother, Joe, the one who walked away from the Mafia. That's when Louie told me that the father's side of his family was involved with the Gambino Crime Family. I turned around to study Uncle Jimmy and I was a little in awe, and a little afraid.

"I came from a household where Italian was the first language. English, broken English, was a very distant second. My father was an elevator operator and my mother was a housewife. I knew nothing about the mob. And as far as my folks knew, Louie was the son of a registered nurse—which they thought was terrific—and a bartender who had died young. They loved Louie, and were glad to see me marrying a solid guy."

LOUIE: "We went for the whole nine yards at our wedding. There was a giant buffet table, with forty lobsters on the half-shell, some dressed in little calypso outfits, the rest done up like Carmen Miranda. We had chefs carving pounds and pounds of striped bass, and turkey, and roast beef. Two stuffed pheasants stood at either end of the buffet table. They had been carved out, and their meat was steaming on plates in front of the dressed birds. And that was just during the cocktail hour.

"We invited two hundred and twenty-five people. And there was one Organized Crime table right up front. I could not disrespect my own family at my wedding. The hell with whatever the Department thought. Uncle Jimmy sat with my grandfather, and Todo, and Bath Beach. My father's friends. Right next to them was a tableful of cops. It was great. I had to warn the wedding photographer about which table to avoid.

"I slipped the bandleader a request, and midway through the reception he made an announcement: 'By special request of the groom, this song is dedicated to James and Dolly Eppolito.' Then they played the theme from *The Godfather*. It was tremendous."

FRAN: "It was really funny. *The Godfather* movie had just come out a year or two before, and while we were making out the guest list Louie told me he really wanted his father's side of the family invited, but he wasn't sure if they would come, what with him having avoided them for all those years.

"But they came, all right. The owner of the Pisa even flew back from vacation to make sure he showed Uncle Jimmy the proper respect. We told the photographer, 'No pictures of that table,' and of course he wanted to know why. One look from Louie stifled his curiosity. Uncle Jimmy never got up. Didn't dance one dance. He just sat quietly through the entire reception.

"When Louie asked the bandleader to play the theme from *The Godfather*, the two of us got up and

swept over the dance floor alone. It was terribly romantic. And when the song was finished, we strolled over to Uncle Jimmy's table arm-in-arm. He kissed us, wished us luck, and handed us an envelope bulging with cash. My family still didn't know why we danced solo to that song, what it really meant, and I felt like a little girl keeping a secret. But Louie's side knew.

"And I didn't see my new Uncle Jimmy after that for years."

16

In January of 1973 Louie Eppolito was transferred from East Harlem back to Brooklyn. His new house was the Seven-one, which encompassed the predominantly black neighborhoods of Bedford-Stuyvesant, Crown Heights, parts of East New York, and, ironically, East Flatbush, which had recently "gone over to the other side"—that is, blacks had moved into Pigtown proper.

"All the time I was in Harlem I pleaded with them to transfer me back to Brooklyn. Brooklyn was my home, and I never felt entirely comfortable working in any other borough. Finally, my prayers were answered and I was asked whether I preferred a good house or a shit house. A shit house, I told them. I loved the heavy work, the feeling of working in scum holes. It was like World War II. You saw a Jap and you shot him. No questions asked. What I liked best was that there was no sanity in the Seven-one.

"The Black Liberation Army was at its destructive peak. Their agenda of killing a cop a month was damn near meeting its quota. In my mind, places like Khe Sanh and Pleiku had nothing on Bed-Stuy. I mean, it was a war. A buddy of mine on patrol stopped to check his tires and Black Muslims came up behind him and nearly hacked his head off with machetes.

"Snipers were everywhere. My squad car was hit on two separate occasions. And once when my partner and I took a metal garbage can through the windshield—it had been heaved off the roof of a tenement —we counted ourselves lucky that the bomb was big enough to see coming.

"That year, more cops were shot, stabbed, wounded and killed in the Seven-one than in all other New York precincts combined. And cop shootings throughout the city were up two hundred percent. It couldn't have been a nicer homecoming. I was young and I was tough and I loved what I was doing."

There were blocks in Bedford-Stuyvesant where radio patrol cars refused to respond to emergency calls. One, Union Street between Schenectady and Utica, was nicknamed Ho's Alley, in homage to Ho Chi Minh. Of course, knowingly shunning this street broke all kinds of departmental regulations. The police were, after all, being paid to protect the citizenry, even those who were unfortunate enough to live in Ho's Alley. But, unofficially, the unlucky and few law-abiding citizens who lived on those blocks were left to fend for themselves. As the saying went in the Seven-one, 'You go to Ho, you go to the hospital.'

It was shortly after Louie's transfer to the Seven-one that he met Jimmy McCafferty. Phil Contronio, the Seven-one's duty sergeant, pleaded with Louie to take McCafferty as his "temporary" partner until he could find someone else to fill the permanent slot.

"Contronio warned me that McCafferty was a foul-mouthed, hot-headed Irishman, a former Marine, and basically a cop that no one else wanted to drive with. He told me I'd probably hear a lot of 'guinea-this and guinea-that,' and asked me to just put up with it until he could find me a permanent replacement. Contronio promised me that McCafferty would only be riding with me for a couple of weeks, 'at the most.'

"I wanted no part of this. Hell, I was already getting a reputation as one of the department's stars. I told the sarge that I didn't need this Irish headache for even one tour. But he talked me into it.

"Jimmy and I partnered together for the next four years, and I came to love him like a brother."

Patrolmen Eppolito and McCafferty quickly established a violent, if effective, reputation throughout the borough. They became known as Atlas and Little Jim, as McCafferty was lucky if his five-foot-eight-inch frame tipped the scales at 160 pounds (even if he did, as Louie would later put it, "have two hundred pounds of balls"). By this time Louie's weightlifter's body was facing the inevitable strains of gravity, but what he lacked now in mobility he made up for in firepower. Plus, he had a partner he trusted to watch his back.

"I figured this little Mick must have had some Sicilian blood dumped somewhere into his ancestral gene pool. He was one tough sonofabitch, maybe the only cop I've ever met who threw as good a punch as I did. And if we got out of the car, when the smoke cleared, there were a lot of people hurt. Christ, we were Maris and Mantle with nightsticks."

The two once answered a disorderly call in a bar and ended up padlocking the joint and putting eleven people in the hospital. For their batting averages on that particular occasion they were given community service awards. It was a bad bar, they said, when questioned about their methods by some of the neighborhood's "liberal agitators," and it was necessary to break a few heads. Atlas and Little Jim feared nothing when they rode together, and if any "citizen" dared file a complaint with the Department's Civilian Complaint Review Board, they did the expedient thing.

"We lied. Both our daddies had taught us that. No one can expect any kind of civilian court to understand what it was like out there on the street. The tension. The split-second decisions. Jimmy and I didn't break any heads that didn't need to be broken. There's a lot of black grandmothers and bartenders and bodega owners out there who will attest to that. And along the way we managed to get in a few laughs."

Humor, of course, is a relative thing. Thus it was that only Eppolito and McCafferty could find laughs in a deadly hostage situation that earned Louie his second Medal of Honor nomination.

"It was a stickup at a candy store, and when we reached the location the perps were still inside, guns drawn. It was raining hard and as we bolted from the patrol car Jimmy slipped, banged into a street lamp, and went down. One of the skels ran out a side door and stuck a shotgun in his face. 'You are one dead pig,' the guy screamed.

"I was in the vestibule of the store by this time, so I wheeled and told the guy to freeze. Jimmy, who was a little woozy, began murmuring to me, real soft, 'Louie, don't turn around. Do not turn around!' I thought he was playing with my head, like in the movies. So when I glanced over my shoulder and saw the other perp covering me with his sawed-off, you might say I was a little surprised.

"They marched us both into the store, and the guy with the bead on me put me up against a wall and stuck the gun in my mouth. 'You think you're fucking tough, pig,' he said, 'but I'm going to show you how to die. But, first, I'm going to kill a kid just for your benefit.' Then his partner dragged a thirteen-year-old boy out of the stockroom, where they were holding half a dozen people hostage. I still remember the kid's name, Mark Bracey.

"He took the gun off me and put it in Bracey's mouth. I grabbed it back. 'What the fuck you going to hurt the kid for?' I said. The two perps were Puerto Ricans, and the one with the gun in the kid's mug looked at me and laughed. 'This kid's only a fucking nigger,' he said.

"As my bowels weakened, I grabbed the barrel of the shotgun and stuck it back in my face. 'If you're going to do it, pull the goddamn trigger,' I told him. 'I get paid for it. But don't hurt the kid, he didn't do nothing.' Throughout this conversation, the other guy's got Jimmy covered.

" 'Why do you give a shit about some black, you stupid fucking cop?' the guy on me asked. Then he cocked the trigger. 'We're gonna splatter these walls with this black kid's brains.'

"I told him I even gave a fuck about him. 'Let me let you in on a secret, smart guy,' I chattered. 'You may not know it, but you're a dead man right now. You can kill me, and you can kill my partner, but you can't kill the seventy or so people waiting outside to tear you apart. You see, this here is a numbers joint you're sticking up. And that mob out there is going to peel the skin off your body. Now you tough guys have a choice. You can do your three years for armed robbery standing on your head. Or you can face that angry neighborhood. It looks to me like I'm the only chance you got.'

"Incredibly, these stupid morons fell for it. Nobody

ever said you had to be a rocket scientist to stick up a bodega. They handed over their weapons! When we cuffed them and took them outside, there wasn't a soul on the street. They called me every name under the sun, names in Spanish you wouldn't call a dog in Chile, I think. Jimmy and I were laughing too hard to kick the shit out of them.''

Once, on McCafferty's day off, Louie was assigned a tour of duty with a rookie partner whose entire patrol experience consisted of forty-eight hours behind a desk. When they answered a sick call not three blocks from the station house, Louie advised the rookie to lock and cock his police-issue .38 Special.

"He couldn't believe it. Unholstering your weapon on a sick call isn't in anybody's rule book. But he followed my orders. Of course, there's no sick woman in the apartment building, and when we come back out onto the street, all four of our tires are punctured and the entire radio car's on fire. Someone poured gasoline over it and lit it up.

"Now a crowd's gathered around us, laughing their asses off. And my partner's starting to shake like a leaf. The fire went out without burning the interior. But instead of calling for a road tow, I told the rookie to get in the car. We drove on drums back to the precinct, with the paint on the car still smoldering. I refused to allow anyone to get the better of me." To Louie, it was as important not to make *una brutta figura,* a bad showing, as it was to uphold the standards of a New York City police officer.

Louie Eppolito's daddy had indeed taught him well. He was a hard case and reveled in his borderline tactics. He might be wearing a blue uniform, but he remained the son of a Mafia soldier who pinned his concepts of honor and respect to his sleeve as surely as he pinned his badge to his chest. And there are many who would argue that the streets of Bed-Stuy were better off for it. Louie's ethic applied to all he came in contact with, cops and citizens alike. Or, as Louie often said, "Sometimes it's good when 'right' takes it on the arches."

One of those times occurred during a bitterly cold January night in 1974, when Patrolmen Eppolito and McCafferty were assigned to assist a New York City marshal in a dispossession. This pro forma police procedure usually entails making sure whomever the marshal is dispossessing does not turn around and decide to dispossess the marshal of his senses.

But both Louie and McCafferty found it a bit odd that the notice to dispossess arrived at the station house at 10:30 at night. Dispossessions were normally handled during the 8 A.M.-to-4 P.M. day tour.

"It doesn't take us long to figure out what's going on. The marshal, a Jamaican immigrant with a real heavy West Indian accent, tells us that he wants us to 'throw them people out on their black asses, mon' while he appropriates all their furniture.

"I reminded him that city marshals were only allowed to dispossess furniture and the like, and he answered that he was not only a marshal but he owned that piece of property. So my eyebrow went up. This creep was using his office as an extension of his prick. And his plan was to use Jimmy and I to throw these people out on the street like washrags."

When Louie, McCafferty, and the marshal reached the second-floor apartment, they found a young mother and her two infants living in squalor.

The windows were broken, the winter wind was whipping through the two-room flat, and despite the fact that the woman had strung towels across the gaping window frames, her two children were huddled before an open gas stove.

The woman explained to Louie that she was only three months behind in her rent, had managed to give the marshal some money every month, and finally produced a letter from a secretarial service confirming that she would be beginning a new job in two weeks.

"One look at those poor freezing babies and suddenly this lady's not talking to Louie the cop, she's talking to Ralph Eppolito's kid. While she's explaining about the job she's got coming up, the Jamaican butts in: 'Mon, this is all bullshit. The fucking nigger here is ruining me house.' I let that one slide, and Jimmy told the guy to calm down.

"But as the woman pulls out a ledger and begins explaining to me how, once she starts her new job, she has a plan to fork over the back rent, the marshal pipes up again: 'Mon, this is all bullshit. What's gonna get this matter corrected?'

"The Jamaican was a big guy, six feet, two hundred pounds, and I hit him with my right hand so hard in the chest that he couldn't breathe. Then I grabbed his coat, pulled him across the room, and told him that throwing him out the window was what was going to get the matter corrected. This was no bluff. I wasn't trying to scare the guy. I fully intended to throw him out that fucking window and let him bounce to the pavement. If he lives, he lives; if he dies, he dies.

"It was his word against mine. I would have said he slipped. I was not afraid to see this guy fly, and I was not afraid of the system. But as I'm wrestling him across the windowsill, Jimmy grabbed me and convinced me that it wasn't worth getting all jammed up over this piece of scum."

And, with that, McCafferty slapped the marshal across the face and began a lesson in etiquette.

"This young lady is a mother of two who's trying to make ends meet," McCafferty continued. "*You* have no right to be calling anyone a *nigger*. If anyone in this room is going to be called names, it is you, *mon*. Your attitude is getting you nowhere."

After a little more of this collective bargaining, the two cops convinced the marshal/landlord that it was in his best interests to allow the woman and her children to remain in the apartment for another week *and* forget about the back rent. After Louie and Jimmy departed they called a local television reporter who ran an "Action Line," and within three days the reporter had found another apartment for the family.

"I didn't care who I had to take on," says Louie. "There are some things that you're taught as a child that stay with you the rest of your life. It's like a code you can't break. In my case, a Cosa Nostra code. And if following that code means having to face the consequences, even among friends, then so be it."

Never was Louie's adherence to his family's "Cosa Nostra code" more troublesome than when he found himself pitted against his co-workers. There was, for instance, the day he entered the Seven-one to find half a dozen officers crowded into a holding cell, working over one of the skels from the neighborhood, a black man in his twenties. As much as he liked a good brawl, Louie sensed that this wasn't so much a fight as an execution. There was no honor in this beating, and when he noticed that the perp was still handcuffed, he went ballistic.

A white rage grew in him as he began peeling cops off the pile, "like so many artichoke leaves." Naturally, his fellow officers took special umbrage at one of their own taking the wrong side. They informed Louie that their prisoner was the worst kind of perp, a cop fighter who had not only mouthed off, but had struck his arresting officer with the fellow's own night-stick. Surely Louie, of all people, could understand their reaction.

"But their excuse didn't matter, which only goes to show how little these cops understood about me. 'You got a beef with this guy, then you do the manly thing,' I told this one beet-faced sergeant. 'You take off the cuffs, you bring him into the fucking bathroom, and you punch him out. This here, seven on one, this is bullshit.'

"Then I picked the guy up, brought him into the bathroom, and began washing his face. I wanted to know what he had done to provoke the whole pre-cinct. When he explained that he didn't mean to hit the arresting officer, that he was only going for his girlfriend, I told him he was an asshole, but added that if he stayed cool, I'd try to square it with the mob outside.

" 'Why are you doing this for me?' he asked. 'I ain't nothing but a nigger.'

"Memories of my father flashed through my mind. 'You're a man first,' I blurted out. 'After that you can be a nigger, after that you can be any goddamn thing you want to be. But first, be a man.'

"Now there are cops who are wrong, cops who shouldn't be cops. But there are also people out there on the streets who shouldn't be people, who should be locked away from society like animals. I didn't get the feeling that this guy was one of the latter. And when I went back out to the muster room I tried to explain it that way. Plus, I was angry that my guys, the goddamn people who represented my profession, had acted like the mutts my old man had always warned me about.

" 'If you're tough, be fucking tough, but be tough with honor,' I told the guys. 'If not for the badge, at least show a little respect for yourselves.' I don't think my speech went over too big."

Two months later Atlas and Little Jim picked up a call about a "disturbance" in the Melody Bar, a Bed-Stuy tavern that was a halfway house to hell. The two pulled up, walked in, and immediately realized that they in trouble. The dispute was a drug deal gone sour, and there were at least twenty players inside this bar, all of them flashing iron. Louie and Jimmy had unsheathed their nightsticks, but they were useless. The two were engulfed by the crowd the moment they walked in.

"I heard the door lock behind us—we'd left our portable radios in the squad car—and then I heard one or two people debating what to do with us. The consensus seemed to be to kill us on the spot. You may not be able to understand this, but we didn't go for our guns. You put your hand on your gun in front of two dozen people who don't like you in the first place, and you're going to get killed.

"We were pushed to the back of the bar and brought face to face with this bald guy with one earring who looked like he sailed under Captain Blood. 'I'm not taking shit from nobody,' he declared. 'And if I got to kill a cop, I'll kill you right here.'

" 'Listen,' I said, 'we got a call about a dispute. We're not here to search people. We're not here to look for guns. But I don't mind telling you right now, I ain't fucking afraid of you or anybody in this bar. If you want to do it, let's do it, 'cause we ain't going down like no pussies.'

"Now I didn't know who wanted to kill me more, Captain Blood or Jimmy McCafferty. I'd given them something to prove, and the mood was ugly. Suddenly somebody lets go with a shotgun blast and I feel like my heart just ripped through my chest. I turned and it was the guy from a couple months back, the guy who was catching the beating in the cell. 'Your beef ain't with these cops,' he shouted. 'Eppolito, take your fucking partner and get the fuck out of here.'

"He didn't have to tell us twice. Out on the street we called for backup, surrounded the joint, and stormed back in. I had the rear door covered, and if a couple of guys got away, including one with a shotgun, well, it was just one of those things that happen in the confusion of a raid. Sometimes it paid to live by the law of the street rather than the law of the Department. That's how you make friends, and that's how you earn respect."

17

Louie surely could have been suspended, dismissed, or possibly even arrested for a goodly percentage of his departmental "heroics." Yet, he never did anything "I thought was wrong." There were, in fact, scores of incidents involving Louie that weren't sexy enough to make the papers yet helped to define his complex nature. Once, after apprehending two teenagers who had defaced a Brooklyn synagogue, he became so outraged over the "so-what" attitude the criminal justice system had taken toward the crime that he organized—on his own time—a daily private bus shuttle that filled the courtroom with Hasidic Jews.

"Sure, maybe to the average citizen a few swastikas spray-painted onto a building was nothing in comparison to the murders and rapes and armed robberies filling the news. But to these old Jews, a lot of them Holocaust survivors, it was a lot more than a prank. It was a desecration, a warning, and an assault all rolled into one. I wanted to make sure the judge trying the case understood that these people were very, very interested in his ruling. I just felt that I had a moral responsibility to help these people out."

Louie's sense of morality, like his sense of humor,

was relative to his own actions and not society-at-large. Following Ralph's dictum, he found it extremely difficult to turn the other cheek. Nowhere was that more evident than in his description of an off-duty, barbaric police vigilante raid.

"There was a group of junkies, Rastafarians mostly, who hung together every night in one corner of Prospect Park, the largest park in Brooklyn. These hard cases would hook up about one in the morning, get rowdy, and cause all kinds of problems.

"One summer night we were cruising and received a ten-thirteen call, a cop in distress emergency, going out for that corner of the park. By the time several patrol cars had converged on the site, there was no one around except the bloody remains of what, a few moments before, had been a Transit Police officer. The cop wasn't dead, but his spleen and kidneys were ruptured, seven of his ribs were broken, and his collarbone was smashed. The junkies had nearly kicked him to death.

"The next day, cops from the park's three surrounding precincts—the Seven-one, Six-seven, and Seven-oh—had an unofficial meeting. Half a dozen radio cars pulled up behind an abandoned warehouse, and the vote was unanimous. We were going to mete out some justice on some junkies.

"It was decided that after the six-to-two shift—six P.M. to two A.M.—we'd all meet back behind the warehouse in street clothes. Radio dispatchers sent out a coded borough-wide warning to all on-duty patrol cars to avoid the park area between two A.M. and dawn. By the time I got to the prearranged meeting place, there were close to two dozen cops on the scene.

"Someone ripped open a carton of pantyhose, and

we all covered our faces. Then we walked to the park, stopping along the way to pick up any weapon we could find—bottles, tree branches, two-by-fours, bricks, garbage can lids, anything. At a given signal, we turned into a Mongol horde.

"We broke their hands. We broke their arms. We broke their legs. And we did it viciously. I had one guy on the ground, a tough guy whom I knew was a cop-hater, and I whaled him, twice across the face with a board. He was barely semiconscious when I sat down on the curb, picked up the biggest rock I could find, and crushed every one of his fingers, one by one. I could feel the bones smash. Then I went to work on the other hand. Finally, I snapped both his wrists before cracking him over the head with a brick.

"We put thirty-seven people in the hospital that night, and not one radio car responded. There were ambulances galore, and several of the junkies, including the guy whose hands I mangled, ended up crippled for life. And I didn't give a fuck, and I still don't. I know he won't be hurting cops anymore. In fact, I never heard of another attack on a policeman in that corner of the park.

"Sounds wrong. Sounds scary. But I considered it meeting fire with fire, like my old man had always taught me. And it worked. When you work for a bank, you abide by the law of the banking commission. When you work on the street, you abide by the law of the street. And if that means dealing with some drugged-out psycho on his own level, then you have to become a psycho yourself to survive."

That off-duty Pickett's Charge was by no means an isolated incident. Yet it seemed that the two sides of Louie's soul were constantly at war. Shortly after the Prospect Park incident, for example, rough, tough

Louie Eppolito refused to arrest a purse snatcher on the grounds that the teenaged black thief "reminded me of my father."

"Jimmy and I were on patrol, turning the corner from Flatbush onto Linden Boulevard, when we saw the kid push a woman from behind and grab her purse. The perp wasn't even looking behind him, and Jimmy, who was driving, pulled right up on his tail and followed for a few blocks. Finally, he let me out, and zipped ahead to cut him off. The perp spotted Jimmy, ducked into a closed alleyway, and ran right into me."

Louie had his gun drawn and was ordering the felon to drop the handbag when he got his first good look at the child's face. The thief couldn't have been more than thirteen, and an eerie feeling washed over Louie as he examined the child more carefully. There was a white foam frothing from the boy's mouth, and gobs of dried mucus stuck to the side of his nose and the top of his upper lip. His arms were toothpicks, his belly was distended, and Louie felt as if he were looking at a Biafran.

"It looked like this poor kid was in shock. He was out of emotion, out of steam, and when I pulled him by his shirt he offered no resistance. Like a rag doll. Nothing. I made eye contact with him for the first time and he was like a frightened deer caught in the headlights. That's when that sixth sense I have started tingling. I knew right then that he'd never done this before. When I asked him, he said, 'No,' and I believed him."

When Louie asked the boy how he could have been so stupid as to snatch a purse right in front of two uniformed cops, the child's answer chilled him: "Because I got my mother at home and four little brothers and sisters and nobody's eaten in three days."

Louie and McCafferty put the kid in the back of their squad car and concocted a story for the snatcher's victim. They explained to her that the child had thought he was playing a trick on his aunt, whom, they said, the woman resembled. When the boy realized he hadn't grabbed his aunt's handbag, he panicked and ran to the police to explain. It worked. The woman declined to press charges. Both cops had seen the same thing in this youngster's eyes, something that told them he did not belong behind bars.

"I asked this kid where he lived and he gave me an address on Caton Avenue. We decided to take a ride over there. I told that kid if he was lying to me I'd give him a crimping he wouldn't forget for the rest of his life."

The boy hadn't lied. When the two cops arrived at the apartment at 10 Caton Avenue they ransacked every kitchen cabinet and found nothing. No milk. No bread. No cereal. "There wasn't even a half-empty jar of mayonnaise in the refrigerator. Who's ever heard of a refrigerator without a half-empty jar of mayonnaise?"

"Now, by law, I see this kid commit a felony right in front of my eyes and I'm supposed to let a judge decide if his story has any merit. But—and this is a crazy but—the part of me that witnessed the purse snatching was Louie Eppolito the Cop, and the part of me that looked into that kid's eyes was Ralph Eppolito's son. I remembered a conversation with my father, where he sat me down, stared into my eyes, and said with this cold hard voice, 'I will do anything to support my family. Anything.'

"When that sore spot has been hit, your memory will jump right back ten years, in my case to that particular conversation with my father. I didn't think this kid had done anything wrong. I didn't think he had done anything I hadn't been taught to do."

Louie and McCafferty guessed that the child's mother was in her mid-thirties, and she weighed no more than one hundred pounds. When they opened the door to the one bedroom in the flat, they were struck by what Louie calls "the most heart-wrenching sight I've seen in all my years on The Job." Crowded onto the lone mattress on the floor were two little boys and two little girls. Layers of clothes—pants, shirts, tops—were piled over the children to keep them warm. Louie asked the woman if she was on welfare. She answered that her religious values precluded her from accepting public assistance.

With that, McCafferty and Eppolito made a decision. They returned to their radio car and called Central Communications. They asked that all available cars in the Seven-one meet them at their location. Within five minutes there were seven squad cars at the scene, including a cruiser carrying a lieutenant who was the patrol supervisor for the shift.

"I asked these fourteen guys if I had backed up every one of them on their calls. When they answered, 'Yes,' I told them it was payback time. I explained the situation upstairs and asked everyone to dig deep into their pockets.

"Now these guys were tough, hard-nosed cops who hated the whole fucking world. They hated blacks, they hated whites, they hated ballbreakers, they hated pimps, they hated guys that drove their cars too fast and they hated guys that drove their cars too slow. See, when you're working in a shithole for all those years, you learn to tolerate things. People will say, 'Do you mind if I park here?' and their answer will be, 'I mind everything, but I'll tolerate it.'

"But these guys reached into their pockets, and if one guy had eighteen dollars, he gave me sixteen. If another had twenty-five dollars, he gave me twenty. One guy had eighty dollars, and he threw me seventy. Out of those fourteen cops I wound up with about a hundred and sixty dollars."

Now it was time for a supermarket sweep. The male version. Louie and McCafferty found an all-night bodega and began to shop for the penniless family as only two men who have never grocery-shopped in their lives can.

"We bought cake and cookies and cornflakes and Twinkies and candy. I mean, it was two cops doing the shopping. I bought ten bags of popcorn. When the Puerto Rican who ran the bodega found out what we were doing he threw in a couple bottles of Scope mouthwash and some nacho chips. Real useful stuff, right? But it was the thought that counted. He had a brother who ran a supermarket in the neighborhood, and when we told him about the woman, he arranged to get her a job as a checkout girl."

When the two cops returned to the woman's apartment with their bags of goodies, the children were still asleep in the bedroom. Louie awoke a six-year-old girl. She had that sleepy look on her face that assures an adult that a child is still in dreamland. Suddenly, still half-asleep, she threw her tiny arms around Louie's bull neck and whispered, "I love you."

"I know she doesn't even know what she's saying, or who she's saying it to. But I had my own two little girls at home. Show me the man that can't be moved by that and I'll show you a stiff."

That was the way Louie worked his beat. And the mention of his name, even today, elicits a "Mad—do you hear me?—mad" look in the eyes of former co-workers.

"When I first met Louie Eppolito, my initial thought was, 'How did this guy ever get on The Job,' " says Deputy Inspector Michael Julian, a twenty-two-year veteran who began his career in the Seven-one and now works in the Police Commissioner's office. "I mean, he was one of these loud, obnoxious cops. Always bragging. Always threatening to fuck somebody up. There's more cops like that than you think.

"But you learned soon enough that this guy could back up his brag. So after a while I didn't doubt the war stories I was hearing. He was like a crazy Audie Murphy. If Louie said he did it, I believed he did it, no matter how outlandish the tale. Plus, he was a good cop. He made the collars. He ran a good investigation. And he was one of those lucky son of a bitches who always seemed to be in the right place at the right time. Bank robbers seemed to just appear in his rear-view mirror."

Like many of his co-workers, Inspector Julian, who at the time knew nothing of Louie's Mafia background, nonetheless sensed that there was something "a little off" about him. "He went through life with something to prove. And it was obvious that someone had taught him to think quick on his feet."

Indeed, Louie was a master at turning the Department's inevitable red-tape frustrations to his advantage. Several former co-workers, for example, repeated the story of Louie and the "cop hater" known only by his street name of Captain Hook. Captain Hook was a fixture in Prospect Park in the early 1970s. He was said to have acquired the name in Attica State Prison, where he'd put someone's eyes out with a bent knife. The cops all knew Hook was bad.

And they knew, as only cops can "know," that he was behind several armed robberies in the neighborhood. But they could never hang anything on him.

Captain Hook was, in essence, the perfect foil for Louie Eppolito.

"So one day Jimmy and I made a rather violent arrest of a felony rapist who hung out with all the junkies in the park. A crowd of fifty or sixty gathered as we took this guy down. After the brawl was over I walked over to Hook, shook his hand, and thanked him, rather loudly, for the phone call. Told him his reward would be coming soon. His own kind took care of Captain Hook for us that night. We never saw him again.

"That's the law of the street in action."

By the time Louie had been on The Job for four years his reputation had spread. He'd been involved in half a dozen shootouts, numerous "star-maker" investigations and arrests, he had tiers of medals and commendations pinned to his chest.

Yet he would have gladly traded all his medals for one piece of metal, the gold shield of a New York City detective.

There is an air of mystery to the New York City Detective Division that goes beyond Hollywood and affects even those uniformed patrolmen who work in conjunction with them. Cops like Louie would often be the first to show up at the scene of a homicide, for instance, before handing the case off to the gold shields. The patrolmen, their jobs done, would have no more involvement in the case until they read about its disposition in the papers. But Louie was always more curious than the average foot soldier.

"So a few weeks later I'd make it a point to run into one of the detectives on a stairwell, or in the can, and ask how things were going on such-and-such a case. 'Oh yeah,' he'd say, casual as can be. 'Remember that woman who went out the window? Well, we got the guy.' And I'd be amazed.

"Detectives fascinated me. I'd bring my lunch into their squad rooms, sit back, and just listen to their stories. Well, sit back for a while, anyway. Because I'd be so full of questions. 'Where do you start? How do you know where to go?' Naturally, they'd appear as mysterious as possible.

" 'It's hard to explain, kid,' one of them would inevitably tell me. 'You sort of have to be there.' I dreamed about how fabulous it would be to break those kind of cases. But there was one big impediment to my promotion. The mob."

There is a certain career path every dedicated cop follows in order to get ahead on The Job. And one stop along that path is a hitch in the "glamour puss" Narcotics Division. But drug-busting was not for Louie. By the mid-1970s the Gambino Family's involvement in the drug trade was a matter of record. For Patrolman Eppolito, the Narcotics Division reeked of too many entangling alliances.

"I didn't know exactly what my Uncle Jimmy was up to, or Todo, or Johnny Bath Beach. But you didn't have to be a brain surgeon to figure out that Detective Eppolito would be stepping into a snake pit if he started investigating Jimmy 'the Clam' Eppolito. I could feel those Shooflies down at Internal Affairs just rubbing their hands together in glee. But avoiding Narcotics really hurt my chances of getting the gold shield.

"For three years, every time promotions rolled around, I was given the unofficial word by some well-meaning superior that it was finally my turn. I had enough recommendations from superior officers to fill a shoebox. But every year, when the list was posted, my name wasn't on it. I ended up canceling three promotion parties.

"At the time I thought maybe that people just didn't like me. My name had made the paper and television news a lot, and the brass hates that shit. And I wasn't ignorant of the fact that there were people in the Department who remembered my roots, where I came from. Still, I was naive enough to figure I could overcome my father, my uncles, my family.

"Finally, in 1977, I made the list. But by now the gold shield had lost some of its luster. I took the whole affair rather matter-of-factly. In my mind, I was being promoted three years too late. And I never forgot the snub."

V

THE GOLD
SHIELD

18

Most New York City police officers would rather bathe a leper than talk to the press. But not Detective Louie Eppolito. He delighted in his first-name relationship with most of the city's crime writers, and they returned the favor in spades.

No New York City newspaper morgue is complete without at least one bulging file attesting to the loquacious detective's street feats. Not surprisingly for a tabloid town, the stories written about Louie took on a breathless, overwrought tone. Even his promotion was deemed newsworthy enough to be captured in headlines:

For Louie Eppolito
Tin Turns to Gold

A sampling of the reams of copy filed about Louie throughout the seventies attests to the mythic status the detective had acquired.

"A tough cop's persistence and skill with gun, muscle and handcuffs were credited yesterday with the arrest of three Brooklyn men accused of stabbing, beating and kicking a spunky pharmacist who refused to turn over his stock of narcotics," begins one *New York Daily News* account.

"In a series of spine-tingling events rivaling any Hitchcock thriller, a lone detective chased three hardened criminals through the streets of Flatbush and captured them without harm to passersby despite the fact that they were armed," reads another.

The art-imitates-life motif is a recurring theme in the Eppolito chronicles, such as this one (*New York Daily News*, July 18, 1977). "Every Saturday night cop buffs tune in to 'Starsky and Hutch' to watch the super sleuths collar criminals by taking bold action like leaping onto the hoods of cars and pointing the barrels of their .38 S&Ws at the bad guys. The producers of the show, however, should follow the act of one of New York's Finest if they really want to see action—Detective Louis Eppolito."

Finally, no doubt running short of panting prose, exhausted headline writers were content to let the feats of the local legend assume the commonplace, as in the sweet and simple: EPPOLITO DOES IT AGAIN (*New York Daily News*, November 30, 1973). Ironically, no reporter was aware of Louie's Mafia background, and he made sure to keep it that way.

"My family background was nobody's goddamn business."

By the late 1970s, Atlas and Little Jim had joined two other Brooklyn detectives to form the undercover Senior Citizens Robbery Unit. Louie racked up so many medals, awards and commendations that his fellow detectives dubbed him the Field Marshal. His fame followed him when the Department broke up the team and promoted Louie to the Brooklyn Armed Robbery Squad. In fact, his previously recorded achievements paled in comparison to the one big case that (Louie admits, tellingly, with a common Cosa Nostra phrase) "really made my bones."

They crawled up from the city sewers in 1979, and they were known as the Disco Gang, as a result of their penchant for sticking up danceterias. Toting shotguns, they blew people away for no reason, they raped indiscriminately, and they dared the police to catch them with a series of taunting telephone calls. They were the Brooklyn Armed Robbery Squad's number-one priority.

As each new report on the atrocities of the Disco Gang filtered into the Robbery Squad, one thought kept popping into Louie's head: *For all the dirt the Cosa Nostra was involved in, they never treated innocent people like this. When they killed people, it was for a reason. You never heard of the Mafia whacking innocent bystanders.*

One by one the squad rounded up the members of the seven-man crew. They were black gangsters, and all the joints they hit were black-owned. So, against form, the ghetto community opened up with invaluable tips and leads. Louie and his new partner, Steve Caracappa, also used their brand of gentle persuasion to glean scraps of information from stoolies busted on minor raps. Finally, only two members of the Disco Gang remained at large. Louie and Caracappa knew them by their street names, "Bugs" and "Big T."

"One day Steve and I got a line that Bugs had a steady poke in Bed-Stuy, so we staked out the girl's apartment. He never saw us coming. But Bugs was one tough sonofabitch. Steve grabbed him and disarmed him—Bugs never went anywhere without his handy sawed-off—and he fought like hell even when I had him on the ground with my thirty-eight stuck halfway down his throat."

Back in the precinct's makeshift interrogation room, Louie gave Bugs the standard Eppolito options: drop a dime on "Big T" or kiss his ass goodbye.

"Do what you gotta do, pig."

Wrong choice of words. Yet, to Louie's astonishment, for the first time in his career his interrogation methods were having no effect.

"I must have punched Bugs forty times in the head. But he wasn't talking. The guy wore out my arms. My hands were swollen. And he just sneered.

"Finally I took him into a back room and filled a bucket with the hottest water I could find. I emptied half a jug of ammonia into the bucket. I couldn't even put my face near it without my eyes burning. Then I grabbed Bugs's head and dunked. He came up screaming. His face was mutating into a giant purple blotch. But when he caught his breath, he turned to me and told me to, 'Fuck off.'

"So I dunked him again. And again. 'I've always been known for my balls,' Bugs said between dunks. I couldn't disagree."

In a morbid way, Bugs had gained a glimmer of Louie's respect. Ralph had taught his son well. Louie hated rats as much as his father. He had often been sickened while interrogating suspects who had given up their accomplices faster than he could write down their names. His respect for Bugs's tenacity, however, only went so far.

"I didn't think of myself as a cruel person. I still lived by my father's axiom that every man was a human being and should be treated like one until proven otherwise. But not giving up his partner was the only human characteristic I could attribute to Bugs. He was a cold-blooded murderer and rapist who had once grabbed a woman in an elevator, forced her to have anal sex, and then made her lick the shit off his dick. If he was a dog, he'd be the type you'd bring to the ASPCA and say, "Put him to sleep.' And I'd have gladly volunteered."

Louie was so rattled over Bugs's ability to withstand his tender mercies that after dumping him back into the holding cell he committed the cop's cardinal sin. He called Fran "within earshot" of the cell, and asked her to hold his baby daughters, Andrea and Deanna, up to the receiver. Cooing to his girls over the phone was Louie's way of letting off steam. Plus, Bugs's arrest would be big news on the television. Louie wanted to make sure Fran knew he was safe.

He didn't give the phone call another thought until the following day, when David "Big T" McCleary called the Robbery Squad and asked for him by name. McCleary's message was succinct.

"Hey, Eppolito, I heard what you did to Bugs. I always figured the real tough cops like you are the ones whose mothers got fucked by police dogs. Is that true?"

"Right away I can see that my relationship with the Big T is getting off on the wrong foot. In that situation, a cop is supposed to somehow talk the guy in. Dare him. Promise him. Plead with him. But stay professional. Instead, what went through my mind was, What would Ralph do? Or Todo? Or Bath Beach? Big T hurt his case every time he opened his mouth, especially when he brought up my family by name.

"He told me he was going to find Fran and fuck her up the ass in front of Andrea and Deanna. Dina he called her. Then he said he was going to blow Fran's head off in front of the kids, but not before he peeled the skin from their heads. 'I might even fuck them, too, Eppolito,' he said. 'Do you think their little snatches are big enough?' "

If it hadn't been personal before, it was now. Louie informed McCleary that he could forget about any arrest, or trial, or anything, for that matter, that touched upon normal criminal procedure. "Because I was going to find him and administer my own justice. I was going to kill him on the spot. 'You know I'm a shooter, Eppolito,' he told me. 'I got guns and I got balls.'

"Even match, I figured."

Over the next six days Louie and Steve Caracappa worked round-the-clock shifts, sleeping in the squad room, rousting every source, interrogating each minor bust until their zeal was rewarded with a tip on David "Big T" McCleary. It was a snitch, a hooker they knew from the street. McCleary, the hooker said, was on his way to meet a girlfriend in Crown Heights. She even had the address.

Eight detectives piled into four unmarked cars. Louie somberly informed his partner that if he reached McCleary first, "he was going to eat his heart."

"As we pulled up to the brownstone, I looked up to a second-floor window. McCleary was staring down at me. Laughing. I knew him from a mug shot. I burst out of the car screaming, 'You're a dead motherfucker, Big T. I'm Louie Eppolito, and I'm coming for you.' Because the rest of the squad took a moment to don their bulletproof vests—I left mine in the car out of sheer stupidity—when I kicked in the front door I had a thirty-second head start on the posse."

It was more than enough time. Adrenaline surging, Louie shouldered through a second locked door, blew it right off the hinges, and fell into a bedroom off the second-floor landing.

"There was McCleary. Lying in bed. Balls-ass

naked. A huge grin on his face. He was unarmed. He smiled and said he was ready to come peacefully.''

A body bag was Louie's idea of "peacefully." He broke his knuckles on McCleary's head, and would have choked the man to death right there on that bed if Caracappa hadn't pulled him away. "Without Steve, I guarantee you David McCleary would be six feet under right now instead of doing three consecutive life terms upstate."

But from Louie's point of view, nothing ever came easy. Two weeks later McCleary's girlfriend filed a grievance against him with the Civilian Complaint Review Board for breaking down her doors. Disposition: exonerated.

Despite these minor brushes with officialdom, Louie was well on his way to becoming *the* star of the borough. Young detectives sought him out, asking for tips. He had even stored away the snub of waiting so long to wear the gold shield. He was doing what he felt he was born to do: chasing people on the streets and beating them up. Of course, sometimes they were the wrong people.

Cruising Bed-Stuy, he once leaped from his car and drew a bead on a seedy character he suspected of casing a bar. The crowd in the street scattered, leaving rookie Detective Louis Scarcella pleading for his life.

"I was in plain clothes, working undercover, and dressed real scruffy," Scarcella remembers. "In about one second he was on me like white on rice. His thirty-eight was six inches from my nose, and since I knew who he was—every cop knew who Lou Eppolito was—there was no doubt that he was going to shoot and ask questions later. That was his rep."

Scarcella began screaming that he was also a cop. After pinning him to the sidewalk, snatching his service revolver, and inspecting his credentials, Louie finally holstered his gun.

"Then he began screaming at me for looking so much like a skel," Scarcella recalls with a laugh. "That's all right, though. It was a pleasure getting reamed out by a legend like Eppolito."

At home he left his rage on the doorstep. His family, and especially Fran, was Louie's emotional outlet. His daughters adored him, and Louie spent nights on end cradling an agitated Andrea in his arms, rocking her to sleep to the strains of "The Sleepyhead Song." The image of Louie Eppolito crooning "There were five sleepyheads all tucked into their beds; as I sing this lullaby, one got dream dust in her eye," was foreign to anyone outside his immediate family.

One night, as the Eppolitos were entertaining a fellow cop and his wife, Andrea's insomnia struck. Detective Jerry DeMarco* watched, dumbfounded, as Louie lifted her out of bed and began singing a lullaby.

"This is the same animal I watch prowling the streets of Brooklyn?" he whispered to Fran.

"What did you think, he comes home and throws us all up against a wall?" she answered.

"In one sense Louie brought his job home with him," says Fran. "But not in the bad sense, like other cops I'd heard about. He saw nothing wrong with hurting the bad guys, even shooting the bad guys, and then telling us all about it, down to the tiniest gory

---

* DeMarco left the police force in 1990 to open a florist shop on Staten Island. He cited The Job's increasing violence as the reason for his retirement. On Mother's Day 1991, DeMarco was shot dead in an armed robbery of his store. His wife and two children witnessed the murder.

detail. The only thing that bothered me, at first, was his language. I mean, Louie can be a talking sewer. I flinched every time the girls listened to Daddy's dirty stories at the kitchen table. But he can't help it. That's the way he is, and that's the way he'll always be. So we learned to live with it.''

"It was,'' says Louie, "the happiest time of my life. Sometimes, like with Bugs, I went overboard. But I'm a human being, Ralph Eppolito's son, and sometimes my emotions just have to blow full. I guess it's in the genes. So I use a few too many curse words in front of the kids. Sue me.

"The public will never understand the mentality of a cop—a good cop, anyway. In a way, it's very similar to the mentality of Organized Crime. You do what you have to do and don't think twice about consequences, because when you gotta go, you gotta go. A lot of guys couldn't hack it. Just like a lot of guys can't hack the mob.

"Ever since my rookie tour in Marine Park I had shied away from units like Narcotics or Homicide, places where I was likely to come into contact with Organized Crime figures. My world was the slums of New York City. But where I thrived, I saw a tremendous amount of cops lose their families. The drinking, the whoring, the drugs. I vowed that would never happen to me.''

Louie knew cops who floated through their shifts chewing cotton wads dipped in liquid cocaine. He worked with a detective who had a beautiful wife at home—"a twelve on a scale of ten"—and who was shot by a pimp for copping freebies from his two skanky heroin hookers.

He freely admits that he worked with dozens of men, badge-abusers, he calls them, who had somehow slipped past the Department's psychological screeners. One of the best investigators he knew in the Seven-one was a nuclear bomb waiting to explode, "the sort whose eyes twirled in his head when he spoke to you."

The blast finally ignited one night in Prospect Park. The plainclothes officer, off duty, pulled his car over in the park when his tire went flat. Two muggers approached. He collared one and gave him a choice: a bullet in the head or the polar-bear cage. The next morning the papers reported that a junkie had accidentally fallen into the polar-bear cage and been eaten alive.

Amid such physical and emotional carnage, it was only natural for cops to turn inward, to circle the wagons. Some officers found solace in "cop bars," where The Job's triumphs and tragedies could be replayed over and over, like highlights from a football game. "Real people" were discouraged from butting into these circles. Off-duty brawls were easy to cover up.

But Louie found that he got his fill of fights on duty, and taverns had never been his style. That left family as his only anchor. Fran never failed to lend a sympathetic and unquestioning ear after a particularly tough day. Louie treated her as part mate, part psychologist, and part sounding board.

More and more he found himself calling Fran near the end of a tour. Could she meet him for a late dinner? It was one such rendezvous that led Louie into his first serious encounter with Internal Affairs, the Police Department's internal watchdog agency.

Smashing doors from their hinges could be overlooked. Consorting with the enemy was an entirely different affair.

"As I got older, the mob guys I knew as a kid became more important in their Families. That worked against me. On occasion Fran would meet me in Brooklyn for dinner after a shift, even after we moved out to Long Island. We'd pick out an Italian restaurant —try getting a good marinara sauce on Long Island— and once in a while it would happen that at the end of the meal I'd be told that the check had already been picked up by somebody at the bar. That occurs a lot with cops. But I rarely let anyone pay. Some people think they can buy the badge.

"So, on one of these occasions when the waiter said the check was paid, I got uppity, stalked over to the bar, and there was old Todo Marino, grinning like a jack-o'-lantern.

"Naturally, out of respect, I gave him a kiss. That's the greatest honor you can offer these guys. A handshake is nice, but a kiss means respect. And frankly, I wasn't being a hypocrite. This was one of my old man's nearest and dearest, my Uncle Jimmy's compatriot. I did respect Todo.

"Todo came over to the table to say hello to Fran, we had coffee, and I let him keep the tab. On the way out I tried to explain to her what a headache this was for me, what shit I was going to have to take 'back at the office.' At first she didn't get it.

"I explained that there were hundreds of FBI agents whose sole job it was to follow people like Todo. There was even a good possibility that they had filmed us. She refused to believe The Job could be that picky.

" 'So?' Fran asked. '*All* you did was say hello.'

"I tried to make her understand that I wasn't even supposed to know these guys, much less be caught smooching with them. But she was just too logical for me.

" 'How could you not know these men,' she said.

'How could you be raised by Ralph Eppolito, meet all his friends, and then pretend not to know them? What are you supposed to say: I don't know these people anymore because my father's dead? Don't the police know about respect?'

"Actually, they had no idea. Those redneck, low-life FBI agents who trailed these mobsters couldn't find their dicks with a map. Things hadn't changed since they were threatening me on the street corner as a kid. They all had tunnel vision. They saw things one way, in black and white. It was like giving an accountant a gun and a badge."

Inevitably, one week after his chance encounter with Todo Marino, Louie was summoned to the FBI's Manhattan headquarters at 26 Federal Plaza. The Feds showed Louie a picture, blown up to nearly poster size, of him bussing the Genovese Family capo on the cheek. When Louie tried to explain to the agents that he had known "Uncle" Todo since childhood, that the man had once bounced him on his knee, the federal agents were unimpressed.

"Do you know what this means?" one asked.

"Sure I do," Louie answered. "It means that I've known the man my entire life. I have pictures at home of me as a seven-year-old sitting on his lap. That's what it means."

Then Louie got nasty. He'd had enough. "And let me answer your next question before you even ask it," he told the G-men. "Of course I knew at seven years of age that Uncle Todo was a wiseguy. So throw me in jail."

He didn't care anymore. Either they believed his story or they didn't. "Had I known Todo was going to be there," he told the agents, "I would have gone to the trouble of picking another restaurant. But once in that situation, I couldn't disrespect the man.''

He could tell by the look on their faces that he was preaching an alien concept. They shooed him out of their office as if he were a bum who was wasting their time. Not unexpectedly, several months later Louie was called down to the Internal Affairs Division. They showed him the same picture.

''Don't you guys talk to each other?'' he demanded. ''I already went through this crap with the FBI. Jesus Christ Almighty, for a lousy plate of pasta I have to put up with this shit?''

IAD was not pleased with the detective's attitude. But, as he had not broken any departmental regulations, they sent him off with a warning. They'd be watching. On the drive home that evening, Louie mused about the differences in attitude between the career he had chosen and the one he'd forsaken.

''It's funny, but guys like Todo had the decency to come over and say hello, make polite conversation for a moment, despite the fact that we were on opposite sides of the fence. I only wished that my fellow cops had given me the same benefit of the doubt. But they didn't. And then they wondered why I was always so sarcastic with them.''

In time, that sarcasm would curdle into pure cynicism, and, finally, hatred. Several years later, for instance, Louie attended Todo Marino's wake. Afterward, he was again summoned to Federal Plaza. The FBI wanted to know what the hell a cop was doing at a mobster's funeral service. Louie gratuitously informed them he was sure each gangster in attendance would slip a few dollars into Todo's casket, ''to ease his journey to the happy hunting ground.'' Louie said his plan was to hang around until the funeral home emptied, at which point he was going to rifle the cadaver's pockets.

"You know how cops are," he sneered on his way out. But that was still several years down the road.

But Louie was not naive. He didn't think the Internal Affairs Division ever let anything rest. He became more cautious, avoiding bars and restaurants with even a whiff of Mafia connections. And despite the fact that whenever he bumped into one of his father's old friends he continued to offer his "respect," there were no more incidents.

19

On October 17, 1978, the former Luigi the Nablidan, master watchmaker and consort of Lucky Luciano, died in his sleep at the age of ninety-one. The wake provided his grandson with one of his rare opportunities to see his family.

"I walked into the funeral home and the first person I saw was my Uncle Jimmy. He was surrounded by his cronies—Joey "Piney" Armone, Joey Gallo, Pete Piacenti. Two bodyguards stood discreetly behind him. It had been six years since I had spoken to him last, and suddenly this warm feeling kind of washed over me. He looked more like my father than I remembered. They could have been twins. I walked straight over to him, hugged him, kissed him. I almost cried.

"He began ribbing me good-naturedly about never calling. 'All I do is read about the big hero in the papers.' He turned to my Aunt Dolly and told her that his nephew seemed to have no problem talking to newspaper reporters, but it was another story when it came to his uncle, his own flesh and blood. Then he took me aside, lowered his voice, and told me how proud he was of me for being such a good cop.

"I was thinking to myself, *Yeah, I'm sure you're real proud of me*. But we ended up in the back of the funeral parlor, laughing and talking for the next hour. As we sat there, literally dozens of wiseguys walked into the funeral home, spotted Uncle Jimmy, and walked straight up to kiss his cheek or his hand. They never even went to the body to acknowledge the dead. They just acknowledged Uncle Jimmy. It was obvious that he had really made his mark in the Gambino Family.

"Uncle Jimmy didn't even know how many kids I had, and when I told him I had two little girls he made me promise to come and visit him. That wasn't the best idea in the world, what with surveillance and all, but a promise is a promise.

"So, a month later, Fran and I decided to take a ride to Brooklyn to let Uncle Jimmy see Andrea and Deanna. The first thing he asked us was if we had taken the kids to Disneyland. Not on a cop's salary we hadn't—I cleared eight hundred dollars every two weeks.

"We had coffee and cake, and on the way out Jimmy slipped Fran an envelope without telling me. She opened it on the drive home. It contained three thousand dollars in cash, along with a note: 'Take the kids on vacation.' I almost drove off the highway.

"I didn't want the money. I didn't need the money. I didn't visit him hinting for a gift. And the thought flew through my mind to turn the car around and return it. Just as quickly, I realized that that would be showing the highest form of disrespect. Fran helped me rationalize. 'He was just making up for the fact that he hasn't seen you in six years,' she told me. There were missed Christmases and birthdays and christenings. I was, after all, his brother Ralph's only son."

The brief encounter at his grandfather's wake broke

some of the ice. Afterward, Louie began dropping by his uncle's house regularly, sometimes as often as twice a month. To hell with the brass. To hell with IAD. Didn't his service to the City of New York count for anything?

"Uncle Jimmy and I would have coffee, even though I hated the stuff, and he'd drink a little Sambuca. I didn't give a shit about the surveillance. I'd played by the Department's rules long enough. I was a good cop, and my attitude became that if they didn't like my family, well, the hell with them.

"Uncle Jimmy never talked business, and I never talked about The Job. Mostly he'd tell old stories, Lower East Side stories, about Ralph and Freddy. Or we'd talk about the Giants, or the Mets. I felt like I was part of a family again.

"It was during one of my last visits that Uncle Jimmy broke our private agreement about shop talk and explained to me about Jim-Jim, the scamming of the charity, Rosalynn Carter, and what kind of trouble the family was facing. He didn't say it in so many words, but I knew. It killed me that there was nothing I could do.

"A month later Uncle Jimmy and Jim-Jim were both dead."

Jimmy Eppolito's assassination marked a change in Louie. He described the feeling as being "shipwrecked," his police ethic blown apart. If Detective Louie Eppolito had always thought of himself as the clenched fist at the end of the long arm of the law, there was now a defiant middle finger protruding from that image.

The sniping from his fellow officers, the sly looks and cynical remarks overheard in the squad room, the suspiciousness that followed him left him feeling dismal, as if *he* were the mob guy, on the outside looking in. Before he left the station house on the night of the hit, for instance, after his argument with Joe Strano, Louie was visited by two agents from the FBI's Organized Crime Division.

They told him they were "investigating" the murders. Still upset, Louie found their investigation more akin to an "interrogation." Offended, he lashed out. Their brief conversation ended with one agent advising Detective Eppolito, "The apple don't fall too far from the tree." Louie, not surprisingly, countered by instructing the Feds in their family genealogy. His enemies list was lengthening.

The FBI agent, however, was not alone in his analysis. There were forces within the Cosa Nostra itself who were also wondering just how far Ralph Eppolito's apple had fallen. Specifically, the Gambino Family feared a vendetta from "Jimmy the Clam's crazy cop nephew."

What Louie didn't know was that his Uncle Jimmy's power had waned since Paul "Big Paulie" Castellano had succeeded his cousin and brother-in-law Carlo Gambino as head of the Family in 1976. While Don Carlo ruled the clan, Jimmy Eppolito's crew held ascendancy over a rival group headed by the capo Nino Gaggi. But Gaggi and Castellano were related by marriage, and Nino had petitioned his new Don for more power, specifically in the neighborhood numbers banks on Eppolito's turf. He also wanted a piece of Jimmy Eppolito's lucrative heroin distributorship, for by now, each of New York's five Mafia crime families —bylaws be damned—was actively engaged in cramming dollars into its vaults from the sale of white powder.

Jimmy Eppolito had gotten wind of Gaggi's plans for a coup, and had asked Castellano for permission to whack Gaggi. Castellano's answer was, technically, noncommittal. But he secretly warned Gaggi that he was in danger of being hit. Using the pretense of Jim-Jim's embarrassing public involvement with John Ellsworth, Rosalynn Carter, and the International Children's Appeal, Gaggi struck first. Pete Piacenti, investigators later learned, was an innocent dupe in the setup.

Castellano, who was also known as "the Pope," was not sure how much Lou Eppolito knew of this intrigue. But to hedge his bet and forestall any notion of revenge, Big Paulie devised an innovative, if unprecedented, plan. He would call for a sit-down with the hotheaded detective to insure that he wasn't taking his uncle's murder too personally.

Exiting the church after Uncle Jimmy's funeral, Louie was pulled aside by his cousin, Frankie "Junior" Santora,* and told to expect a phone call in a couple of days. Santora, who had made his bones doing five years for bank fraud at Allentown (Pennsylvania) Federal Penitentiary, had been Jimmy Eppolito's bodyguard. He was also a made member of the Gambino Family. He didn't say from whom the call would be coming, only that "somebody important's got something to say to you."

Three days later Santora followed up with another

---

* In 1988, while ambling down Bath Avenue with Gambino Family soldier Carmine Veriali, Frank Santora was gunned down by hit men executing a contract on Veriali. Santora was shot four times. He was not the actual target of the gunmen, as even Brooklyn Rackets Bureau Chief Mark Feldman admitted, "Junior was, unfortunately, in the wrong place at the wrong time."

message: Tommy Bilotti wanted to speak to Louie. Bilotti was Castellano's bodyguard and right-hand man. Although he was known in law enforcement circles as a vicious, loudmouthed braggart, Louie nonetheless swears that no one he knew "ever had a bad word to say about Tommy Bilotti." Well, no one, perhaps, except John Gotti, who was to have Tommy whacked along with Big Paulie when he took over the Gambino Family. But that was still five years down the road.

"Tommy set up a meet for that night, in Bensonhurst, and it was all pretty cloak-and-dagger. I was sure nervous about it, and Fran was a notch from hysterical. She's the only one I told. It wasn't my style to go to the Department with something like this. For one, I didn't want any clowns from the Organized Crime Division making like Eliot Ness and getting me killed. Secondly, I was bitter, and my faith in the NYPD had just about flown out the window.

"Truthfully, I expected a boss like Big Paulie to treat me more honorably than anybody on The Job. I thought about going to Steve Caracappa for advice, and maybe some backup. But in the end, I really didn't want Steve involved in this. It was a family thing. And, Christ, it was bad enough that I had to go. I was scared shitless."

When Fran asked Louie what could happen, he gave her two scenarios. The first was that she'd never see him again. If the Gambinos were planning on whacking Louie, they certainly weren't going to leave a dead cop littering the streets. It would bring down too much heat. So, tactful husband that he is, Louie told his wife that they'd probably chop him up and dump his body in a place where he'd never be found. Not for nothing did Big Paulie list his occupation as "butcher." The second option, he told Fran, was that he'd be home for breakfast.

At two in the morning Louie edged his blue Chrysler New Yorker into a parking lot on the corner of Eighteenth Avenue and Eighty-sixth Street. He parked in the shadow of a bank, and waited. Five minutes later a stretched black Cadillac pulled up beside him. The car door opened and Louie peered inside. There was no Tommy Bilotti.

"Some monster gets out of the car. He's right out of Francis Ford Coppola's imagination. Ugly, but dapper. It's pitch-black outside and he's wearing a pair of wraparound sunglasses. 'Come on, Louie,' he says. 'Get in the car.' And I'm thinking to myself, *It's over, I'm fucking gone*.

"There's an expression in organized crime, it's called cleaning house. If you whack somebody, then you have to whack everybody who's going to cause you any trouble for whacking the first guy. Now it looks like Louie Eppolito is part of the housecleaning. So there was nothing I could do but brazen it out.

"It sounds stupid in retrospect, but everything my father taught me about being a standup guy flashed through my mind. I could walk away like a pussy, or I could get in the car. Forget about calling for help. As soon as I agreed to that meeting I stopped being a cop. Flashing a badge or pulling any kind of official stunt was out of the question. 'Fuck you,' I said to the monster. 'Move over.'

"I climbed into the backseat, and another Lurch type comes out of nowhere to slide me over into the middle. I handed them my gun without being frisked. I figured, what's the use? I'm sitting between the two of these guys now, and they ask me if I want a drink.

What I wanted was to never have shown up for this meeting. I told them no, thanks.

"We're driving and I'm trying to appear like I'm not real interested in where we're going, and at the same time I'm wondering if I looked as nervous as I felt. And it's funny, but suddenly this serene feeling washed over me. I was pretty sure I was a dead man, so I sat back and started thinking about my father. I actually had it in my mind that if they killed me, at least I'd get to see my old man again. And it seemed like my father was with me for the entire ride."

The Cadillac slipped onto the west-bound Belt Parkway, exited at the ramp for the Verrazano Bridge, and continued west into Staten Island. Maybe, Louie thought, they were going to do him in Jersey. There was no conversation. Louie had never seen either one of these guys before, and nobody was making any introductions. His racing heartbeat slowed a bit when the limo pulled off the Staten Island Expressway and the car began climbing Todt Hill, the highest elevation in New York City. The mound had been named Todt Heuvel (Death Hill) by the original Dutch settlers, and over time the name had become Americanized.

"Every cop in the city knew that 'The Pope' lived in the big white mansion, the White House we called it, at the top of Death Hill. There was no way they were going to whack me at Paulie's home.

"The Caddy pulled into Castellano's long horseshoe driveway and cruised right up to the open front door. Tommy Bilotti, God rest his soul, was standing in the vestibule. I'll never forget the image. He had on blue slacks and a white polo shirt with two blue stripes. His toupee was impeccable. Like a day at the fucking beach. He was smiling as he walked over to kiss me on the cheek.

" 'Louie, Louie, how long's it been? Three, four years? Whatcha doin'? How are ya? Louie, sorry I couldn't meet ya personally, but I had some things I had to take care of for Paulie.'

"Me, too, I thought, but let it go. I told Tommy I was fine, and asked what was going on.

"Very matter-of-factly—too matter-of-factly?—he replied, 'Nothing, Louie, honest. No problems at all. When you get in there, Paulie just wants to talk to you.'

" 'What can I tell you, Tommy, it's an unfortunate thing about Uncle Jimmy,' I said. 'But things happen.'

" 'Hey, Louie, that's what it's all about,' he said. 'We all pick and choose our directions. Unfortunately, some go the wrong way.' Then he walked me between the two massive pillars on the portico of the White House, and introduced me to Big Paulie Castellano.

"I had seen Castellano dozens of times, but I had never actually met the man before. He was wearing gray slacks, a gray button-down shirt, and a gray cardigan sweater with huge, shiny gold buttons. Since he was in his home, he was obviously in an informal mode. We sat across from each other in these two ornate brocaded gold wingback chairs. Everything was gold, even the lamps, which were shaped like Renaissance sculptures. Big Paulie got right to the point."

With an avuncular shrug, Castellano explained to the detective that the Family's recent "problems" hadn't specifically been the fault of his uncle, but of Louie's cousin Jim-Jim.

"I knew your Uncle Jimmy for a long time," Castellano said in a raspy voice. "I had the utmost respect for him. But, Louie, as I'm sure you know, he could not see his son put to rest while his eyes were open. He made that clear in the few talks we had with him.

"Now, Louie," Big Paulie continued, "I know a lot of people who speak very well of you, who have a lot of respect for you. And that means I have a lot of respect for you. What I don't want you to do is get bent out of shape over this incident, to begin thinking that you have to hurt somebody who hurt your family.

"No one has anything against you, Louie. No one is threatening you. No one will hurt you. It's just that you don't need the aggravation, and we don't need the aggravation. I just wanted to let you know that the thing was more with the kid than with the father. The kid did a lot of bad things wrong."

"The Pope" sat back, finished, trying to read the detective's face, awaiting his response. Louie began by addressing him as "Godfather," but Castellano cut him off with a short laugh and a brusque wave. "I'm not Don Corleone," he said.

Choosing his words carefully and adopting the grave, Mafia-ese appropriate to such formal occasions, Louie replied, "Look, Mr. Castellano, there's nothing you can say that's going to make me leave here thinking that it's okay that you killed my uncle and my cousin. They were my blood. And the reasons they had to die, however right you may think they are, are not important to me.

"But I'm in a unique position. Yes, I am a police officer, but I also come from a family like yours. So I understand the rules that govern the life my uncle and cousin chose. I'm tremendously honored that you've chosen to respect me by bringing me here tonight. But I'm not impressed, nor can you dissuade me from any personal feelings of loss that I have.

"It's not for me to say what is right and what is

wrong in this matter. But I can say that I am not look-ing to hurt anyone. I'm not looking to come after any-one. I'm not looking for revenge. I just want the dead to rest in peace."

Big Paulie stood up and shook the cop's hand. "That's all I wanted to know," he said. Then he asked if there was anything he could do for Louie. Any favor, any treat—now or, perhaps, in the future. His implication was clear. Another cop on the payroll never hurt.

Louie was offended. He knew what Castellano was offering, and he felt that before he left the "White House" he had better make his position perfectly clear.

"What I would like in the future is to be left alone," he told Castellano. "I don't want to see anybody else hurt. And, frankly, I don't think that this meeting was necessary. I'm a cop, not of your world. And there's no way on earth I can sit here and say that if you needed help in the future, I'd help you. Because I wouldn't. I expect no less from you."

Castellano's bearing tensed a little at that. He'd made a play for Louie, and the detective had shot him down. It wasn't overt, but then the Mafia style is never overt. In Louie's mind, what Big Paulie Castellano was asking him to do was "bend over and take it up the ass for a few bucks."

"If my old man had taught me anything, it was never to whore myself out for a dollar. That lesson had stayed with me, and what better person to show how well I'd been wiseguy-trained than the Godfather himself?

"When I climbed back into the car I began to see my life, my father's lessons, the Police Department, with a whole new perspective. I was also extremely happy just to be getting out of there alive. Three days later I ran into Tommy Bilotti on the street. He told me what a hit I'd made with the Godfather. Paulie, he said, liked the fact that I was a stand-up guy.

"And I never reported my meeting to the fucking cops."

20

FRAN: "I saw changes in Louie after Uncle Jimmy died. He went through a long period of mourning, and I started to get scared that he was going to get involved. I begged him to stay out of it. I knew what was in his blood, and I knew how hurt he was.

"After the kids went to bed at night we'd sit around the dinner table and he would tell me how he couldn't believe his uncle's best friend, Pete Piacenti, had set him up like that. Of course he didn't know then that Pete had been used to set up his uncle. And then when that phone call came, and he told me some important people wanted to talk to him, I nearly went to pieces. I didn't need to know names. I only had to hear the tone of his voice to realize this was heavy. I mean, I had never seen Louie scared before. Ever.

"At first I told him not to go, but he just gave me a look that said, 'You know better than that.' Same when I pleaded with him to take someone, anyone, with him. I waited up all night for him, not knowing who to call if he didn't come home. And when he did walk in, and told me what had happened with Big Paulie, I couldn't believe it. It was like something you see in the movies.

"All I wanted to know was, 'Is it over?' He assured me it was.

"But from that day on Louie was a different person. It was like he now had a little more pride in what his uncle was. Maybe Uncle Jimmy's death, and hearing what cops were saying about him behind his back, made Louie stand up a little taller. He wasn't ashamed of his family background any longer. He never apologized for it. If anything, he would brag to our friends, 'That was my uncle.' That sort of thing.

"Then I noticed that he began picking up some Italian mannerisms that he never had before. Before Uncle Jimmy's murder, I didn't oversee what you would call an Italian household. Louie didn't drink that black coffee they all drink. God, he even hated the smell of it on my breath when we kissed.

"Now, suddenly, I was being told to make him a cup of espresso. Or to put some wine out on the kitchen table. Huh? Plus, he started talking with his hands, like my parents did when I was a kid.

"Then I noticed that he also began talking about his Italian heritage all the time. Bragging about how Italians did this, Italians did that. He started taking me to clubs to hear Italian singers, like Jimmy Roselli, the Italian Tony Bennett. Of course, Louie didn't understand a word he was singing.

"All this was fine with me. I grew up in that kind of atmosphere. My Italian was rusty, but at least I understood Jimmy Roselli's lyrics. And there had always been a bottle of wine on my parents' kitchen table. I felt right at home, even if I did find Louie's new persona a little weird.

"I mean, when Steve Caracappa came over you'd think there were two Godfathers sitting at our kitchen table. The talking with the hands. The drinking of the double espressos. '*Salud*'-ing each other to death after every sip. And now Louie was starting to kiss everybody on the cheek. Before he'd just kiss the family, and shake hands with anyone else. Now it was Kiss City.

"He told me about the comments he was hearing at work, and suddenly it seemed to dawn on him that not everybody who wore a badge was his true friend. He didn't attach that much importance to his work anymore. His whole being was still centered around being a cop, but now it was a job instead of 'The Job.'

"His family became the focus of his life now. I used to laugh as he sat the girls on his knees and told them stories about their great Italian ancestry, or about how important family ties were. The kids were babies, and they looked at him like he was nuts."

Louie Eppolito was caught in some moral twilight zone. He was no longer a cop, at least in spirit. The cutting remarks after his uncle's murder had left wounds that wouldn't close. Nor was he a member of his family's criminal society.

In May of 1980, eight months after Louie's uncle and cousin were killed, New York City's fiscal crisis forced the consolidation of many of the Police Department's specialized agencies. The Brooklyn Armed Robbery Squad was disbanded, and its detectives were divvied out to precincts across the city.

Louie was ordered by Richard Perio, the borough of Brooklyn's Chief of Detectives, to put in for the three precincts, in order of preference, to which he wished to be transferred. He'd had it with "ghetto blasting." He was also through running from his past. His three preferred choices were all in South Brooklyn. Organized Crime territory.

"I was called into the Borough Command and told everything was set, that I'd end up in a 'good house' for the first time since my rookie year. Two weeks later everything changed. Suddenly I was going to the Seven-seven, the hellhole precinct of New York City.

"The Seven-seven was in the middle of Bed-Stuy, and it was a dumping ground for bad cops, lazy cops, crooked cops, and generally the dregs of the Department. It was the NYPD's Tasmania. And it still is. Even the 'Buddy Boys' scandal that rocked the Seven-seven hasn't changed that. Of course, I was livid.

"I barged into the Chief of D's office the next afternoon wearing war paint. I told him I had put twelve fucking years of my life into the shit holes of the City of New York, and there was no way I was being transferred to the worst one on the planet. I was a good cop, at the crossroads of my career, and the brass was shoveling me bullshit. I demanded to know why. Deep down I knew what was on their minds. Uncle Jimmy. Uncle Freddy. Ralph. But I wanted to hear *them* admit it.

"At first Perio tried stroking me, telling me how much the Department needed a good detective like me in the Seven-seven. Hello? When persuasion didn't work, I figured I was in for a ball-busting contest. But, to my amazement, the Department backed down. Later that same afternoon I was transferred to the Homicide Squad of the Six-two in the heart of Bensonhurst. I felt like I was home."

Only yards from the precinct, Paul Castellano himself operated his legitimate business, one of the neighborhood's many *macellerie,* or meat markets, copiously stocked with miraculously inexpensive (translation: hijacked) cuts of veal and racks of lamb.

Louie was forever bumping into the Pope, and Todo, and Bath Beach. "Christ, the station house was on Bath Avenue, the street that gave Johnny Oddo his name."

There were nightclubs and pizza stands and coffee shops owned and operated by figures from out of his past. After answering a disturbance call at one social club along Eighteenth Avenue, he was taken aback when the manager, Ralph Polito, invited him to stay for dinner.

"You don't remember me, do you?" Polito asked the detective. "I used to blow up balloons for you while your father did his business with Todo. I own a joint down the street. Come on in any time you want."

"And I did," says Louie. "I'd get anything I wanted to eat, and it was for free and I loved it. I didn't care who was watching."

Frank "Funzie" Tieri lived three blocks from the precinct. Tieri had taken over the Genovese Family when Tommy Ebboli was whacked in 1972, and he wore his button proudly. Louie had known Funzie since childhood. He remembered his father sharing espresso with the young soldier who, everyone said, was just ruthless enough to be destined for big things.

Invariably, whenever Louie and Funzie met, the mob boss would ask the detective into his house for coffee. Louie never accepted, because, he said only half-jokingly, he was afraid one of Tieri's daughters would take a liking to him.

"Funzie's daughters could make a fucking onion cry. One day Funzie walked into a club called the Hollywood Terrace and, seeing how Funzie was the second-most powerful gangster in the country behind Big Paulie, the joint's manager fell all over himself trying to do the right thing.

"Now this manager was a real dashing, debonair ladies' man. Full head of black hair, white sideburns, polished fingernails, the whole bit. He was also married to a woman who had to be one of the hottest lookers in Bensonhurst. Funzie had brought one of his daughters into the club with him, the one who'd entered a beauty contest and come in second. Everybody else came in first. The story on the street was that when she was a baby they had to tie a pork chop around her neck to make the puppy play with her.

"So anyway, the club manager is falling all over the daughter, wining and dining her, figuring he'll get in tight with Funzie. When Funzie finds out about the affair, as the story has been told, he heads down to the Hollywood Terrace with two leg breakers. He sits the manager in a chair and informs him that he'll be divorcing his wife Friday and marrying his daughter the following Monday.

"I heard they lived happily ever after. But still, I wasn't taking any chances over coffee at Funzie Tieri's house. In an odd way, though, the fact that I knew all these bad guys sometimes worked to my advantage.

"Carmine Lambordozzi, the elder statesman of the Gambino Family, was another regular on my beat. Because of my family, he had the highest respect for me. If I had a problem, say, with a wiseguy investigation, I thought nothing of going over to see Carmine. Sometimes he could help, sometimes he couldn't. It never hurt to try. And one time I had a bad problem. But it wasn't with a homicide. It was with one of Carmine's nephews.

"This nephew was all mobbed up, and just loved acting the part. He saw me once on Eighteenth Avenue and tried to hand me a few bucks. 'Here ya go,

Louie,' he said. 'Why don't you take a couple of dollars.' Then he made a remark about my mother. It was not a flattering remark.

"Instead of ripping this guy's face off, I went to see Carmine. I explained that his nephew was disrespectful, that he didn't know how to talk to people. He didn't know how to show respect. I told him that I didn't take that kind of shit from anyone, but because it was Carmine Lambordozzi's nephew, the kid got the benefit of the doubt. For now.

"The next morning the guy walked into the precinct house. 'Detective Eppolito, I'm so sorry,' he said, 'I didn't know who you were. I thought you were just another cop.' There was no use trying to talk like a man to this guy. I warned him to never embarrass me like that again.

"This was the kind of shit 'New York's Finest' had to put up with. These guys just hated cops. But with me, they didn't know who they were dealing with. I was almost one of them. Which is how I took part in my second 'sit-down.' "

It began with a complaint to the police from the ex-girlfriend of a wiseguy wannabe named Frankie Carbone. By this time, Louie had a reputation throughout the Six-two precinct as the detective to see when you had a problem. Big problem, small problem; Detective Eppolito would at least listen and do what he could.

Frankie Carbone's ex approached Louie and complained about being beaten. She wasn't talking about the occasional smack. She meant he had broken her jaw. Then he threw a few shots at her car. While she was driving it. So Louie went to Carbone's house, left his card with the gangster's mother, and asked her to tell Frankie to give him a call. Frankie called all right.

"Let me tell you something, you douche bag," were

the first words out of Carbone's mouth. "Somebody should have taken a shotgun to your mother's twat before she had you, you scumbag cop bastard. You gotta lock me up, then you do what you gotta do, and I'll do what I gotta do. But leave my mother out of it."

Another tough guy, thought Louie. He informed old Frankie Carbone that "doing what he had to do" would be no problem, and hung up the phone.

"The following morning a little detective work led me to Spiro's, a mobbed-up social club on Eighteenth Avenue that was Frankie Carbone's hangout. I kept a sawed-off shotgun in my locker for just such occasions. It fit snugly under the folds of my trench coat. I spotted Frankie sitting at a card table, walked up behind him, stuck the barrel in his mouth, and ordered him to his feet. 'By, motherfucker,' was all I said, and he lost his whole insides. As I backed him into a wall I watched the stain in his pants get bigger and bigger.

"Suddenly I knew what it felt like to be my father. I was walking like a wiseguy, talking like a wiseguy. The power surge was comparable to what I had felt, at times, as a cop, yet somehow different. As if the police worked on an AC current, and the Mafia on DC. I cocked both barrels. 'Please,' he begged. 'Please.' For one instant, I had this wonderful, heady urge to pull the trigger.

"Meanwhile, nobody in the club is saying a word. I'm sure they thought it was a professional hit."

When Louie pressed Frankie Carbone up against that wall, it was as if Ralph Eppolito's spirit passed out of his body. He was back to being a cop. He identified himself, and told Frankie he had until two the next afternoon to report to the station house to answer

216

the assault complaint. And then he sat Frankie down and said he wanted to tell him a story.

"Frankie," he began, "my entire fucking family were members of Organized Crime. All except me. But I learned a lot from them. So, Frankie, let me tell you what's going to happen if I don't see your ugly face at my desk tomorrow afternoon. First I'm going to throw you in the trunk of a fucking car. And then I'm going to blow your fucking brains out. Then, I'm going to park that car by the precinct before I go home for the weekend. Give you enough time to get ripe.

"Two days later, before I come back to work, I'm going to stop and make an anonymous call to 911 saying that there's a weird odor coming from this particular car. And when I get back to work, guess whose job it's going to be to find out who killed you? Mine, Frankie. That's what's going to happen unless I see you tomorrow."

Frankie Carbone was at Detective Eppolito's desk when he walked into the precinct the following afternoon. Louie made him wait three hours before filing the complaint.

"But they were all bullshit charges. Harassment was the heaviest. We couldn't even get him on the gun count. He had witnesses who swore it was only a BB gun he used on his girlfriend's car.

"But it wasn't over between me and Frankie. I had embarrassed him in front of his peers. He'd been angling to get made in the Colombo Family and when he'd shit his pants he'd lost respect. The word went out on the street that Frankie had vowed to put two in the back of my head. Frankie Carbone I could deal with. But Frankie had big friends, including Alphonse Persico, the son of Carmine 'the Snake' Persico, boss of the Colombo Family."

Like the sons of so many Mafia bosses, Alphonse Persico had surrounded himself with a coterie of hop-heads, thugs, and flakes that in his father's heyday would have been used for no more than fish bait. Frankie Carbone fit snugly into this category. But Allie Boy was, nonetheless, still "the Snake" 's son, and Louie saw no need to be looking over his shoulder for the rest of his life. So he made a call.

"Sally Bonagorra, a knockaround guy I'd known since I was a kid, was a soldier in the Gambino Family as well as an old friend of the Eppolito family. Sally and my Uncle Freddy had done business way back, and he had been close to both my old man and my Uncle Jimmy. I also knew Sally sometimes did some hijacking with one of the Colombo crews. I figured he was the perfect mediator.

"So I called Sally and asked him to represent me at a sit-down with the Colombo people. It was set for the following Sunday afternoon, at the Nineteenth Hole, another mob joint on Eighteenth Avenue.

"There were only four of us there: me, Sally, Frankie Carbone, and a capo from the Lucchese Family whose name I didn't know. He didn't introduce himself, either. He was representing Frankie Carbone. Somebody told me later it was 'Christy Tick' Furnari, who ran the joint and was a mob mediator par excellence, but I never found out for sure. I was, after all, a detective. It wasn't like the Luccheses were going to ask me over for cappuccino after the meet.

"Sally began the meeting with a little speech. 'I admit this is unusual,' he said. 'In fact, sit-downs with people outside the Family are not allowed. So maybe, technically, this isn't a sit-down. But I've known Louie all my life. I know his family. And there seems to be a fucking problem. We'd like to settle it right here.'

"So far, so good. Frankie Carbone told his side first, describing how I had 'disrespected' him in his club. Then I gave my brief. The girlfriend's complaint. My visit to his house. The insulting phone call.

" 'Nobody,' I said, 'not him, not you, nobody talks to me like that. You know my family. I got my bones. Being a cop is only a job. Before I'm a cop I'm a man, and I don't need this kind of bullshit in my life, where I have to call for a sit-down when somebody says they should have stuck a shotgun in my mother's pussy. But I'm here out of respect for my people. There's just no reason for a shithead like this to be breaking my balls. He's out of line.'

"Frankie didn't appear amused, but I seemed to be getting through to Christy Tick.

"Frankie's sponsor said that he'd like to see the entire mess cleared up, and rather than turning to Sally, I looked him square in the eye and told him I was willing to abide by any ruling he put out. I knew how to play their game. By addressing the Lucchese capo instead of Sally, my sponsor, I was showing my respect.

"It worked. Frankie's people ordered him and Allie Persico to steer clear. I agreed to do the same. Now I only had one more problem. On my way out with Sally, I wondered how many federal agencies had recorded our conversation."

21

In fact, there were several branches of law enforcement that were beginning to take an active interest in the comings and goings of the burly homicide detective from the Six-two Precinct. The FBI had kept a wary eye on Louie since his uncle's assassination. And not a few of his fellow homicide detectives marveled at his bounty of knowledge regarding the dead mobsters who littered South Brooklyn.

"I wondered about Eppolito the way the old-time cops wondered about marijuana," said one. "They didn't know much about the stuff, except that it kept bad company."

Foremost among the curious were investigators from the Brooklyn District Attorney's Organized Crime Unit, who couldn't help but notice that Lou Eppolito's name turned up in an inordinate amount of surveillance reports.

As Louie suspected, his personal visits to Carmine Lambordozzi, his friendly conversations with Funzie Tieri, his general lurking along the edges of Bensonhurst Mafia circles were generating more than a few questions. It was not unusual for detectives reporting for duty to find their mob collars uncuffed, uncaged, and sharing coffee and old times with the gregarious

Detective Eppolito. And on one occasion Louie actually escorted Todo Marino into the Bath Avenue station house. He wanted the ancient *caporegime* to hear for himself how a group of would-be extortionists were taking his name in vain.

"We'd arrested three thugs for trying to put the arm on a sandwich shop, and while they were in the cage all they could talk about was Todo this, Todo that; how many people they'd whacked for Todo. I mean, I knew the law, I knew the mores of Organized Crime, and I knew that remarks like the kind they were making led to guys like Todo getting nailed in conspiracy cases. Now, it would be one thing if the comments were true. But this was all hot air blowing.

"Finally, one real tough guy dressed in an Italian tuxedo—that's the white, sleeveless T-shirt—started bragging about how he had the okay from Todo to whack anybody he wanted, including any cop with the nerve to lock him up. He looked right at me as he said it.

"That was it. I got in my unmarked car and drove straight to Todo's hangout, the Esplanade Lounge on Bay Fiftieth and Cropsey. I interrupted his meal—and it had better be for something important if you were going to interrupt Todo's meal—and brought him and his bodyguard right up into the squad room, but out of sight of the cage, to let them listen to these punks jabbering away.

"When Todo finally stepped out into view I thought they'd all die of cardiac arrest right there in the cell. Then, despite his protests, I chauffeured Todo and his man back to their club. He was afraid, you see, that I'd get in trouble."

Todo wasn't far wrong. Not surprisingly, an Eppolito rat trap was baited by the boys from the District

Attorney's Mafia squad. The cheese was bogus information.

On several occasions in late 1982, the DA's investigators nonchalantly fed Louie misinformation. Because he was such an active cop, involved, by his count, in over forty Cosa Nostra–related homicide cases, Louie was a regular visitor to the DA's mob bureau. "One of the reasons we all knew Louie so well," says Mark Feldman, who ran the Brooklyn DA's Rackets Bureau at the time, "was because his relatives kept turning up dead."

Thus, it wasn't hard for Organized Crime investigators to stop Louie in the hallway, in the can, or over coffee, and drop an interesting Mafia tidbit under the guise of casual conversation.

"If that kind of gossip bounces back to you through wire taps, or informers, you can be sure it only came from one place," says a mob specialist still on The Job. "But I have to admit that none of the bogus stuff passed to Louie ever came back to anyone."

One former head of the DA's Organized Crime Unit recalls that there was an ambivalence in his squad with regard to Detective Eppolito. "If you asked me, personally, if Louie Eppolito was mobbed up, my gut feeling would be yes," he says. "He worked his way all through those people. But, professionally, there was never one shred of evidence that linked Louie to any Organized Crime activities. And believe me, people tried."

That perseverance was certainly aided and abetted by the know-it-all homicide dick's absolute refusal to mask his disdain for the Department's so-called "mob experts."

"Most of the Organized Crime murders I did involved guys on the Mafia fringe. Low-level hijackers, punk extortionists, maybe a numbers runner skimming off the top. But every once in a while we'd turn up a boss, a capo, with three in the head. That's when you'd see the big-time investigators come out of the woodwork. The Organized Crime Task Force. The boys from the Eastern District. All kinds of Feds. And, I mean, these jamokes really annoyed me.

"I'd walk onto a crime scene, the body would be slumped over the steering wheel, and there'd be a conspiracy circle jerk going on around the car. It would sound something like this:

'Well, let's see, in 1957 he owned a pizza joint, but his pies weren't that good. Everybody thought the sauce was bad so they were staying away until he got a better sauce man, so maybe the first sauce man came back to clip him, because he's with the Antonio crew now. Or if not that, we know his friend Ziggy just bought four pairs of shoes but he only paid for three and since the guy who owns the store is Fatsy Funzie's cousin, maybe he put the hit out on him.'

"Ridiculous! These guys would name every Italian they could think of, and the motives were always a hoot to listen to. If a guy was busted for selling Tuinals three decades ago, for example, they always classified the murder as drug-related.

"Finally I'd get tired of listening to all this conjecture and I'd pull the boss aside and ask if anyone bothered to find out if the deceased was poking somebody's else's wife? Or had anybody taken the time to check if maybe this stiff got drunk the previous night and gave some lip to a made man in a bad mood?

"I mean, sure, there were a lot of Cosa Nostra whacks that never got solved. Intricate, conspiratorial whacks. But there were just as many that had the most mundane motives sitting right in front of your nose, if you'd only put away the heavy theories. It made me laugh.

"I have to admit though—and this is a terrible knock on me—I didn't work as hard when somebody I knew from the old days turned up dead. Most of the time I managed to wangle myself off the case. And when I couldn't, I'd merely go through the motions. I'd walk into a club I knew was wired, for instance, and make a big deal out of questioning some crew member. Meanwhile, as I'm shouting at the guy to answer my questions, I'd be nodding and winking to show that it was all a big joke. Sometimes I'd even go as far as to call ahead to let them know I was coming. For all my time on The Job, I never really lost my old man's credo that nobody got killed for no reason."

In some respects, there was an irony to Louie's Bensonhurst assignment, primarily because he related so well to, in cop vernacular, "the regular citizens." Most of the neighborhood's residents were straight, hard-working Italian-Americans. They set tile, or washed windows, or picked up garbage. Louie developed a real rapport with them.

The way he saw it, being a cop was similar to being a made man, in that favors were the coin of the realm. He respected the currency. If the Six-two's detective squad room received fifty phone calls a day, Louie guesses that, conservatively, forty of them were for him. If Frankie "the Nap" could give him a lead on an unsolved homicide (as Frank DeNapoli once did), then Louie deduced that it wouldn't kill him to put in a call to the Queens precinct where, he was told, the Nap's teenage daughter had recently been hauled in with a group of kids, one of whom had some pot on him. But favors were by no means reserved for made men.

"Once, this little butcher right off the boat from Sicily walked into the squad room crying that his eight-year-old kid was missing. He didn't know what to do. After a half-hour of conversation in broken English, it came out that the butcher had taken his son to Coney Island the previous night.

"I asked him if the boy had liked the amusement park, and as soon as he answered, 'Yes,' we got into my car and drove over. Sure enough, there was the kid, standing on the boardwalk staring at the Ferris wheel. The guy was so grateful that the next day he brought me over a bottle of homemade Italian wine. That's when it felt awful good to be a cop. When it felt bad was when Internal Affairs hassled me about accepting gifts—in this case, the wine—from civilians.

"And it felt worst of all when we got a new commanding officer, a guy named Bill Juliano. The manpower shortage had thrown a lot of old-time desk jockeys back into the street, and Juliano was dusted off when our CO retired."

Juliano, a former Brooklyn detective who'd been working over on Staten Island, came storming into the precinct on January 1, 1983. On his first day he gathers the detectives for a pep talk on graft, threatening to personally lock up anyone who takes so much as a department-issue pencil.

"He went on to give a little hard-ass, drill-sergeant speech about how he didn't believe in being pals with his men, how it was his way or the highway, the usual bullshit from guys who are in over their heads.

"Juliano was the type of cop who thought everybody but him was on the pad, especially if their name ended in a vowel. I didn't like the guy from day one, and he didn't like me. In fact, after his little holier-than-thou speech, I made it clear to the other detectives that I thought we were now working for a loser. Word must have gotten back to our new boss about me opening my big yap. I had bad-mouthed him. Nothing like getting off on the right foot with the new boss.

"From that day on, I was assigned every piece-of-shit case that came into the Six-two. Guys blowing themselves up with gas grills. Drunken-driving deaths. Domestic homicides. Real heart-stoppers. Yet one of them, what initially looked to be a cheap murder, was about to turn my life upside down."

VI

BETRAYAL

VI

BETRAYAL

22

The victim's name was Albert Veriali. Albert and his brother, Patty, were a pair of teenage extortionists who terrorized South Brooklyn's merchants. They must have found an old Mustache Pete handbook, for their credo was as simple as it was unsophisticated: "Pay up, and your windows—and maybe your legs—remain unbroken."

The Veriali brothers were the constant clients of officers from the Six-two, primarily for gun charges. Their yellow sheets read like an armory's inventory list. In the spring of 1983, Patty Veriali's corpse turned up in a remote corner of the precinct. Apparently, these thugs had pushed the wrong people too far, for some of the merchants they were attempting to bleed were already under the mob umbrella. Four months later, on July 1, somebody finished the job. Albert was gunned down, in broad daylight, on the corner of Twentieth Avenue and Eighty-sixth Street, in the bustling heart of Bensonhurst.

"Albert Veriali had eighteen holes in him, but, true to form, nobody saw a thing. Every shopkeeper, every bartender, every Chinese busboy in the neighborhood was in the john at the exact time the hit went down. Grandmothers, shoe clerks, gas-station attendants, they all heard the shots fired just moments after they decided to go to the bathroom. It's a wonder the pipes didn't burst. South Brooklyn must have the best plumbing in the world.''

Louie had been vacationing when Albert Veriali bought it. He returned to duty three days after the murder and was told that the only lead the investigating officers had was a witness from out of town, a teenager, who had been standing next to Albert when the hit went down. The witness, unaware of the neighborhood's unofficial toiletry ordinance, told the detectives that he thought he could identify the shooter's face.

"Since I knew the locals, the sergeant from Borough Homicide in charge of the investigation, Jimmy Shea, asked me to go over mug shots with the kid. When that went nowhere, Sergeant Shea requested that I accompany the kid to Intelligence Division headquarters in Lower Manhattan, on the good chance that their mob picture books were more complete than ours.''

The Intelligence Division is the NYPD's organized crime epicenter. Shea was fairly certain Albert Veriali's killer was mob-connected, and he thought his witness might spot the shooter in their OC mug shots. Louie had never been to the division's Hudson Street headquarters before—in fact, he wasn't quite sure exactly where it was located. So Shea ordered another detective, Louie Rango, to escort Louie and the teenaged witness.

Intelligence headquarters is a warren of dusty old rooms devoted exclusively to the mob. Getting into it is like signing into Fort Knox. They take your fingerprint. They take your thumbprint. They double-check your badge number. Then you're allowed to sign in and receive a numbered pass. The number on your pass is marked down next to your signature on the sign-in sheet.

Once inside, Louie was a third wheel, "sitting there with my thumb up my ass," while the teenager and Rango perused the division's mug-shot albums. At one point, Louie happened to notice a cluster of wanted posters tacked to a hallway bulletin board. One of the flyers featured a Sicilian gangster named Rosario Gambino, who, despite being the late Don Carlo's nephew, was not a member of an American crew.

"The Sicilian and American Mafias have evolved into two separate entities. It had once been common for made men, whether Italian or American, to cross lines, so to speak. It was similar to being a Mason. But over the years differences arose between the home-grown Cosa Nostra and the European branch, and today they very much go their own ways.

"The Sicilian Gambinos in the States are strictly drug dealers. They stay out of the Americans' shylocking and gambling operations and even have their own hangouts along Eighteenth Avenue. The Cafe Italia, Alba's, the Mille Luci. They are their own people and they run their own mob.

"About three weeks previous to the Veriali homicide I'd been cruising on patrol when this greaseball steps out of the Cafe Italia, spots me, and grabs his crotch. It was Rosario Gambino. He put his hand right between his legs, grabbed his prick, and shook it at me.

" 'Stop the fucking car,' " I shrieked to my partner. I got out, walked across the street, threw my hand around this skinny little guy's throat, and lifted him off the ground. Diplomatically, I explained my chagrin: 'Let me tell you something you slimy greaseball prick. People don't do that to me.' I was about to break his hand in three different spots when he began begging.

" 'Please, I don't mean no problem,' he said. 'I was just fixin' my pants.' I told him that if he fixed his pants like that in front of me again I'd fix what's inside his pants, and started to walk away. Halfway across the street I was stopped by two Organized Crime Control Bureau detectives, Frankie Pagola and Kenny McCabe. Kenny McCabe was known city-wide as the most respected mob investigator on The Job.

"McCabe told me I was on surveillance film, 'and things like that don't look too good for you. You can't be slapping these guys around like that.' I just laughed as I walked away.

"So anyway, down at Intelligence Division I'm recounting this story to Louie Rango, when an OC detective named Bill Sweeney passes by. I asked Sweeney who was handling the Rosario Gambino* case. He said the Feds had it on hold because Rosario was in Sicily. I told him that I didn't know where the Feds were getting their information from, but if they wanted to nail Rosario Gambino, they'd find him sitting every day in the front window of the Cafe Italia on Eighteenth Avenue. Then I gave him a description, and a make on Gambino's car.

"That was it. A two-minute, off-the-cuff conversation that was about to ruin my career. Talk about life playing its desperate little tricks on you."

A month later, on August 15, Louie caught a routine homicide: white male confirmed dead on Bay Parkway. When he arrived at the crime scene he recog-

---

* The younger Gambino was wanted on a drug rap.

nized the corpse as William Hunt, a harmless old man who frequented the Six-two's squad room with complaints that his son-in-law was using him as a heavy bag. The murder was gruesome. Hunt had been hacked up with a carving knife, and his body was so punctured that his liver was oozing out onto his kitchen tiles.

When Louie interviewed Hunt's daughter, Margaret Vasile, she seemed more resigned than horrified. "I guess my common-law husband, Herman Penny, did it," she sighed. "I got two kids by him, and he's a nut."

After the interview, Louie handed Margaret Vasile his card. When she read his last name, she brightened and asked Louie if he was any relation to Jimmy Eppolito, the murdered mobster. It was a small world. Patrick Penny, Herman's son from a previous marriage, had been the teenager who'd been necking in the car and witnessed the shootings of Uncle Jimmy and Jim-Jim.

After a routine investigation and cut-and-dried arraignment, Herman Penny was indicted on charges of manslaughter. Bail was set at $100,000. Penny couldn't raise it, and Louie assumed Herman Penny was out of his life. He was dead wrong.

Four months later, on December 12, 1983, Margaret Vasile stopped Louie as he was stepping out of his car in the Six-two's parking lot. She handed him a letter from her common-law husband.

Dear Margaret:

As you know, I will soon receive $175,000 from the insurance company because of the car accident I was in. Since my bail is set at $100,000, I am currently making arrangements to borrow the bail money from two Mafia shylocks I know, using the insurance money as collateral. I hope to be out of jail by December 15th because by Christmas Day I have plans to kill you, the two kids, and myself. After all, I told you I was going to kill your father, so who cares what happens.

Louie was as shaken as Margaret by the matter-of-fact tone of Herman's letter. So shaken, in fact, that he called the District Attorney's office that afternoon. Mark Feldman—"a tough Jew if I ever met one"—he was sure, would know how to handle this situation.

After getting a synopsis of the problem, Feldman suggested that Louie drive over to the Intelligence Division to see if there was a file on Herman Penny. Perhaps they could track his loan sharks and nip this thing in the bud. On December 13, Louie signed the Intelligence Division's entrance sheet for the second time in his life. He found no file on Herman Penny.

On his way out, Louie was spotted by Detective Sweeney, who asked him if he had ever heard from the Feds regarding the Rosario Gambino case. Louie told him he hadn't, but that he continued to see Gambino hanging around the Cafe Italia. The two talked for a few minutes, and then, as an afterthought, Sweeney asked Louie if he could pin a name to a surveillance photo related to the Gambino case.

"I didn't recognize the guy in the mug shot, but told Sweeney I'd ask around about him. Then Sweeney handed me a file folder full of copies of old arrest records, fingerprint records, newspaper articles, and Rosario Gambino's Family tree. None of this stuff was up to date. All in all, nothing of importance.

"Sweeney suggested I take the folder with me— 'There's nothing but bullshit in here,' were his exact words—and, after conferring with another detective, he handed it to me. On the way back to the precinct I swung by Feldman's office to drop off the Herman Penny letter, and then stopped off at the Cafe Italia. After copying several license-plate numbers onto the outside of the Gambino folder, I stuck my head in the joint looking for Rosario. He wasn't there. I thought nothing about it and left."

Only once over the next ten months did Louie give a passing thought to Rosario Gambino. When the Sicilian was convicted in October of 1984 for conspiring to sell forty kilos of heroin to an FBI undercover agent, Louie clipped the story from the *Daily News* and crammed it into the disorganized cabinet drawer that passed for the precinct's Organized Crime file.

A week later, the Six-two's civilian office manager informed Louie that he had been summoned to an Internal Affairs hearing on November 1, at IAD headquarters in Brooklyn Heights. "They strongly suggested that you bring an attorney," the clerk added.

Ironically, Detective Eppolito's first instinct was that another cop was in trouble, and he was being called to testify for the defense. His long list of commendations and awards made him the ideal character witness for any cop caught up in the petty feuds of the police bureaucracy.

Nevertheless, he placed a pro forma call to Steve Gardell, the South Brooklyn Trustee for the Detectives Endowment Association. It was standard rank-and-file procedure to contact a union representative when Internal Affairs was involved. Curiously, Gardell had also that morning received a call from Detective Pete Furtado, another member of the Six-two

PDU. Internal Affairs also wanted to interview Furtado on November 1.

As Furtado had done, Louie explained to Gardell that he was completely in the dark as to the nature of IAD's summons. Gardell saw nothing unusual in that. He knew of Louie's reputation, and he knew Internal Affairs. It was, however, customary for the Shooflies to at least give the union delegate a hint as to the nature of their hearing's agenda. Gardell's antennae shot up a few inches when several phone calls to a friendly IAD investigator went unreturned. They went on full alert when a Department source told him that an inspector was scheduled to preside at both the Furtado and Eppolito hearings.

"Louie, usually there's only a sergeant at these things," Gardell informed his new client. "Something has to be up with you. Think back. Isn't there anything you can remember?"

Louie's mind was a blank. As a precaution, Gardell contacted Howard Cerny, a white-shoe attorney whom the Detectives Union kept on retainer. (Cerny represented, among others, the singer Michael Jackson and oil magnate Leon Hess.) Cerny, with contacts throughout the Department, also attempted to get a handle on the nature of the complaint. A brick wall went up. All the lawyer could learn was that Louie was the target of the investigation. They would all walk into this one blind.

The type of IAD hearing to which Louie was summoned is designated G.O. 15s, after the Police Department's General Order empowering the hearing officer to suspend a cop on the spot for refusing to answer questions. Furtado's G.O. 15 was short and sweet. He was asked vague questions about Organized Crime activity in and around the Six-two, and

finally about a collect telephone call he made to his squad room from Atlantic City on March 12, 1984.

Furtado explained that he and his wife had been celebrating their wedding anniversary in the New Jersey gambling resort when he called the office regarding a scheduled court appearance. The interviewers thanked Furtado and excused him, but the odd question about the phone call left Gardell with a queasy feeling. Somehow, it didn't fit.

At 9 A.M. on November 1, 1984, following Furtado's appearance, Louie, Gardell and Cerny met for breakfast at the Brooklyn Heights Coffee Shoppe. There was not much conversation. Louie appeared a bit too unconcerned to Gardell, who was aware of his client's explosive temper. Gardell had passed this bit of information on to Cerny. Before paying the check, the lawyer cautioned Louie to answer the investigator's questions as moderately as possible. No one wanted a scene.

STEVE GARDELL: "I'd known Louie professionally for seven or eight years. We'd worked in adjoining precincts—he in the Six-two, me in the Six-eight—and every so often we'd share a homicide. They'd shoot them in his precinct and dump them in mine. Plus, the guy was in the papers all the time. He was a reporter's dream.

"I pulled double duty with the union—we only had five union officers for the four-thousand-man Detectives Endowment Association—and as the Brooklyn South trustee it was natural for Louie to call me when he got the notification to show up at IAD.

"I'd been through these hearings hundreds of times before. I knew the routine. First you call down to IAD to find out exactly what the beef is. But when some sergeant tells me he can't 'disclose the charges,' right away I know we have a problem.

"Now you have to understand, ninety-nine percent of these beefs are minor stuff. A detective seen in an off-limits restaurant or bar. An off-duty cop drinking too much and pulling his piece on a neighbor. Piddling shit like that. Even though IAD is a very closed-mouth division, they usually told me over the phone what kind of G.O. 15 my guy was facing. That was just the rapport I had with them.

"So when the sergeant wouldn't give me any information, I kind of pursued it a little further through back channels. I called a captain I knew and he apologetically tells me that if I need to know anything about Eppolito's beef, I have to get it from this Inspector McCormack. I didn't know McCormack well enough to call him out of the blue, plus I'm getting vibrations that even if I did, he wasn't going to divulge anything.

"That's when I called Howard Cerny. When Howard called IAD, and they wouldn't tell *him* word one about the beef, I knew we were going from 'problem' to 'big problem.'

"I called Louie back, trying to jump-start his memory a little bit. But he tells me, 'I don't know, Steve, it could be a hundred and one things.' I know exactly what he's talking about. Louie was such an active cop, and this is not something unusual for an active cop. I had an instructor in the Police Academy, a street-smart lieutenant who warned our class that one of the primary lessons we were going to learn on The Job is that you only get in trouble if you do the work.

"You can put in twenty years, not do a thing, and you'll never see the inside of an IAD office. But you become a good cop, an active cop, and they're going to muck with you. This was Louie to a tee. He was doing his job. He was out there on Eighteenth Avenue, harassing the bad guys, trying to mingle with the mobsters, sniffing around for information.

"Of course, it didn't help that his old man was Fat the Gangster and his uncle was Jimmy the Clam.

"So there's nothing to do but show up and see what they got in store for us. Louie met Howard and me for breakfast in downtown Brooklyn after Furtado's hearing, and the three of us walked over to IAD in the Heights. IAD is housed in the old Eight-four Precinct, and the place has an adverse psychological effect on a cop the moment you walk through the front door.

"It has a hollowed-out look to it, like you're walking into a haunted house. I swear they left it that way for that reason. You get in there and immediately you're overcome with this dreary feeling, like they're coming to take you to the guillotine. That's exactly how Louie felt when Inspector McCormack walked down the stairs to greet us, with a Lieutenant Henris and a Sergeant Penzes trailing behind like satraps.

"Now, an inspector rarely sits in on these hearings, and Cerny and I knew it. We throw a glance at each other on the way up to the hearing room that more or less says, 'What the fuck did Eppolito do, murder the Pope?' "

23

So we walk in and they put me at a desk facing a long table, the type you'd see in Nuremberg, Germany, around 1946. Gardell, Cerny, and I sat facing this Deputy Inspector McCormack, a Lieutenant Henris, and a Sergeant Penzes. They'd hauled out the big guns, and I felt like there was a target painted on my face. After the formal introductions were read into the minutes, they began their little dance.

"Which Organized Crime cases had I worked on lately? What was their nature? How many were still pending? How did I feel about investigating the Mafia? Did I socialize with members of the Cosa Nostra?

"After about a half hour or so of this bullshit, they finally got to the point. Christ, these guys were worse than the mob when it came to getting to the point."

Transcripts can never catch the true flavor of any conversation—inflections and tones of voice flatten out on the printed page—but the minutes of Louie's G.O. 15 more than imply the IAD investigators' bias. Subtle trick questions were posed. Louie was repeatedly asked the same question in several forms. His answers were jumped on before he finished.

By the time the investigators got to the meat of the Q & A, their direction was clear. The hearing had something to do with the Rosario Gambino file, the file that had been passed to Louie at Intelligence headquarters, and which had now magically appeared and was pushed across the "Nuremberg" table for Louie to inspect. Deputy Inspector Robert McCormack apparently found it incredible that Detective Sweeney had *just given* the Gambino file to Louie, and demanded to know why.

With that, Louie breathed a little easier. This had something to do with the Sicilians, he thought. And aside from busting a few "greaseball *guyones*" along Eighteenth Avenue, he hadn't tangled with the Sicilian Cosa Nostra in any shape, manner, or form. Louie gave McCormack a long and convoluted explanation of the Albert Veriali hit, his chance meeting with Detective Sweeney, and the process by which the Gambino file wound up in his hands.

"I never wanted the goddamn thing to begin with," Louie explained. But, flustered, he erred on his dates. In his memory, he merged the two trips to Intelligence Division headquarters. Sweeney gave him the file, he said, while he was with Louie Rango and the teenage witness to the Veriali murder.

"I just completely forgot that the Veriali visit was in July and that the December visit involved the hassle with Herman Penny. That's when the inspector jumped all over my case.

"They had facts, dates, and sign-in logs. They had *proof* that I had actually taken the Gambino file on December 13. What, they asked, rapid-fire, was I doing at the Intelligence Division on that date. What commander had ordered me over there? There was no notation on the Six-two's destination log. Had I taken it upon myself to visit the Intelligence Division and request the file on a member of Organized Crime? Had I knowingly violated departmental regulations?

"Now I was sweating. I couldn't remember. I checked my memo book—every cop keeps one—for 12/13/83. In my scribbled handwriting there was an entry marked 'BDA.' I assumed it stood for Brooklyn Detective Area. Every detective in the county stopped by the Brooklyn Detective Area, an administrative center at Borough Command headquarters in East Flatbush, on a nearly daily basis. It's where you took witnesses, it's where you got papers signed, it's where you could pick up your paycheck. But there was nothing to indicate why, or even if, I went to the Intelligence Division.

"Christ, how was I supposed to remember what I was doing on a Thursday morning nearly a year ago? I gave them an honest answer, my only answer: I couldn't recall."

At this point Louie assumed that he was being investigated for removing files from the Intelligence Division without going through proper channels. A heavy charge, but nothing he couldn't live with. More bureaucratic nonsense. He wasn't prepared for the trap that was being baited.

With a series of seemingly innocuous inquiries, McCormack established that Louie was the unofficial Organized Crime officer of the Six-two detective squad, in charge of the handling of Mafia files. Would anyone else possibly have access to them, McCormack asked? (He had put the same question to Furtado.) The cabinet was unlocked, Louie explained. It was a mess. Anything is possible. But, he admitted, he didn't know of any other detectives who consulted them regularly.

Reading the transcript at this point, one can almost

envision the rope, Louie at one end, twisting in the wind.

DEP. INSP. McCORMACK: "So Detective Sweeney gave you this information, gave you that material, gave it to you in a folder. Is that correct?"

DET. EPPOLITO: "Correct."

Mc: "All right. Now what did you do with it?"

E: "I brought it back to the Precinct, put it into a file marked Gambino. File 12-12-83 . . ."

Mc: "That's all?"

E: "Yes."

Mc: "Did you ever use it again? Did you ever add anything to it?"

E: "I added this piece of paper the day I saw it in a newspaper."

CERNY: "Let the record reflect that he's showing an article entitled *Gambino Convicted*."

Mc: "You added that last Tuesday?"

E: "Yes."

Mc: "Did you ever add anything else between the time you got it and last Tuesday?"

E: "To the best of my knowledge, never."

Mc: "You never touched that [file] at all?"

E: "Right."

Mc: "I just want to get this clear. . . . You got it from Intell, apparently it was their file. . . . You brought it back to the Six Two PDU. . . ."

E: "Made a folder. . . . "

Mc: "Made a folder, put the [Gambino] material in a folder?"

E: "Yes."

Mc: "Put it in a file cabinet . . . and never touched it again until last Tuesday when you added that [article]. Did you ever make any copies of that folder?"

E: "None whatsoever."

Mc: "All right, Detective, then how do you explain the fact that on March 16, 1984, copies of exactly what you have there in front of you were recovered by the Federal Bureau of Investigation and the U.S. Attorney while executing a search warrant at Rosario Gambino's residence in Cherry Hill, New Jersey? Can you think of any reason why that should have gotten out there? Do you have any idea of how it was out there at all? Can you, in your experience as a detective, think of any reason how it might have gotten there?"

The words reverberated like the clang of a sword. Louie had no answer. McCormack augered in.

Mc: "Okay, did you ever make a copy of that material?"

E: "Not once."

Mc: "Not once? No, you didn't make a copy?"

E: "No, I did not make a copy of that material."

Mc: "All right. Would it interest you to know that the copies that were found in Gambino's house were run off, according to laboratory analysis, from the precinct copy machine in the Six Two precinct. You have no explanation for that at all?"

Now, finally, McCormack applied the coup de grace.

Mc: "Detective, I have one more question."

E: "Surely."

Mc: "The laboratory analysis of the material that was found in Gambino's house—the copies of the information that was from the Six-two PDU—also have

your fingerprints on it. Can you tell me how those fingerprints got there? Do you have any idea at all?"

Louie was struck dumb. Cerny and Louie exchanged puzzled looks. Louie felt Gardell slump down in his chair, as if recoiling from the charge.

"Recess," Cerny choked out. "Louie, let's step outside."

In the hallway, Louie told the attorney that he'd never made copies of anything. As far as he knew, the Rosario Gambino file was still buried among the papers in the precinct's haphazard Organized Crime file, where he'd thrown it ten months ago. Louie had no idea how IAD had retrieved copies of the file with his fingerprints on it.

All he could do was venture a guess: "Mr. Cerny, there's nothing but bullshit in that Gambino file. Pictures. Rap sheets from a decade ago. Old newspaper clippings. Somebody is setting me up."

When Louie, Cerny, and Gardell returned to the hearing room, any pretense of decorum swiftly disintegrated. Cerny wanted to know about these fingerprints. Were they originals? Xeroxed copies? He warned the investigators that Louie was finished answering questions for the day until he got some answers. Inspector McCormack nearly jumped out of his chair, bellowing something about "Eppolito and his kind." G.O. 15 was in effect, he said. Louie would answer their questions or face suspension immediately.

The hairs stood up on the back of Louie's neck. After years of faithful service to the NYPD, after a lifetime of burying his past, here was the eleventh-most-decorated officer in the history of the police force once again being accused of being that apple that didn't fall far from that tree. Louie didn't need this crap.

"Let me tell you something," he told the inspector. "I never gave nobody no papers on Rosario Gambino. You tell me that the FBI has had this file for six months. What the hell have they been doing with it for all that time?"

McCormack's answer chilled Louie. Agents from the Federal Bureau of Investigation had been tailing him. Internal Affairs had even subpoenaed his phone records, from his home and his office. Over the past six months, McCormack admitted, the Shooflies had been interviewing Louie's co-workers, and even his friends. The ultimate indignity. Louie had been treated like a "goddamn perp!"

"And what the fuck did they find in six months?" Louie demanded. "Do you have any tapes of me calling anyone in Organized Crime? Of anyone in Organized Crime calling me? Any pictures? Any evidence whatsoever?"

His questions were greeted with silence. When it became obvious that the only answers he was going to receive were stony glares, Louie continued. He reiterated that other than adding that one newspaper clipping, he hadn't given a thought to that Gambino file since he'd stuffed it in his file cabinet. Nobody from the Intelligence Division had ever contacted him about the case, he explained, and he had decided that if it wasn't that important to them then it wasn't that important to him. He harped on the fact that the FBI had gotten nothing on him in six months, not a whiff. What made IAD think, he wanted to know, that they could accuse him of being mobbed up?

"Because of the phone call from Atlantic City on March 12, 1984," Lieutenant Henris had answered.

He continued, condescending, to state that four days before Rosario Gambino had been collared, someone had made a collect call to the Six-two station house from an Atlantic City pay phone. A telephone records search had discovered that the same pay phone had been used to place a call to Rosario Gambino's New Jersey home.

Louie's head was spinning. He'd never been to Atlantic City in his life, and told his interrogators so.

"You're full of shit," Sergeant Penzes said.

That was it. Louie erupted.

"Fuck you," he screamed. "Fuck all of you."

Howard Cerny tried to calm him down. Louie ignored him.

"Wait a minute," he said. "I'm here under oath and I waived my right to remain silent and when I give you an honest answer you tell me I'm full of shit. I don't get it. Or maybe I do get it. This is a witch hunt, and I'm being hung out to dry here. You say I was in Atlantic City on such and such a date, and you don't even want to know if I can prove that I wasn't there."

"I was getting the drift now. They weren't doing this to me because I was a dirty cop. They were busting my balls because of my family, because of my background, and because I'd been giving desk humps like them shit for my entire career. I had no idea how that file got into Gambino's hands. It almost didn't matter. I thought of that line from the movie *Raging Bull*, when Jake LaMotta lost the title fight and turned to his brother: *Joey, I don't deserve this. But I did a lot of things wrong. Maybe it's all coming back now.*

"Maybe it was all coming back to me now. I'd been an arrogant cop, not a crooked one.

"Suddenly I was calm again, like on the ride to Big

Paulie's. I decided to take a final shot at straightening this thing out here and now.

"I admitted I was reacting terribly. I volunteered to take a lie detector test, to be hypnotized, to be shot up with sodium pentothal. 'I have nothing to hide,' I told them. 'And you had better be ready to back up these charges with facts, and not just the fact that my old man and uncles were made men.'

"My little speech went unanswered. Finally, I turned to Henris and asked: 'Tell me straight, are you doing this to me because you think I'm a bad cop, or because I'm an Italian cop?'

" 'If the shoe fits,' Henris said, 'wear it.'

" 'Go fuck yourself,' I told him.

" 'Eppolito, you're in a world of shit.' "

Hearing adjourned.

STEVE GARDELL: "One thing you have to understand about Internal Affairs: they scare me because they don't have seasoned investigators. No good cop makes his reputation working the street only to suddenly decide he wants to become a Shoofly.

"What I'm saying is that their investigators don't know how to look for the nuances. They jump at things right away. Something that another cop might recognize immediately as circumstantial evidence, they race right into without ever taking off the blinders.

"There's a lot of cops that do things wrong. I know that. I've defended them. But these guys from IAD are notorious for locking onto an idea and never letting go, like no-brain pit bulls. Which is what they did with this Gambino file. But Louie is answering their questions real good. He's steadfast and they don't rattle him, on the outside at least, until they accuse him of being in Atlantic City four days before the Feds nail Gambino.

"We can't figure out what being in Atlantic City has to do with Rosario Gambino and the missing file. Obviously they see some link between Atlantic City, Furtado, and Louie. But I can't figure it. They don't have to answer our questions at these hearings. And despite Cerny's objections, they didn't. All they would say was something about Louie making a phone call from the Tropicana Hotel. But Louie is denying it. His day book showed he was out sick on the day they say he's in Atlantic City. But so what? The guy says he's never been there, I'm willing to believe him.

"But what really killed me was when McCormack blurts out that Louie's fingerprints are all over this file they found in Gambino's house. He says it like we're all supposed to fall down with heart attacks. What do we have to say about that?

"Howard Cerny calls for a quick recess. Louie tells us he has no idea what the fuck they're talking about. And after we came back in Cerny and McCormack are going at it pretty good. All Cerny wanted to know was if the fingerprints they found on the Xerox of the file in Gambino's home were actual prints, or photocopies of prints. And they refused to answer that question. This back-and-forth went on for a good half hour.

"We're trying to explain to them that any mutt could have walked into the Six-two's squad room, copied the files, and got them to Gambino. Hell, says Cerny, somebody could have copied the file, put the copy back into the cabinet, and given Gambino the original. Anything could explain the fingerprints. And if Louie's prints are photocopies, what's their beef? Because Louie doesn't deny having the original folder. Then one of them made a comment about Louie, 'and his ilk.'

"That was it. I thought Louie was going to overturn the table on them. It was 'fuck this,' and 'fuck that,' and for a split second I even looked down to see if Louie was carrying his piece. It's funny, but none of that stuff made the transcript. That's how out of control he was. He wanted a lie detector test. That was unrealistic. But he was so adamant and so angry that I really felt for the first time that he was getting Rembrandted. They were framing this poor schmuck because he was an Eppolito. They basically said as much, in attitude and words.

"Louie was mixed up about certain dates. And they had him signing into Intelligence Headquarters on a December day that he didn't remember. But what do you expect when you walk in cold to one of these hearings? I was sure that, given some time, the whole puzzle would have fallen into place.

"But the hearing went nowhere after the outburst. As we walked out, Cerny and I both told Louie that we thought they were full of crap. The following afternoon I even called up and spoke to a source in IAD who told me Louie was going to be okay.

"The hearing took place on November 1. And for the next couple of weeks I was getting nothing but good vibes from people who were in a position to know. I called Louie once or twice a week to tell him not to worry about a thing. And after a couple of shaky days I'm pretty sure I've got him calmed down. I mean, word was out all over the borough that Louie Eppolito may have been a pigheaded cop, but he was a good cop.

"I coach a boys' soccer team on weekends, and on Saturday, November 24, I got up early and went down to the corner candy store for coffee and the morning paper. As I was sipping my coffee, I reached for the stack of papers. *The Daily News* was buried under a pile of *Post*s. When I pulled it out, the headline just jumped off the page in big, bold type:

MOB BIG GOT DATA FROM COP

MOB BIG GOT DATA FROM COP
By MURRAY WEISS *
(POLICE BUREAU CHIEF)

A veteran detective passed confidential Police Department intelligence reports to a member of the Sicilian Mafia who was convicted last month as a major heroin trafficker, sources told the Daily News yesterday.

The detective, who was not immediately identified, made photocopies last December of the intelligence files on mob figure Rosario Gambino and passed them to Gambino while he was under federal investigation, according to an informed source in the Police Department.

Gambino is a nephew of Carlo Gambino, the late "boss of all bosses," who reputedly was the most powerful crime figure in the United States before his death in 1976.

The detective, a 16-year veteran assigned to a Brooklyn stationhouse, is being investigated by the department's Internal Affairs Division. He is expected to be brought up on departmental

---

* *New York Daily News*, November 26, 1984, p. 3.

charges and suspended, possibly next week. He may also face criminal charges.

The officer has denied passing the files to Gambino, the source said.

He said the detective and Gambino apparently are friends and that they often were seen together at a cafe in the Coney Island section of Brooklyn.

"Internal Affairs investigators believed that their case against Louie, although circumstantial, was smooth and solid. And Louie, they were sure, had brought it all upon himself."

"The thing with Todo Marino, bringing him into the station house, was the last straw," recalls one Shoofly. "I mean, who does the guy think he is, bringing wiseguys up into the squad room. There's lots of cops in the city who know mobsters. You're going to have a pretty eclectic mix when you got thirty thousand guys on the force. But Eppolito just flaunted it. We kind of enjoyed seeing him squirm."

In the six months prior to Louie's G.O. 15, those "no-brain pit bulls" from Internal Affairs had put together an impressive array of so-called evidence. Fat the Gangster's kid was a big target.

In an interview conducted with Louie's old boss, the recently retired Lieutenant Juliano, one week before Louie's hearing, Juliano told IAD's Lieutenant Lawrence Henris that he would never have sent Detective Eppolito to Intelligence Division headquarters, "for fear that Detective Eppolito would spend the whole day and accomplish nothing."

Henris noted in his report that "it was clear that [Juliano] did not like or trust Detective Eppolito, and that he broke up the team to which he was assigned."

And as early as June 4, 1984—two and a half

months after the FBI discovered the copied file in Gambino's New Jersey home—an internal security report fingering Louie as the detective who had walked out of Intelligence headquarters with the Gambino papers was delivered to IAD's Inspector McCormack. It was based on an interview with Detective Sweeney of the Intelligence Division. Thereafter, from IAD's point of view, all the loose ends began to be woven into a case. Apparently, it mattered not that during the time period between the discovery of the file in Rosario Gambino's New Jersey home and Louie's G.O. 15 they could find no hard evidence with which to indict the detective. They smelled blood, and as one IAD investigator recalls, "they were determined to nail Eppolito one way or the other."

On June 6 the Office of the State Special Prosecutor for Corruption was notified about the investigation and advised of Louie's involvement. Sensing a political hot potato—the Special Prosecutor is a government appointee—his office passed on the case, while asking to be kept abreast of future developments.

A week later, while Louie was off duty, Lieutenant Henris and Sergeant Kenneth Penzes visited Sergeant Thomas Dowd, the second whip in the Six-two PDU. Dowd and Louie hated each other, and the sergeant gleefully handed over the Gambino file. Internal Affairs sent the fingerprints of four "primary suspects" to the police lab for comparison to the prints found on the file. Tellingly, according to an IAD report, all four suspects were detectives with Italian last names—Miciotta, Sasso, Furtado, and Eppolito.

The lab sent their results back on July 30, four days after McCormack put in a request to subpoena seven months' worth of the Eppolito household's telephone records. It "appeared," the report said, that two of the prints matched those of Detective Louis John Eppolito. Now it was merely a matter of closing the trap. As far as IAD was concerned, the other three "primary suspects" were in the clear.

A week prior to his G.O. 15, Detective Pete Furtado was met at the Six-two by Henris and grilled about his trip to Atlantic City. He made sure to tell Louie about it.

Henris also questioned the precinct's phone operator, police officer Angotti. "[Angotti] was asked if Detective Eppolito was with Detective Furtado when he made that collect call from Atlantic City," Henris wrote in his official report. "To this [Angotti] replied that to the best of his knowledge he was not." Furtado had told Louie about his interview with Henris and, recalled Louie, "swore up and down that I hadn't been with him."

On November 5, four days after Louie's hearing, Detective William Sweeney was summoned to his own G.O. 15. According to IAD's after-action report, "Det. Sweeney stated that Det. Eppolito visited the Intelligence Division sometime during the month of December, 1983, by himself, *and only on one occasion.*"

The investigators were now sure Louie was lying about shepherding the witness of the Veriali murder to Intelligence headquarters in July. To be sure, however, the following day they dispatched two officers to check the Intelligence Division's log books between January 1983 and November 1984. The two reported back that Louie's signature could only be found once on the entry log, on December 13. (Interestingly, in the box marked "Time Spent" on their report, the officers filled in "15 minutes.")

During this grilling, Sweeney—naturally defensive,

for he was still in the dark as to the nature of the investigation—challenged Louie's version of their meeting. He recounted, "I showed him a folder and *he asked* if he could have some information from it. So I gave him copies of reports on Cafe Italia which also included reports on Rosario Gambino."

Sweeney added: "Detective Eppolito mentioned that he had seen Rosario Gambino in the Cafe Italia prior to coming to the Intelligence Division office." This chance remark was obviously the source—via IAD's interpretation—of the *Daily News* article's contention that Louie and Gambino "are friends and that they often were seen together at a cafe in the Coney Island section of Brooklyn."

As Inspector Robert McCormack, since promoted and transferred to head the Department's Fourteenth Division in Brooklyn, recalls, "we all thought we had an airtight case."

24

On Friday night, November 23, 1984, Fran and
Louie went to a late movie. When they returned
home, they both stayed up past 3 A.M. watching television.

The ringing telephone awoke Louie at seven the
next morning. It was his old partner, Steve Caracappa. Caracappa asked if Louie had seen the Saturday paper yet. When Louie replied that he hadn't,
Caracappa turned cryptic. "It's going to be a tough
day, Louie, a tough weekend. Just get the *Daily
News*."

Louie thought it was some kind of prank. Steve
knew he liked to sleep late on his off days. Awake
now, however, Louie grumpily trudged outside and
snatched the newspaper from his mailbox. His first
thought upon reading the headline was that there were
nearly two million copies of the *Daily News* sold every
day in New York. *Una brutta figura*. His second was,
"a hangman's noose."

"I knew my life as I had known it was over. I mean,
the reporter didn't even use the word 'alleged.' Every
scumbag perp that shoots somebody in Times Square
in front of fifty witnesses gets the word 'alleged' in
front of his name. Not me. I 'passed confidential infor-

mation' to Gambino. These guys had already convicted me.

"I slid down onto our front steps, dropped the paper, and kind of cradled my face with my hands, trying to figure out what this all meant. I was sick to my stomach. I realized then and there that my life would never be 'normal' again. There was no way in the world that this would ever balance itself out.

"There were cops all over the city who were reading this paper. The Job can be one huge hen party, and even though my name wasn't mentioned, every cop in New York knew who this story was about. I could almost hear the comments.

Eppolito, I told you he was bad. Fucking Eppolito, they finally nailed him.

Ralphie's kid.

The Clam's nephew.

"I couldn't help but think that no matter what I did for the rest of my life, I'd be classified as a member of Organized Crime."

A version of an old Greek proverb he had once heard on the street crossed his mind: "It is the sins we don't commit we regret." He wondered if he just should have thrown in with his Uncle Todo or Uncle Jimmy when he was a kid and saved himself the trouble. No, he thought, not with his temper. "I knew that had that been the case, I'd be dead by now. I was too stubborn, too hotheaded, and the Mafia doesn't hold much truck with General Order Fifteens.

"Throughout my entire career the only person with big enough balls to offer me a bribe had been Big Paulie, and I think that was because he felt it was his duty more than anything else. Everyone knew I was a clean cop. That was something that had to do with character, integrity, honesty. I was known for my principles—well, okay, I was pretty notorious for my temper, too—and I took a lot of pride in that reputation. That was gone now."

As Louie walked back into his house, the phone rang again. It was Steve Gardell.

"Louie," he said, "it's obvious that they've leaked the story."

Not to Louie it wasn't. "Who are 'they'?" he demanded.

"Who do you think?" Gardell replied. "Internal Affairs." Gardell suspected that it might have been Inspector McCormack himself who funneled the story to the *News* reporter.

Louie was at sea. Regardless of who it was, someone at IAD must have betrayed him. Hadn't he cooperated? Hadn't he sat at that table in IAD's top-secret dungeon and tried to tell these people everything they wanted to know? Who would possibly have the nerve to leak something like this after all he'd done? Who would have the balls to breach the department's Blue Wall of Silence?

"IAD had to, because they got bubkes," Gardell laughed. "They're fishing, Louie. The Feds, the state, NYPD Intelligence, they've got phone taps and wires on mob guys all over the city. They're trying to stir some shit to see if your name comes up in any conversations. They want to generate some gossip about you in the mob crews."

Gardell appeared elated at the turn of the events. *Sure*, thought Louie, *it isn't his name plastered all over the* Daily News.

"What killed me was the part that said I knew Rosario Gambino well, that I hung out with him in Coney Island. They couldn't even get the neighborhood straight. Where were they getting this stuff? Gardell offered to head out to Long Island and meet me for a cup of coffee. I couldn't see that. What was the guy going to do? Drive sixty-five miles just to stare at me in my anguish? I didn't need nobody holding my hand."

That day was the longest of Louie's life. When he showed the newspaper to Fran, her mothering instincts took over. "Light at the end of the tunnel, darkest before the dawn, all that crapola." Although Fran tried hard, it didn't work. Yet, at least Louie was relieved to see that she was taking it so well. He instructed her not to speak to any reporters who called, and walked back out to the front stoop. She followed him out, slumped down next to him, put her arm around him, and rested her head on his shoulder.

"I love you very much, Louie," she said. "The Job, the reporters, they might not think very much of you, but I think the world of you. You're the father of my children, and I just want you to know that whatever happens, I don't care. I know you're going to do okay with this. Nothing can happen to us, Louie. Nothing can hurt us. Nothing."

FRAN: "That morning I felt like the house just crumbled on my head. When I read that newspaper story, when I saw the devastated look on Louie's face, my knees started to get weak. But I couldn't show it. For so long he had been the strength of our life, and now he just looked absolutely beaten. I figured it was payback time for me. I owed him that.

"I hugged him and kissed him and told him everything was going to be all right. I just hoped I didn't sound as hollow as I felt. It wasn't like I was lying. I didn't believe for one moment that he had done any of the things he was accused of. If someone had told me

Louie was being investigated for shooting eight junkies, or for punching out a couple of his bosses, well, *that* I would have believed. But passing information to the Mafia? No way. Not from a man who went out of his way to avoid his family for eight years.

"I think what galled me the most was the wiretap. Ironically, I'd received the notice that they'd subpoenaed our phone records on November 1, the day Louie was called in by Internal Affairs. By law they have to tell you about it after ninety days. But I was sure they'd also been listening to our phone conversations. I mean, I was married to a cop. I know how they work when they want you. I felt violated.

"After the initial shock of the wiretap, and Louie's explanation of what went on at the Internal Affairs hearing, things seemed to quiet down. Everyone—the union people, Louie's partners—everyone was telling us what a big mistake IAD had made, and how the whole thing would blow over. We went about life as if there was nothing to worry about.

"Now, suddenly, here's this newspaper story saying that Louie would most likely be suspended, and possibly arrested. Arrested? My God, it was hell, the whole weekend was hell. Saturday afternoon we took the girls to Tess's apartment to spend the night. Little Tony, our third child who was just three, was still too young to understand what was going on. After we put him to bed, Louie and I just sat in the living room staring at each other. I'd never seen my husband so helpless. I was used to big, rough, tough Louie Eppolito. I only hoped that I could be big enough and rough enough and tough enough for the both of us.

"He was off Sunday, then, Monday night, before he left for work, he seemed to snap out of it. Or he tried to make me believe he had snapped out of it. But I

knew deep down he was just concerned about protecting me and the kids. 'Don't worry,' he kept repeating, 'I'll handle it.' "

LOUIE: "I left for my tour that Monday night plotting strategy. All the advice I was getting, from Fran, from Gardell, from Caracappa, was of a type: sit cool and let this thing play out. But I had my own ideas, and they had nothing to do with sitting cool. Okay, I thought, in the beginning I was humble with these Gestapo fucks. I was nice and I tried to cooperate and what did it get me? Just what they said it would: a world of shit.

"It was obvious to me that these people had no intention of finding out whether I had actually climbed into bed with the mob. They were just out to hurt me. They wanted a vendetta? They would get one. I made a promise to Fran that I wouldn't raise my hands to anyone. But I'd sure as hell go nose-to-nose, eyebrow-to-eyebrow with anybody trying to give me shit. There would be no more 'Yes, sir,' and 'No, sir.'

"I was sure something would happen this week. When you've worked it long enough you have a sixth sense about the politics of The Job. The bosses throughout the Department would have read the Saturday *Daily News*, and would come to some kind of face-saving decision quickly. I'd hear about it soon.

"Sure enough, after an uneventful, if stressful, Monday-night tour, I got home and climbed into bed about six A.M. Fran woke me at eight-thirty to tell me she was taking her mother out. The telephone rang just as I was dozing back off. It was exactly nine A.M. when Sergeant Dowd called.

"If I searched inwardly until I scraped the bottom of my soul, I couldn't find a nice word to say about

Sergeant Dowd. The man had no redeeming qualities whatsoever. He had a rodentlike personality, he was an ass-kisser I've seen call his captain every ten minutes for instructions. In my opinion, the only thing he had going for him was his uncle, a good cop who had played an integral part in the Son of Sam investigation.*

"From what I've seen of him, Sergeant Dowd couldn't find a Chinaman in Chinatown."

During his conversation with Dowd, Louie was sure he detected an uncharacteristic glee to his sergeant's tone of voice. Dowd ordered Louie down to the Six-two by 10 A.M. in order to turn in his guns and shield. He added that Louie should prepare himself to be "arrested."

"That woke me up."

Louie explained to Dowd that he lived sixty-five miles from the precinct. It would take him at least thirty minutes to shave, shower, and dress. And perhaps another hour to drive in. He told Dowd there was no way he'd make it to Bensonhurst in an hour. A shouting match ensued.

Finally, Dowd threatened to call the Suffolk County Police and have them take Louie into custody. It was the wrong time to make such a threat.

"I want to tell you something, Sarge, something you should have on your mind while you're dialing the

---

* David Berkowitz, aka Son of Sam, gripped New York City—and especially its tabloids—in 1977 with a string of serial lovers-lane murders. He was captured after a months-long manhunt and declared mentally incompetent to stand trial. Berkowitz remains incarcerated in a New York State mental institution.

Suffolk PD," Louie replied. "Nobody, and I mean *nobody*, is coming into my house to arrest me. You want a hostage situation? Fine. I'll give it to you. But don't you threaten to send cops to my home to arrest me and embarrass my family. Because I'll hunt you down like a dog and kill you."

Louie assumed he had just added another charge to his file: threatening a superior officer. No matter. As usual, it had been worth it. He hung up on Dowd and immediately dialed Gardell, who set him straight on at least one aspect of this nightmare. He was being suspended, not arrested. Dowd, "that wishful-thinking weasel," had jumped the gun. Gardell went on to explain that Police Commissioner Benjamin Ward had seen the *Daily News* story and decreed that *something* had to be done, and IAD had complied by ordering Louie's suspension.

"Gardell told me to take my time. He'd meet me at the Six-two. He added that he'd try to get some kind of modified assignment, like working in the department's motor pool. They won't let you carry your gun or badge on modified, but at least you still have a paycheck coming in.

"After I dressed I sat down to write Fran a note:

Dear Fran,
  We expected this and it's happening. I'm getting in the car and I'm driving sixty-five miles into work as a cop and I'm coming home suspended, not as a cop anymore. I'm sorry. It may look as though I let you down, but I haven't done anything. It's a bad one for me because life for us will never be the same. I don't know what's going to happen, but I apologize. I love you and I love the

263

children. Just don't feel that this is anything that's happened between the family.

It's not the truth, Fran. I never did what they say I did. So just bear with me and everything will be okay. Again, I'm sorry, and I love you.

FRAN: "I wasn't home the morning he got the call from Dowd. I had taken my mother to the doctor. It was Louie's day off, and Louie's not an early riser, so I figured by the time I got back he'd probably just be getting up.

"So I was a little surprised when I walked through the front door—I guess it was around eleven—to find him sitting at the kitchen table in his suit and tie. He was writing me a note. I greeted him with a perky, 'Hi, darling.' When he turned to look at me his eyes were moist.

"I'd only seen Louie break down once before, back when we were engaged and he was talking about losing his relationship with Louie, Jr. But this was so different. He turned to me and his voice kind of creaked. 'I'm so sorry that I did this to us,' he said. 'I've been suspended.'

"My knees just buckled.

"There was nothing I could say at this point to ease his pain. All I could do was beg him to let me come with him into the city. 'Nope,' he answered. 'I'm a man. The kids need you more.' When he walked out I just broke down sobbing.

"All sorts of crazy thoughts were running through my mind. I mean, suddenly I found myself thinking about our financial situation. We had no savings at all; we lived from paycheck to paycheck. Weird thoughts go through your head in times of crisis, I guess, because I started thinking about Christmas. I resolved to start returning presents we'd bought for the kids. I'd sell my jewelry. Louie was always big on Christmas. He showered the kids with toys and presents. Not this year, I decided. I knew he'd give me a hard time about it. But I meant to put my foot down.''

LOUIE: "I was impressed with Fran's toughness. During the drive to Brooklyn all I could think of was that she was some piece of work. Gardell was waiting for me at the Six-two. Dowd was nowhere to be found. While I was packing up my guns and personal belongings Steve told me IAD would probably set a trial date within three weeks. I'd just have to hang tough until then.

"After I gathered my equipment, Steve and I headed down to IAD headquarters to turn them in. And who should greet us the moment I opened the door but Sergeant Dowd. The bastard was dangling a set of handcuffs. 'Louis Eppolito,' he began officiously, 'I'm here to formally place you under arrest. . . .' The guy was reading me my Mirandas! I was about to rip his throat out when the Shoofly lieutenant, Henris, walked in.

"To my amazement, Henris, who had made that snide if-the-shoe-fits comment at my hearing, began dressing down Dowd. He explained to the sarge that I wasn't being arrested, and that he had no business being there. Dowd persisted, sputtering that it was his understanding that I was supposed to be placed under arrest. Henris finally ordered him off the premises. As Dowd walked out I shook my head and laughed. The rat couldn't even get this right.

"I was halfway enjoying myself as I watched Dowd slink off. That changed in about a New York minute. Henris and a posse of deputies converged on me to

officially inform me of my suspension and relieve me
—a tad nervously, I suspected—of my guns. They
made sure the two cops who disarmed me were Italian
guys. There was no pretense of politeness. In fact, one
of the guys, a sergeant named Donati, told me in no
uncertain terms to drop my stuff off and get out of
their sight. 'Let me voucher this stuff so we can get
this scum out of here,' he said. I had one trick left for
this guy.''

STEVE GARDELL: "The deeper I got into the Eppolito case, the more it stank. On my way to meet Louie
at the Six-two the morning of his suspension I stopped
by Brooklyn Borough Command to have a word with
Frank Schilling, who had succeeded Richard Perio as
Brooklyn's Chief of Detectives. I was fairly friendly
with the chief, but when I explained to him that I
thought Louie was getting railroaded, he sloughed it
off real casually.

" 'Chief, they're taking a guy's guns and badge
away because of a goddamn story in a newspaper,' I
told him. 'He's one of your guys. Doesn't it bother
you?' His answer knocked me for a loop.

" 'You know Louie, right?' he says to me. 'You
know his family. It's in his genes. You can't separate
the mob background, the mob Family, from the cop.
It's in his blood.'

"I extracted a grudging promise from Schilling that
when Louie beat this rap he could have his old job
back at the Six-two, but our conversation ended on an
ominous note. Schilling warned me not to 'stick your
neck out for this guy.' I slammed the door on my way
out. I was pissed. I'm Italian, too.

"I didn't mention Schilling's remarks when I met
Louie at the Six-two. I could see he was uptight, and

I spent the ride down to IAD just trying to calm him down. Then, when we get there, we're met by this guy Dowd with his handcuffs. Louie thought the way Henris handled him was funny. I was beyond appreciating the comic relief.

"Finally they send these two Italian guys down, a sergeant and a lieutenant, to relieve Louie of his guns. One of them looked like he was ready to slip on a banana peel right into the grave, and the other looked like he just stepped out of the morgue at Bellevue Hospital. IAD's Finest. They took his stuff very gingerly. I think they were afraid he was going to do something violent.

"Louie turned over his weapons without a problem, but I'm looking at his face, and I see that every ounce of blood in his body has risen to his cheeks and neck. He looked like a red balloon. After he's disarmed, they give him a voucher receipt for his weapons and shield, and this sergeant begins telling him what a disgrace he is to the Department, and how he can't stand to look at his face anymore because he's scum.

"With that, Louie turns to the sergeant and asks him if he doesn't want all his guns. The sarge, who was so brave when he thought Louie wasn't carrying, looks a little confused. He begins fumbling with the receipt. 'You didn't take this one,' Louie says, patting the thirty-eight service revolver he carried on his hip. The sarge nearly jumped out of his skin. As Louie handed over his piece, I smiled for the first time all day.

"Louie won't admit it, but when we get outside I can tell that the guy is upset. I mean, his face is beet red, and he's got this faraway look in his eyes. He looked like a tire that had been slashed. I offered to buy him a drink, a hot dog, a cup of coffee. But he just wanted to be alone.

"I've seen cops accused of far lesser crimes do some very crazy things. It's not for nothing that the phrase 'eating the gun' has become such a part of The Job's vocabulary. So I don't want to leave Louie alone. Finally, I come right out with it. I tell him I know he's got to have a gun at home. I tell him I don't want to see him do anything stupid.

"So what do you think this crazy bastard does? He flashes a picture of Fran that he carries in his wallet. 'If you had a woman who looked like this waiting for you at home in bed,' he asks me, 'would you even consider blowing your brains out?' Only he didn't use the word 'woman.' I watched as he drove off alone."

LOUIE: "I got in my car and like an arrow I flew to the water. It was brisk out, cold, and I could feel the sea breezes blowing right through my stomach. I had goose bumps on my arms. I walked right along the high-water mark, but the sound of the surf was like it was a million miles away. Each time a wave crashed I repeated the same question: 'How am I doing?'

"I started talking to my father. 'Daddy, I didn't deserve this. Daddy, I need your help.'

"I had no idea what would happen to me now. My father always told me cops were no good. But I thought I'd always be protected by that thin blue line. Was I wrong? Was he right? Where was he now? Since his death he'd been there for me a lot of times when I felt I was in trouble. But now I'd never felt so alone. It seemed like the waves were bringing the entire world crashing down on my head. I didn't even feel like a cop anymore. For the first time in sixteen years I had no gun, no shield. Christ, I was naked."

* * *

FRAN: "Louie didn't come home until eight or nine that night. When he walked in he looked like a drowned rat. I could tell right away that he was off in his own little world. And I even suggested that if he thought he needed some time alone, the kids and I would certainly understand if he wanted to get in the car and just drive somewhere. Maybe to a hotel by the beach. He was always pulled to the ocean when he was troubled.

"I guess out of sheer nervousness I began telling him about all the resolutions I'd made that day. After I'd composed myself that morning I'd sat down and drawn up a budget. Figuring in our mortgage and the like, I was sure we could get by if we did certain things like cut down on Christmas expenditures. I also said I was going to look for a job. I'd work until this thing blew over.

"Well, he would have none of it. We were going to lead our lives exactly the way we always had. Especially Christmas. We were going to have the biggest and best Christmas of all time. This was completely unrealistic. Frankly, we were broke. But the last thing I wanted to do on the night my husband was suspended was begin arguing over Christmas presents. So as we sat on the couch discussing the future, I flicked on the television.

"The publicity caught us completely by surprise. Suddenly there was a newsbreak in some stupid sitcom. In oh-so-very-serious tones the announcer practically ordered us to stay tuned for the big story about the suspended cop. Film at eleven. We both sat there stunned."

LOUIE: "First I put on the ten o'clock news. I was the second story. *New York City Detective Louie Ep-*

269

polito, one of the NYPD's most decorated officers, was suspended today without pay for allegedly passing sensitive information to a member of the Mafia.

"At least the guy on TV used the word 'alleged.' My police ID picture filled the screen as the reporter rehashed the Gambino charges. Then they showed a facsimile of my badge, including my shield number, but it was cracked and tarnished. I turned to jelly. I don't know why my arms didn't fall off.

"The report was repeated in various forms on all of the eleven o'clock news broadcasts. It was completely devastating. In the middle of the final broadcast, our phone rang. Fran reached for it, but my stare stopped her cold. I picked up the receiver.

" 'Hello, Dad.' It was Louie, Jr. I hadn't spoken to him in months. 'I love you, Dad. And I'm in your corner. I know you didn't do what they say you did. I'm with you, Dad, one hundred percent. Just call if there's anything I can do.'

"My heart could have melted."

FRAN: "The day after the suspension, the day after all the television reports, the phone rang off the hook. Most of the callers were well-wishers, but Louie wouldn't talk to anyone except his mother. I knew he was dying inside, but I didn't know what to do.

"I sent the girls off to school and was puttering around in the kitchen when I decided to send little Tony upstairs to spend some time with his father. Tony was the apple of Louie's eye. I figured if anybody could cheer Louie up, Tony could.

"A few minutes later Tony comes running down the stairs with this shocked look on his face. He ran over and whispered, 'Mommy, Daddy's crying.'

" 'Nooo, that can't be,' I cooed. What made it

worse was that Louie was forever telling Tony that boys don't cry. The poor kid was confused and frightened.

" 'He is, Mommy, go see,' Tony whispered again. 'Daddy's crying.'

"I went upstairs and walked into our bedroom. Louie had his hands over his eyes, and his elbows on his knees. He was sobbing convulsively. It took all I could to hold back my own tears. I put my arms around him and tried to tell him everything would work out all right.

" 'It won't work out all right and nothing will ever be the same,' he moaned through these awful shudders. 'Whether I beat this or they prove I'm guilty, they took my career, and they took my name, and they flushed it down the toilet bowl. It's over, Fran.'

"There was nothing I could say. I guess he needed to get that out. It took him about a half hour to compose himself. And that was the one and only time he ever shed a tear about it. That was it. After that it would either be rage, or anger, or silence."

25

Christmas arrived, and the investigation hung over the Eppolito household like Marley's ghost.

Departmental trial dates were set—and postponed —with the bureaucratic regularity for which the New York Police Department was justly famous. As the New Year turned with uncertainty, each delay etched another tension line in Louie's forehead. Fran found herself shooing the kids to their rooms with more and more frequency. "Daddy's not feeling well today," became the Eppolito refrain. Louie's mood swings were greased by an onslaught of cluster headaches that made him feel as though someone was taking brass knuckles to the back of his eyeballs.

Fran watched, bewildered, and not in a little agony, by her husband's mood swings. Sullen evening drives to the beach would segue into jubilant morning pro-nouncements.

"The worst thing that happens is I lose my job," Louie would joyously announce over Italian sausage and peppers. "It's only a job. Not my life. I'll always find work." By noon he'd have returned to being, in his words, "a morose prick."

Louie had not been abandoned. Jimmy McCafferty, dying of cancer, called daily. Steve Caracappa dropped in regularly for coffee. The New York City police community is inbred, tight, and deeply mistrustful of strangers. In the eyes of this clique, Internal Affairs investigators were the ultimate interlopers.

Two days after his suspension, Louie discovered Police Officer Nick Santamaria standing on his porch. Santamaria was a Queens-based cop who doubled as lead singer of the Capris, a fifties group that once topped the pop charts with "Moon Out Tonight" and "Morse Code of Love." Fran and Louie had attended several of the Capris' golden-oldie revivals.

Santamaria handed Louie an envelope. It contained five thousand dollars in cash. "A loan," Nick told Louie, "until things get right." Fran's brother, Angelo, came through with another five thousand dollars, "just so the kids can have a nice Christmas."

Co-workers and relatives were not the only good samaritans. "Plenty" of shadowy job offers poured over the suspended cop's transom.

"It was actually funny how many mobsters called me with offers. It was mostly construction and sanitation. One guy in particular, just trying to do the right thing, wouldn't take no for an answer. Ralphie Denome was his name, and he was an associate with a Gambino crew. Hell of a nice guy. Couldn't get him off the phone. Then there was my cousin Junior's crew. A guy named Red Colder* ran with Junior. He was with the Lucchese Family—the Irish name 'Colder' came from a stepfather. Red ran a garbage

---

* Early in 1991 a passing patrol car discovered Red Colder's decomposed body in the trunk of a car parked under the docks in the Red Hook section of Brooklyn. According to sources, "it was a Family matter."

truck company and said he'd pay me five hundred dollars a week, clear, no taxes.

"I'd ask these people how they could possibly think I could work for them, considering the charges I was facing. But they just didn't get it. They meant well, though."

Twice Gardell applied for modified assignment for Louie. Twice the application was rejected. In a final attempt, the attorney Howard Cerny contacted the department's in-house Trials Commissioner, Hugh Mo, known to the patrol grunts as "the Hanging Judge." True to his alias, Mo left Louie hanging out to dry.

Four days into his suspension, Gardell managed to get Louie a preliminary hearing, a so-called Calendar Call, before Mo. The procedure is more or less the equivalent of an arraignment in a normal court of law.

At 10 A.M. on Friday, November 28, 1984, Louie, Gardell, and Cerny walked into the Trials Commissioner's courtroom on the fourth floor of One Police Plaza.

"The weirdest thing was walking in and going to the table on the right side of the room. I had to catch myself from turning left as we neared the bench. I'd been in court thousands of times as a cop, but my flesh started to tingle when I had to take the defendant's chair."

Technically, Louie faced three charges:

1. Absent without permission or police necessity for two hours;

2. Appropriation of confidential Police Department records without permission or authority;

3. Between December 3, 1983 and May 16, 1984, did wrongfully and without just cause divulge confidential information without permission or authority.

The mere appearance of guilt on any one of the

three was justification enough for the department to dismiss the detective. Criminal charges would certainly follow.

HUGH MO: "I took one look at Detective Lou Eppolito while I was sitting up there on the bench and I just said to myself: *mobster*. The way he looked, with the gold chains and the necklaces and the rings. The swagger to his walk. Even his mannerisms, the chopping hands when he talked to his lawyer. It all convinced me from the start that this guy was dirty. On appearances alone, you could have substituted Louie Eppolito for every other punk wiseguy I'd seen throughout my career.

"Ironically, I was not a totally disinterested observer. When I first saw the name Eppolito in the case file, I was a little stunned. Several years earlier, before I'd been appointed Trials Commissioner, I'd been an assistant district attorney in Manhattan, and I'd crossed paths with the rest of his family.

"I'd prosecuted James Eppolito and his son, James Jr., for working a racket in conjunction with the New York City marshals. The Eppolito crew was muscling in on warehouse owners on the West Side. The city marshals were getting kickbacks from the Eppolito crew to dump repossessed merchandise in these warehouses, and the Eppolitos were selling it off illegally. From cradles to couches. Anything for a buck, you know.

"Anyway, as the Trials Commissioner, I had the option of assigning the Eppolito case to another hearing officer or taking it myself. After reading the prosecutor's brief—and probably with some unconscious thought that it might as well be me who locked up the whole family—I assigned it to myself. The charges against Detective Eppolito were extremely serious. In essence, he was worse than his uncle or his cousin. He was a turncoat.

"It's every police official's worst nightmare to have an organized crime mole in your midst, and Lou Eppolito was that worst nightmare. It was clear this detective had possession of these files, and that the files were found in Gambino's home. The prosecutors from the Advocate's office also seemed to have nailed him locked and cocked. The fingerprints. Absent without leave. They even said they had surveillance photos.

"An in-house, departmental trial is nothing like a trial in the, so to speak, real world. Nothing has to be proven to me beyond a shadow of a doubt. In short, I don't want to smell a whiff of corruption. I can always find some way to justify a guilty verdict. And no one overturns me. There is no appeal. In fact, my reputation preceded me. I was aware that all through The Job I was viewed as running some sort of kangaroo court. I knew about the 'Hanging Judge' nickname. It was deserved. Eighty percent of the police officers who came before me were found guilty.

"Lou Eppolito's case didn't appear as if it was going to break my streak. When Steve Gardell and the attorney, Howard Cerny, requested modified assignment, I nearly laughed them out of the courtroom.

"I called them both to the bench and suggested they advise their client to begin looking for another job. There's no punishment less than dismissal in my court. There's also no mercy. It was a question of me playing God, and from what I'd seen, I thought Detective Eppolito was a goner. The Department Advocate was sitting over at the prosecution table gloating. It was, I felt, like shooting ducks in a barrel.

"Their request for Modified was denied, and a trial date was set for December 12."

Three days after his Calendar Call before Hugh Mo, Steve Gardell phoned Louie with a job offer. He had some friends who owned a Toys "R" Us outlet on Long Island. They'd pay $10 an hour for a security guard over the holidays.

"I couldn't get any lower than that. The eleventh-most-decorated cop in the history of the Department was being offered a square badge* to guard Lionel Trains and Smurf dolls."

Louie respectfully declined. He began feeling even more sorry for himself, moping around the house, driving Fran and the kids crazy. Like a child, he even ran home to his mother, taking her to dinner at an Italian restaurant in Brooklyn during the first week of December. Tess Eppolito seemed to realize, perhaps better than her son, exactly what lay ahead.

"Think of your father, what he would have done," she told Louie. "You're in for some hard times, but you're going to handle them, and handle them well. Because that's how your father and I raised you. The most difficult time, when you want to throw up, when you want to reach out and kill somebody, that's the time you're going to have to dig deep within yourself and remember you're an Eppolito.

"You have strength down there, Louie. I know it's there, because your father and I put it there. You're

---

* "Square badge" is a derogatory term for what city law enforcement officials often refer to as rent-a-cops. It is against New York State law for private security forces to sport the ovate or triangular badge of the NYPD. Thus, the square badge on the *faux* cops.

always thinking about what Ralph would expect you to do. Here's your chance to act. And don't worry about Fran, or the kids, or me. We can handle it, Louie, as long as you can.''

Easier said than done. The suspension was like a virus that seeped through the Eppolito home, infecting Louie's family one by one.

One week before Christmas, Andrea's grammar school principal telephoned. There was a problem. Could Louie or Fran possibly drop by his office for a talk? When Louie arrived, he found his seven-year-old daughter in the principal's reception area, tears streaking her face.

"My cute little angel threw her arms around my neck and pulled me so close I felt like she wanted to crawl inside me. After I calmed her and listened to the principal's story, I was the one who wanted to crawl. Inside a hole.''

The previous evening, the principal explained to Louie, Andrea had listened from the top of the stairs as Fran and Tess bawled in each other's arms. Louie had been in Brooklyn, meeting Gardell, and knew nothing about the incident. When Andrea came to school that day, she began asking her second-grade classmates for donations. Fifty cents, a dollar, anything. She wanted to buy her daddy a pair of suspenders so her mother and her grandmother would stop crying. Andrea's teacher wanted to know what sense Louie could make of the story.

"Of course, I realized right away that Fran and my mom had been crying over my suspension, and Andrea had misunderstood the term. When I walked out of the principal's office Andrea ran up to me and blurted out, 'Daddy, you're too good of a daddy not to have suspenders.'

"The emptiness I felt in my soul that morning, how my little girl cried, and how she tried to collect money to buy me a pair of suspenders, will stay with me until the day I die.

"I came home that day, looked in the mirror, and gritted my teeth until my gums bled. If I had had Inspector McCormack, Lieutenant Henris and Sergeant Penzes in front of me at that moment I would have killed them. Killed them dead. I wanted to put my hands through their chests and pull out their hearts.

"I was full of bitter fantasies. I dreamed of tying all of them to chairs and slitting their throats as their children watched. I wanted to see how they liked it. How did they like their kids brokenhearted over the fate of their fathers? Internal Affairs was trespassing, coming into my home, and the hate I carried in my heart that day I wish on no one.

"But that incident also taught me something. I thought my family was strong. I thought I could carry this burden with no one else being hurt. I was wrong. My wife and mother were merely holding back their tears until I was out of sight. My children were becoming victims. Somebody, I vowed, would pay. I felt for the first time the true meaning of the word vendetta."

Gardell called the next afternoon. The trial had been postponed, from December 12 to January 13. "They say they're not ready," was the union representative's embarrassed explanation. Louie felt trapped.

"Christmas was coming. No job. No income. Nothing. I thanked God for friends like Nick Santamaria. On the day I was suspended I had a total of three hundred dollars in my bank account. The funny thing about Nick's loan was that on the morning he handed it to me, the day after my suspension, I hadn't even looked in the envelope. I'd just thanked him kind of sheepishly and stuffed it into my pocket.

"After the December 12 postponement I pulled out Nick's envelope and nearly fainted when I ripped it open.

"I went out and bought two trunkfuls of toys and presents for the kids. I bought a beautiful diamond ring for Fran, and told her to begin planning a huge Christmas Eve party. Friends, aunts, uncles, cousins, we'd show them a shindig they wouldn't forget. I knew it was like throwing the money to the wind, but for me it was a kind of therapy. The party alone cost about a grand, but it was worth every cent. For one night, at least, I didn't want to tear anyone's face off. Merry Christmas!"

On the afternoon of Christmas Day, as Fran and Louie entertained her brother Angelo and his wife, Sheila, a phone call came in from a former NYPD detective named Bart Rivieccio. Rivieccio had quit The Job several years before, and struck it rich in the real estate business. He'd made millions buying, restoring, and reselling old homes. Louie had a passing acquaintance with Bart; they'd worked a few homicide investigations together. But there was a cloud over Rivieccio. There were people who suspected he was mixed up with the mob. He had been raised in a family similar to Louie's. Louie was one of those suspicious people.

"I've been doing some business out of town," Rivieccio told Louie. "Is this true what I'm hearing about you being jammed up?"

When Louie explained his fix, Rivieccio advised him to forget about it. "Come down and see me tomorrow. You start working for me for more money than you ever dreamed of getting from The Job."

"I can't say I wasn't tempted. But I couldn't throw in with Bart any more than I could have gone over to Toys "R" Us. He left the offer open. At least until he was nailed for bank fraud. He ended up doing time for some kind of shaky financial deal.

"Bart Rivieccio's phone call only served to remind me that every single thing my father had taught me about respect had been right on the mark. Except when I was arresting them—and sometimes even then —I always treated the men of the Cosa Nostra with honor. I always did for them. And now they were offering to do for me. That thought fed me strength. It was fantastic."

So fantastic, in fact, that shortly after Christmas a "new Louie" emerged.

"Bingo, bango, like somebody waved a magic wand over him," says Fran. "Suddenly he's not feeling sorry for himself anymore. The moping's gone. He's not yelling at the kids. He's sitting at the kitchen table all day, going over his case papers, looking for leads, calling Steve and the lawyer with tips on who to inter-view, what questions they should ask, who to call as character witnesses, that kind of thing.

"Don't get me wrong," Fran added. "He still wanted to kill people over this. But the old Louie always wanted to kill people too."

26

Another delay. January 13 arrived almost before Louie realized it. So did yet another excuse. The prosecution still wasn't ready. They requested a stay until February 15. It was based, they told Gardell, on the fact that the FBI still hadn't provided them with "enough stuff."

Despite the gifts from Nick Santamaria and Angelo Todisco, the Eppolitos were going broke. Louie was even beginning to regret his Christmas Eve extravaganza. Steve Gardell made another request to place him on modified assignment. Forget about it. Louie found his only solace in the loyalty of his former coworkers.

As he put it, "The brass may have been humping me, but the mud soldiers rallied around their own."

Several detectives from the Six-two pitched in and rented a Brooklyn catering hall, the Bay Ridge Manor. A racket was planned for January 24. A racket is what cops call a party, usually given as a going-away bash for a retiring officer. Flyers circulated through the department, announcing a "10-13 for Det. Louis Eppolito" (10-13 is the department's emergency radio code number for a cop in distress).

The Bay Ridge Manor could accommodate close to

150 people. The organizers, Detectives Paul Frommer, Billy Mulligan, and Pete Furtado, estimated that half the proceeds—ten dollars' admission, cash bar, live music courtesy of Nick Santamaria and the Capris —would cover expenses, with the other half going to the sardonically titled "Louie Eppolito Defense Fund."

"If it works for Huey Newton and Abbie Hoffman, why not for Louie Eppolito?" Steve Caracappa asked. Free the Eppolito One! But there was a problem.

Old friends suddenly began calling Louie about the fete. Internal Affairs, they told him, was putting out the word that they'd be looking cross-eyed at anyone attending a racket in a crooked cop's defense, especially any officer over the rank of detective. The higher a cop rises in the chain of command, the easier it becomes for the brass to exert pressure.

"These Gestapo types from IAD knew that. So I called a few friends—lieutenants, sergeants, captains —and told them I understood how, in their cases, discretion might be the better part of valor."

On the night of the racket, Angelo Todisco insisted on accompanying his brother-in-law. And despite his pleas, Tess Eppolito assured Louie that nothing could stop her from standing beside her son. He drew the line, however, with Fran. It was just too embarrassing.

"I'm not winning the Man of the Year award here," he told his wife. "I'm a cop on my ass and my friends are holding a benefit for me. You don't need to see that."

Louie calculated that the combination of not-so-subtle Internal Affairs threats and the bad blood he'd generated with bosses over sixteen years on The Job would produce a whitewash.

"I envisioned twenty guys moping around this huge, empty catering hall playing with themselves. I was a bit out of line. Five hundred and seventy-five people showed up. You couldn't get in the door. There were captains, inspectors, lieutenants. Even Jimmy McCafferty, his body bloated and ravished by chemotherapy, forced himself to drop by. He was so sick, and I made him leave when I found him throwing up in the bathroom. But talk about sending a message to the Commissioner. I felt like a million bucks. I was too proud to cry, but inside I was bursting.

"When the take came in I had to laugh. Financially, it seemed like I was better off suspended. My end of the racket came close to nine grand. Between Nick, Angelo, and the party, I'd taken in nearly twenty grand in three months. Who would have thought I'd need it all? But I did. February came, and my trial was postponed again, until March 3. March arrived, and a date was set for April 4. This stalling was killing me."

Fran noticed a pattern develop with each new postponement. Louie would sag for several days, then plunge back into the discovery materials, or evidence, Cerny and Gardell were receiving from the prosecution. In late March Louie made a startling find.

In the back-and-forth over the issue of the fingerprints found on the copy of the Gambino file, the investigators from Internal Affairs indicated that they had done their own tests but were also relying on the FBI's assessment that the prints were original.

When Louie's defense team pressed them, IAD advised Cerny to check with the Feds himself. When he did just that, he discovered that the FBI had found *photocopies* of Louie's fingerprints, along with fragments of two original prints whose identifying swirls, according to the federal report, "bore a similarity" to

Detective Louis John Eppolito's. Despite the fact that Louie's defense team was precluded by Department policy from calling in their own fingerprint expert to examine the evidence, Cerny and Gardell were ecstatic.

"But I still didn't understand. Cerny laid it out for me as if I were a school kid: I had admitted handling the original Rosario Gambino file. Naturally, my fingerprints were all over that. But only copies of my fingerprints were found on the copy of the file. They couldn't prove I had ever touched the copied file! The two 'live' prints they found, the prints that 'bore a similarity' to mine, could have literally belonged to anyone.

"Then Steve told me about the Canon Copier in the Six-two. The FBI, he said, had checked the machine and the motor mark left on the copy of the Gambino file. It matched the motor mark left by the Six-two's copier. But Cerny had discovered that all Canon Copiers leave the same motor mark. So the copies could have been made on any Canon machine.

"When we double-checked with the Feds on these inconsistencies in the investigation, they concurred on both our fingerprint findings and our copy machine findings. At first I was euphoric. Then it hit me. Why were we only finding this out now, six months after my G.O. 15?

"I was in a fog. Neither Steve nor I could figure out why they'd jerked me around for six months, when they must have known back in November that they had no case. But, as Gardell put it, 'it sure was getting interesting.' "

The defense team had been in contact with Sergeant James Shea, the Homicide investigator who had originally asked Louie to escort the witness of the Albert

Veriali murder over to Intelligence headquarters in July of 1983. Part of the case against Louie dealt with motive. Commissioner Mo had made it plain at Louie's Calendar Call that even a hint of corruption would swing his scales of justice. The defense team had to answer the question: Why did a Homicide detective from Bensonhurst take it upon himself to start nosing around the Intelligence Division?

Sergeant Shea might have struck Louie as a "thick, cold-blooded Irishman, but he was a cop's cop, and a man's man."

"Over coffee Jimmy Shea told us that after he heard about my trouble he had taken it upon himself to contact Internal Affairs and inform them that he had ordered me to Intelligence headquarters. Then he said he had given a statement to that effect to a couple of IAD investigators who had interviewed him.

"Sergeant Shea's statement was nowhere to be found in the discovery papers IAD had turned over to us. And that is something you just do not do. Every bit of prosecutorial material has to be turned over to the defense.

"It's becoming pretty clear to me by this point that the main purpose of this investigation is to shitcan me. Who? Pick a number. Why? I guess the name Eppolito was enough. Somehow, some way, for all these months I'd been under the mistaken impression that I'd be given a fair shot. Don't ask me why. Weird craziness. But better to find out later than never, I supposed. Two days after I spoke with Sergeant Shea, IAD sent over a piece of discovery material they claimed had been misplaced, and suddenly 'found.' It was the interview with Shea."

Shea's deposition, however, still didn't answer the first official charge against Louie: "Absent without permission or police necessity on December 13, 1983." His second trip to the Intelligence Division.

"I wracked my brain. Why the hell was I in Manhattan that day? After scanning my memo book about three hundred times, I finally noticed the capital letters 'MAR' scrawled into the upper right-hand corner.

"Mar, mar . . . Margaret Vasile. Shit, that was it. The Hunt killing, and Herman Penny. I'd notified Mark Feldman from the District Attorney's office about the trip. The 'BDA' in my destination log didn't stand for Brooklyn Detective Area, as I'd told the investigators at my hearing. It was my shorthand for Brooklyn District Attorney.

"When I phoned Gardell with the news, he thought it would be more appropriate if he confirmed it with Feldman. That way, it wouldn't appear like I was tampering with a witness. Feldman was a sharp piece of work. His daily planner laid it out. The date, the time, even some remarks to the effect that I dropped in on Intelligence headquarters to check out Herman Penny. He didn't hesitate to volunteer his testimony. I felt I'd found the key.

"When I reached out to Margaret Vasile, she also agreed to testify as a character witness. Icing on the cake. Finally, Steve Gardell cracked the Atlantic City phone-call mystery that they'd never explained to us, the weird coincidence of Furtado and Rosario Gambino using the same pay phone.

"When Furtado told the IAD investigators at his G.O. 15 that he'd placed that call in order to find out about a homicide trial in which he was scheduled to testify, they'd followed up and seen my name on the witness list. Putting two and two together, they got five, and assumed I was with Furtado and that he was covering for me. But Furtado and I had worked that particular homicide together, and a paperwork mistake had thrown my name into the witness bin. Pete had called from Atlantic City to straighten out the mistake. I talked to Pete, who told me he and his wife would swear before Mo that I was nowhere near them on the wedding anniversary.

"But none of this really mattered. The harpoons were out for me. The head of the Internal Affairs Division was a tough-talking, hard-ass old-timer named John Guido. He'd been brought in after Serpico and the Knapp Commission hearings had exposed departmental-wide police corruption in the early seventies. And he had a white knight's reputation to live up to.

"On April Fool's Day, four days before the trial, and the night after I spoke to Feldman and Margaret Vasile, the phone rang at home. The caller identified himself as William Flack, Deputy Commissioner of the Department Advocate's Office. That's the prosecution. There was no way these guys should be calling me. If they wanted to talk, Gardell or Cerny were the guys they talked to. But I took the call anyway. Flack offered me a deal.

" 'Lou, consider this call man-to-man, off the record,' he began. 'They think they got you at this trial. They're going to nail you with surprises your side doesn't know about. Now Chief Guido says he's got your record in front of him. Do you know what "vesting out" means?'

"I did. Every NYPD cop has the option to retire at half pay after twenty years on The Job. After fifteen years you become eligible to vest out. A cop can put in his papers after, say, seventeen years, and wait the three years before beginning to collect his pension. I told Flack to continue.

" 'Chief Guido was unaware that you were the eleventh-most-decorated officer in the Department,' he said. 'And he'd like to get this thing out of the way with as little fuss as possible. The chief would consider dropping the charges against you if you decide to vest out. Rather than have you fired after such a distinguished career, he's agreed to let you walk out, in his words, "like a man." '

"I told Flack I'd get back to him that night, hung up, and stared at Fran, who had been sitting at the kitchen table listening to my end of the conversation. 'They want me to vest out, honey. We'd start collecting in four years. It would probably come to about seventeen grand a year. That's almost half a million bucks over the next twenty years. If I'm found guilty at trial, I lose everything.'

" 'Didn't I tell you this mess would have a good end?' she asked.

" 'Yeah, honey, you did,' I answered with a wink."

Then Louie called Steve Gardell and explained Flack's offer. Gardell, Louie decided, would answer for him. He would vest out, Louie told Gardell, on the day that Chief Guido performed a public sex act with his mother on New Year's Eve in Times Square. Anything less than that, and Louie would see Guido in court.

"Guido was right. I was going out like a man. A man with honor, a man with respect, a man who was not going to be run off The Job. When I finished fuming, and Steve stopped laughing, of course he told me he couldn't repeat my offer to Guido exactly as I'd laid it out."

So Louie compromised. He told Gardell to leave out the part about Times Square on New Year's Eve.

27

Chief John Guido was very nearly a caricature of the gruff-talking, cigar-chomping, forty-year veteran of the NYPD. He even had a passing resemblance to a bulldog, which was fitting. For he was not a man to take defeat philosophically. As the top cop in charge of policing New York City's thirty thousand officers, he couldn't afford to be. Unlike most of the Department's top brass, Guido had not had his feet on his desk since he took them off the pavement. He had proven that during the investigation of the fatal shooting of Officer Irma Lozado after the temporary disappearance of her partner, who claimed he hadn't heard the gunshot.

To test the cop's story, Guido stationed fifty Internal Affairs officers ten feet apart along the route Lozado's partner claimed to have taken the night she was shot. Guido wanted to determine whether the cop could have heard the report from a thirty-eight caliber. Based on Guido's investigation, the Police Commissioner wanted to discipline the officer, but no charges were ever filed.

As one of the New York City Police Department's five "Super Chiefs," Guido also wielded enormous influence within the Purple Palace, the sardonic name street cops had bestowed on the One Police Plaza tower across the mall from City Hall.

Like his peer Richard NiCastro, the Department's Chief of Detectives, Guido was the son of Italian immigrants. Both Super Chiefs had clawed their way up from street beats in an atmosphere rife with anti-Italian bias. To NiCastro and Guido, who had witnessed firsthand every kind of urban depravity imaginable, there was nothing worse than a blue-clad *paisan* consorting with La Cosa Nostra. They had their gunsights trained on Louie Eppolito.

In fact, as amusing as Steve Gardell had found Louie's tirade after Deputy Commissioner Flack had offered his deal, the union rep's sixth sense told him that Internal Affairs smelled red meat in this case. Working the corridors of One Police Plaza, Gardell discovered that the Eppolito case had indeed assumed the trappings of a vendetta.

A chance meeting with Sergeant Bill Medican, Flack's hand-picked prosecutor in the Eppolito case, only confirmed what Gardell already suspected. After apologizing for the interminable delays, Medican rolled his eyes toward the twelfth-floor offices of both Guido and NiCastro. "I'm going down with the ship on this one," Gardell recalls Medican saying. "They want your boy bad, and they'll do anything to get him. Upstairs they're already calling him Benedict Eppolito."

When Gardell pressed Medican about the prosecution's strategy, particularly Flack's cryptic references to surprise evidence, Medican raised his hands, palms outward, and turned away. Gardell could get no more.

On the morning of April 4, 1985, as they walked across the plaza leading to police headquarters, Gardell—without relaying his conversation with Medican —gently advised Louie to prepare for the worst.

"I know you didn't do it," Gardell said. "You know you didn't do it. And chances are, they know you didn't do it. But none of that means they aren't going to get you for it."

When they arrived at Commissioner Mo's fourth-floor courtroom, the small, choked space was close to filled. A bevy of Internal Affairs investigators wedged into the pews behind the prosecutor's table. And there seemed to be an inordinate number of Feds present. Louie was seconded by two of the faithful from the Six-two squad room—Frommer and Mulligan. It was a crowd lusting for a heavyweight title fight. Unfortunately, they were forced to sit through an interminable prelim. For Trials Commissioner Mo, having been finally presented with all the Department's evidence the previous evening, had an unusual idea.

Mo ordered both the prosecution and defense teams to convene in his office immediately. As Flack, Medican, Cerny, and Gardell trailed Mo out the door, Louie was left to spend the next three hours sitting in the hallway outside the courtroom.

"While I was waiting, an FBI agent began playing with a long piece of string. He tied it into a hangman's noose, held it out in front of him, and twisted and turned it while he was talking to his partner. He was real nonchalant about it, but he made sure it was right in my line of vision."

STEVE GARDELL: "Right away we know something strange is going on, because before anything begins Mo stands up at his bench and says he wants to see me, Howard Cerny, Bill Medican, and Bill Flack upstairs in his chambers.

"So we leave Louie sitting out in the hallway as the five of us trundle up to Mo's office on the fourteenth floor, right next to the Police Commissioner's.

"Mo is looking kind of agitated, and he starts off by asking Flack just what kind of case they have. Flack doesn't have the words 'mob family associate' out of his mouth before Cerny's out of his seat objecting like a banshee.

" 'What are you talking about?' Cerny demands. 'This man's a detective, he's been a police officer sixteen years. He's made thousands of arrests. He's won scores of awards. Where do you come off labeling him a mob family associate?'

" 'His family has ties to the mob, that's a given. . . .' Flack answered. But Mo cut him off in mid-sentence. He motioned for Cerny to continue, but Howard said he'd like me to speak first. Mo, of course, knew me well from other trials, and gave me the floor.

"I began by saying I objected to Deputy Commissioner Flack's innuendo. It was the same crap I was hearing from guys like Schilling, and it wasn't based on any proof. Yes, I admitted, Louie's family had mob ties. Christ, Louie's family was the mob. But that didn't automatically make him guilty. Then, kind of as a formality, I listed all of Louie's citations and awards.

"When I was finished, Flack butted in, saying something about Louie's commendations being 'all in the past.' But Mo cut him off again, and asked to hear from Sergeant Medican. Medican gave a bare-bones, if halfhearted, chronology of the Gambino file; how it traveled from Intelligence headquarters to Gambino's house via Louie's file cabinet in the Six-two. It seemed like the more he spoke the less enthusiastic he became.

"Then Cerny asked Medican exactly what evidence they had tying Louie to the file winding up in Gambino's hands. Flack jumped in with an answer: 'Because his prints are on it.'

"At that point Cerny repeated the question that had gone unanswered for six months: 'Commissioner Mo, may I ask Deputy Commissioner Flack if these fingerprints that we've been hearing so much about are original fingerprints, or photostats of fingerprints?'

"All eyes turned to Flack. 'Well,' he said, 'it's a photostat of his prints.' Bingo.

"Now it was Mo's turn to come out of his chair. 'Is that all this case is based on?' he demanded. Flack began to say something about more circumstantial evidence. There were two 'good' prints on one of the papers in the Gambino file, he said. But we had that report, too, and the best the lab boys could do was report that the swirls of the 'good' prints were 'similar' to Louie's. Louie's and about twenty million other people's.

"When Cerny dropped that one on Mo, it was over, right then, and everyone in the room knew it.

"We countered all the evidence they submitted. When they hit us with that absent-without-permission garbage, we told Mo we were ready to bring in Sergeant Jimmy Shea to testify that he had ordered Louie's first trip to Intelligence headquarters, and Mark Feldman and Margaret Vasile would explain the circumstances surrounding the second. If that wasn't police duty, what was? Moreover, Mo had had the Intelligence Division sign-in logs subpoenaed. When we turned to July 13, 1983, there was Louie's signature, plain as day.

"If we could find it so easily, how come the two cops from IAD had such a hard time? Mo wanted to

know. Then he made a sarcastic comment about the
'fifteen minutes' the IAD guys had marked in the
'time-spent' box on their official report.

"The second charge—appropriating confidential
Police Department records without permission or authority—would be cleared up by the testimony of Detective Sergeant Sweeney, who, we assured Mo, was
ready to admit that he'd asked Louie to take that
bullshit file with him.

"When we'd talked to Sweeney after his IAD hearing, he told us he'd been nervous and confused—as
any cop would be in similar circumstances—and that
some of what he'd said had been twisted around and
taken out of context.

"When they tried to make an issue out of the Atlantic City phone call, we explained the coincidence, and
told them Furtado was willing to answer under oath
that Louie hadn't been with him. And as for their big
surprise evidence, it turned out to be a fuzzy surveillance photograph of Rosario Gambino and some
skinny little runt talking out front of the Cafe Italia.
They claimed the man in the photo was Louie.

"Now, the guy in the picture looked about as much
like Louie as my mother. But they insisted that it was
Detective Eppolito. Even Mo cracked a smile when
he asked to examine the photo. Louie had about six
inches and eighty pounds on whoever this guy was.

"Finally, they hauled out a recorded conversation,
purported to be two mobbed-up goombahs talking
over the phone about an unnamed cop. The crux of
their evidence was a line from one of the mobsters
saying that they couldn't call their cop source, 'because he's in trouble now.' That was it. It was supposed to be a veiled reference to Louie. But neither

wiseguy ever mentioned a name. Cerny blistered
them.

"In legal terms, all this back-and-forth—their evidence and our arguments against it, including all of the
witnesses we wanted to call and a synopsis of what
they would say—is called making stipulations. And
when the stipulations were finished Mo directed one
final question to Deputy Commissioner Flack: 'How,'
he asked, 'did this case ever reach this point?'

" 'I'm under orders,' Flack replied.

" 'Orders from whom?' asked Mo.

" 'Chief Guido,' said Flack. 'He wanted this case
to go to trial.'

" 'I'm going to tell you something, Mr. Flack,' Mo
said. 'Chief Guido does not control my courtroom.
And neither do you. We've already stipulated everything. There will be no witnesses. And now we're
going to go downstairs and hammer this out. And I'm
going to give you my decision today.'

"Mo pounded his fist on his desk before leaving his
office."

HUGH MO: "As the hearing unfolded it became
more and more apparent that the evidence against this
guy was insufficient. There appeared to be something
missing, a gap that couldn't be bridged in the Department's case. So I'm sitting up there in my office thinking, *unless they span this gap, Lou Eppolito is not
guilty*.

"Of course, I had no official word on why the trial
had been postponed so many times. I wasn't in the
chain of command. But it didn't take a brain surgeon
to figure out that the Advocate's Office had spent
the time digging for something else to hang Eppolito
with.

"As the hearing in my office dragged on, I became more and more irritated. I was outraged at what this man had gone through, the sitting on pins and needles, the toll on his family. I've taken down a lot of cops, and I have little, if any, remorse. But I also know the police mind-set. There's something in there that dictates that once a decision has been made, it's terribly hard to unmake it.

"It's like having a cop cut loose an arrest. It's an ego thing. The cop becomes fixated. Somehow, I got the impression that Lou Eppolito had become somebody's ego thing. He was a fish they were sure had been hooked.

"Given the circumstantial evidence, Eppolito was damned lucky that no one could fill in that one little gap to make that evidence hard. But, the fact remained that, after six months, no one could. It sure looked like someone had set him up. But looking at the case with hindsight, I also feel that if the Department wanted to frame him, they certainly could have done a better job."

When the trial proceedings reconvened down in Mo's courtroom, Deputy Commissioner Flack was noticeably absent. The next three hours were spent reading the stipulations into the record. Mo was bull-rushing this through. With each stipulation, the room emptied of another FBI or IAD officer.

At three-twenty in the afternoon, Howard Cerny rose to deliver a terse, reasoned summation that began with a plea to drop all charges. Ten minutes later Commissioner Mo announced his verdict.

From the trial transcript of Departmental Case #57873/84:

COMMISSIONER MO: Detective Eppolito, it is the Court's opinion that based on the stipulated evidence that the Department has submitted in an attempt to substantiate any charges that have been filed against you, it is crystal clear to me that the Department has failed to substantiate this burden of proof for those charges that have been lodged against you.

"After his first sentence," Louie recalls, "I flew into Gardell's arms. We kissed and hugged like sumo wrestlers. I tried to steady my pounding brain to grasp the rest of what he said. The charges wouldn't technically be dismissed that afternoon. Mo said he would prepare a written opinion for the Police Commissioner. He would have me restored to modified assignment until the written decision came down. Then he concluded:

" 'However, at this time I think it is very clear to this court that there is no evidence to substantiate these charges against you and that the court will communicate that to the Police Commissioner.

" 'And in the meantime I will ask your attorneys to send whatever information they can gather relative to your background to the court.

" 'I will submit a written decision in this case within the next two weeks.

" 'Is there anything else?' "

Louie, never one to leave without the last word, raised his hand. Again, from the transcript:

THE RESPONDENT: Thank you.
I have my scrapbooks here, and the only thing I would say is that after seventeen years I have [elev-

enth] ranking on this job. I have come to work with broken fingers at times in order not to go out sick.

I suffer from an uncommon condition called cluster headaches at which time I get headaches so severe I can't stand up. But I come to work. I park my car on the side of the road at times. I come in on those days with headaches and I come five hours early so I could be at work.

I have never had anybody ever accuse me of something.

I was told from the Internal Affairs Division that they had tapped my phones, had surveillance on me, and nowhere ever have they ever seen me talking to anybody.

I have read in newspaper articles that I am a friend of [Rosario Gambino's] and I have been seen in cafes, and I challenge anybody at any time—I told them that I was willing to let them shoot Sodium Pentathol into me and give me a truth serum. I was willing to go through that.

I am of Italian extraction, but I am American. I don't even know how to speak Italian. I don't know or understand any of that.

Being that I felt that they should have worked a little harder to see that I wouldn't do something like that, that is totally out of character.

Everything I have done for seventeen years —

I have gotten citations from President Carter.

I started the Senior Citizens Robbery Program to stop the senior citizens from being mugged and killed.

I have in these scrapbooks Department changes that I instituted for the District Attorney's office to stop people from waiting around all day in court.

I have dedicated my time and my life to this job. I

like this job. I would never embarrass myself or the
Police Department with something like this.

After the verdict came down, as Gardell called the
Six-two to pass the word around the station house,
Louie dialed Fran.

"It's over honey, all over," he told her. "Not guilty
on all charges, sweetheart. Nothing. They found absolutely nothing wrong. I'll see you in an hour."

Then he phoned his mother.

28

The day after Louie was acquitted of all charges, Steve Gardell and Detective Ed Blasie, the president of the Detectives Endowment Association, accompanied him to "Super Chief" Richard NiCastro's office. Like a beaming child, Louie was toting his scrapbooks. Gardell and Blasie entered the Chief of Detectives' chamber while Louie remained in the outer office.

"What's he up here for?" NiCastro demanded.

"Chief, he's never met you and he just wants to show you his scrapbooks," Blasie replied.

"I don't want to see his goddamn scrapbooks."

As Gardell recalls, "So I said to NiCastro—and I never told Louie this—I said, 'You know, Chief, five months ago when all this started, I went to Chief Schilling and told him Louie didn't do it. And you know what he told me? Chief Schilling told me he had to do it, because the mob's in his bloodlines, in his genes.' "

NiCastro was taken aback. Not so much at Schilling's thesis, Gardell guessed, but at the scary thought that this kind of departmental bias might seep into the newspapers. He asked Gardell who else knew about the conversation. No one, Gardell replied, except the three of them in that room, and Schilling. That seemed to soothe the Chief of Detectives. Then Gardell began pressing about the agreement he had cut to return Louie to the Six-two.

"He's never going back to the Six-two," NiCastro said.

"Fine, Chief," Gardell replied. "But you should at least have the courtesy of talking to the guy. He *was* found not guilty."

NiCastro gave Gardell a brusque wave, an indication to show Louie in. Gardell closed the door behind Louie, leaving Blasie and Louie alone with the Chief of Detectives.

"So I walk in with my scrapbooks under my arm, and he's sitting behind this big desk and he's got this puss on. I introduced myself and start to sit down and he jumps down my throat: 'Don't sit down, I didn't tell you to sit down.'

"I apologized, and told him that I just wanted to let him know how proud I was to be a detective and how I would never do anything to embarrass the Detective Division.

"At that, he stood up, walked around from behind his desk, and pushed his finger right into my chest. 'I know all about you,' he says. 'Your kind, and your family. I knew your old man real well from Grand Avenue.' Then he pushes his finger into my chest again.

"That was it. I told him he didn't know my father. The only cops who knew my old man from Grand Avenue were the cops he was paying off. And I added that IAD might not have nailed me before, but they were sure going to get me now, because if he poked his finger into my chest one more time I was going to smash his face flat. He started hollering and I started hollering and the last thing I remember him saying as I blew out of the room was, 'The next time you see the Six-two Precinct in this Police Department is when you ride through it in a hearse.'

"He was right. I guess if there's a lesson there, it's never to argue with a chief."

One week later Trials Commissioner Hugh Mo paid a visit to the Chief of Detectives. He had heard that Louie was being transferred, against his wishes, to the Seven-one. Mo felt it was his duty to put in a word for the cop. He had also heard through the police grapevine that NiCastro was not at all thrilled with his court decision.

"Dick," Mo said, "I know how you feel about it, but fair is fair. The guy was exonerated."

NiCastro turned and glared. "Exonerated by you, Mo, but not exonerated by me." Mo wheeled and walked out, his conscience salved. The limb for a cop named Eppolito was long indeed.

"A few days went by before I went back into Brooklyn Headquarters to get my new assignment. Gardell was with me. Steve had told me about the promise Schilling had made the morning of my suspension, the vow to return me to my old squad if I beat the rap. That eased my mind a little. As my old man—who could barely read or write—had taught me, a man's word was his bond. So I really figured that it was a done deal as I sat in Schilling's office explaining to the chief why I had to get back to the Six-two. Assignment to any other command would cast a lingering shadow over me. There'd always be a tinge of guilt, despite Mo's ruling. Schilling agreed, shook my hand, and promised me a return to my old squad.

"The following Monday I reported to NiCastro' secretary in police headquarters for my assignmen papers. They said I was going to the Seven-one. Ful circle. Hellhole to hellhole. I told the captain sitting behind the desk that there must be some mistake, tha Schilling himself had guaranteed my return to the Six two.

"Very snidelike, the guy gets up from his desk, mo seys over to a file cabinet, and produces my transfer memo, signed by Schilling himself.

"I thought about Ralph and Jimmy, about Todo and Bath Beach. When the Mafia gave their word, they kept it. If my old man had promised someone a post, the guy would have that post or else someone would get whacked finding out why.

"I drove straight to Brooklyn Borough Command. Schilling was in. He didn't look real happy to see me. I only had one question:

" 'Chief, I know I can go to the eighth floor to get my shield back. I know I can go to the first floor to get my guns back. But can you tell me what floor to go to to get my pride and dignity back?'

"He had no answer."

EPILOGUE

On April 12, 1985, Detective Louis John Eppolito received a written disposition of Case #57873/84. The court found the evidence against him to be insufficient, with the following recommendations:

(A) The respondent be found NOT GUILTY;

(B) The respondent be reimbursed for pay, benefits and service time lost while on suspension;

(C) The respondent be restored to full duty.

As a compromise, the Department had negated Louie's orders to the Seven-one Precinct and instead assigned him to the Six-three. But the detective who returned to work in South Brooklyn in the spring of 1985 remained a bitter man. Louie filed a $5 million dollar defamation suit against the NYPD ("I figured that was a number that would get somebody's attention"), which was thrown out of court.

Finally, heeding the advice of family, friends, and co-workers, who warned him that he was "an ulcer about to happen," Louie at last managed to put his suspension and trial behind him, and in February of 1988 was promoted to Detective, Second Grade.

One year later, while on a stakeout outside a midtown Manhattan restaurant, Louie was approached by a Hollywood casting director, who insisted on introducing him to the filmmaker Martin Scorsese. On the spot, Scorsese hired the grandson of Luigi the Nablidan and the son of Fat the Gangster to portray, ironically, the Gambino Family capo Angelo Ruggiero in the movie *Goodfellas*.

If a star was not exactly born, a new career was certainly imminent.

On the set, Louie struck up a friendship with the film's star, Robert De Niro, who would invite the detective to dine in his trailer in return for tips and anecdotes about life in La Cosa Nostra.

"I told De Niro that it was simple to act like a wiseguy," Louie recalls. "That in my father's day, in my Uncle Jimmy's day, you just lived your life according to the code of honor—respect and loyalty. That code is dead now. Maybe it really never even existed for a lot of mobsters. But it existed for the Eppolito family, and it still exists for me. And that's why I decided to put in my papers. I had lost all respect for the bureaucrats who ran the Police Department of New York City.

"As frightening as it may sound, I found more loyalty, more honor, in the wiseguy neighborhoods and hangouts than I did in police headquarters. The bad guys respected Louie Eppolito. Unfortunately, I cannot say the same for the good guys."

On December 14, 1989, Detective Second Grade Louis John Eppolito retired with full honors.

The New York City Police Department had finally managed to rid itself of one of its worthiest cops.